emotional inflammation

**Discover Your Triggers
and Reclaim Your Equilibrium
During Anxious Times**

LISE VAN SUSTEREN, MD, and STACEY COLINO

sounds true
BOULDER, COLORADO

Sounds True
Boulder, CO 80306

This book is not intended as a substitute for the medical recommendations of physicians, mental health professionals, or other health-care providers. Rather, it is intended to offer information to help the reader cooperate with physicians, mental health professionals, and health-care providers in a mutual quest for optimal well-being. We advise readers to carefully review and understand the ideas presented and to seek the advice of a qualified professional if you have any concerns or if you feel like you're in crisis. The anecdotes in this book are from real people and patients but their names and other identifying characteristics have been changed to protect their privacy.

Published 2020

Book design by Maureen Forys, Happenstance Type-O-Rama

Printed in Canada

Printed on FSC-compliant paper

Library of Congress Cataloging-in-Publication Data

Names: Susteren, Lise van, author. | Colino, Stacey, author.
Title: Emotional inflammation: discover your triggers and reclaim your
  equilibrium during anxious times / Lise Van Susteren, MD, and Stacey
  Colino.
Description: Boulder, CO: Sounds True, Inc., 2020. | Includes
  bibliographical references and index.
Identifiers: LCCN 2019036164 (print) | LCCN 2019036165 (ebook) | ISBN
  9781683644552 (hardback) | ISBN 9781683644569 (ebook)
Subjects: LCSH: Emotions. | Self-help techniques.
Classification: LCC BF531 .S87 2020 (print) | LCC BF531 (ebook) | DDC
  152.4—dc23
LC record available at https://lccn.loc.gov/2019036164
LC ebook record available at https://lccn.loc.gov/2019036165

10 9 8 7 6 5 4 3 2 1

CONTENTS

INTRODUCTION:

LIVING ON

HIGH ALERT

1

HIT THE PAUSE BUTTON on your regularly scheduled life for a moment, and ask yourself: Am I spending a substantial part of my time feeling unusually stressed out and on edge or anxious about the future? Do I feel like I'm being bombarded with bad or alarming news or other people's mercurial moods? Am I experiencing emotional whiplash as my feelings swing from sadness to fear to anger or hopelessness in the span of minutes or hours when I hear about the latest natural disaster, human rights crisis, or political debacle? If you answered yes to any of these questions, you're hardly alone.

A rising number of adults in the US are troubled by a phenomenon they don't know there's a name for. It may be marked by a sense of agitation, foreboding, spiraling negative thoughts, sleep disturbances, and a sense of hardly recognizing the lighthearted, fun-loving people they used to be. It's what I call "emotional inflammation," and when I look around, hear the expressed thoughts of my patients, colleagues, and friends, and even consider times in my own life, it feels like we are in the midst of an epidemic of it. While life goes on, and many of us put on a happy face, our sense of well-being is still badly shaken. Some people suffer from symptoms similar to post-traumatic stress disorder (PTSD)—with worry, disturbing and intrusive thoughts, hyperreactivity, hypervigilance, grief, sleep problems, and nightmares—but in this case the symptoms stem not from a traumatic event or series of events but from how it feels to live in today's world and from anxiety about what it could be like in the future.

The intention here is not to make you feel more demoralized or despondent than you do already but to validate your feelings and show you that you have plenty of company in your emotional unease. When people hear about the concept of emotional inflammation and its symptoms, they often have an "aha" moment of recognition and relatability, one that makes them feel understood and less alone. Knowing there's a name for the way they've been feeling helps it feel less unsettling. And realizing that your distressing emotions are being triggered on a fairly regular basis by the turmoil in the world around you, rather than by something *inside you*, should provide some relief. That doesn't mean you should simply accept your current emotional state as the new normal. On the contrary, you can consciously take steps to ease it and navigate toward steadier emotional ground.

The first step is to recognize emotional inflammation for what it is. Many of us are rattled by the political situations in the US and around the globe, the health of the planet, and even the state of humanity. With all the recent disasters in the natural world—the hurricanes, earthquakes, wildfires, mudslides, searing heat, and bizarre weather—that are linked to the climate crisis, people are starting to wonder if Mother Nature's patience has run out. The fear that no one is really in control in the government leaves us feeling deeply vulnerable. People are shaken by the unrelenting mass shootings, the rise of hate crimes, nuclear missile testing, the stream of sexual abuse or misconduct scandals, and general news about how our health and well-being are threatened by the increasingly degraded and depleted natural world.

Given this, it's not surprising that the prevalence of major depression in the US has risen dramatically since 2005, with the most rapid rate of increase among teenagers and young adults. The World Health Organization reports that both depression and anxiety have risen to unprecedented levels—epidemic proportions—throughout the world. Depression is now especially high among women in North and South America, and anxiety disorders are higher among men and women in the US than anywhere else in the world. The use of antidepressants in the US has nearly doubled since 2000, and nine million people regularly use prescription sleeping pills.

The (mis)use of opioids has skyrocketed, too. Since 1999, opioid overdose deaths have increased *fivefold* among women in the US. In 2017 alone, opioid overdoses killed more than 47,000 people in the US. That's more than six times the number of US military service members that were killed in the post 9/11 wars in Iraq and Afghanistan combined. While some of the factors contributing to the opioid crisis are obvious—overprescribing by physicians and unconscionable and unlawful business practices of pharmaceutical companies and distributors—in my experience other questions beg to be asked, including, *Why do so many people want them so badly?*

One answer is obvious: People are hurting emotionally.

With the threats and worries swirling around us becoming so pervasive—overwhelming, really—our culture has recently coined terms for new forms of fatigue or depletion, including *outrage fatigue, evacuation fatigue, scandal fatigue, compassion fatigue, racial battle fatigue, apocalypse fatigue*, and *eco-anxiety*. Recently, the term *solastalgia*, coined by Australian philosopher Glenn Albrecht to describe the distress of seeing treasured land permanently damaged by industrial activity or extreme weather events, has entered the cultural lexicon, particularly in the mental health field and environmental activism community. This term "speaks to my changing experience in nature," Mark Coleman, a mindfulness meditation teacher and nature guide, wrote in a 2019 issue of *Mindful* magazine. "In the past, nature had always been an unending source of nourishment, joy, wonder, and love. Now, it is often tinged with sadness, grief, or loss" over what is happening to diverse habitats, species, and bodies of water.

Many of these newly named conditions reflect a profound sense of helplessness, hopelessness, cynicism, apathy, or distraction—or a mixture of all of them. These fears and worries are superimposed upon our own personal, day-to-day challenges—coping with demanding jobs for which we may not be sufficiently compensated, the high cost of modern life, raising kids in a world with increasingly challenging obstacles, dangerous temptations, and the like.

If you don't think you're experiencing emotional inflammation, you're probably not paying close enough attention to how you're feeling. As a psychiatrist in Washington, DC, I am increasingly seeing the debilitating effects of emotional hyperreactivity in my patients, as well as in friends, climate activists, political insiders, and media professionals, and even in my own life. In my work with young people, I'm seeing an increase in anxiety and depression—more teens reaching for opioids, and college students showing up at student health centers in overwhelming numbers. They may come in complaining about stress that's related to exams or social pressures, but these issues exist against a backdrop of news that the natural world may be on the verge of collapsing. Besides seeing and treating these variants of psychological and emotional distress on a regular basis, I have become a frequent commentator about anxiety and trauma for television, radio, print media, and other venues. My coauthor Stacey Colino is an award-winning writer specializing in health and psychology, and our combined expertise, perspectives, and experience, I can say with conviction, more than confirm the adage that two heads are better than one.

More and more these days, people are asking, *What can I do about the psychological turmoil that I'm feeling? How can I feel safe and steady myself again? How can I respond to triggers more effectively?* These questions reflect the deepening emotional toll of anxiety, fear, outrage, anger, and sorrow—of a society under stress. It doesn't have to be this way. When we can name and better understand these emotions, some of the intensity of their grip will dissipate naturally. But not all of it will, which is why we have written this book.

Many of the issues triggering emotional inflammation—fear mongering and discord among politicians, extreme weather events, living with a mercurial leader, human rights abuses, natural disasters, and breaking news about widely used chemicals harming our health—feel largely outside of our control. Yet, we do have a *degree* of influence over these triggers because we can better understand how we respond to them and cultivate critical thinking skills and the emotional clarity to keep us from being at their mercy. We can quell our emotional hyperreactivity by creating lifestyles and rhythms that are in sync with the inherent needs of our bodies and minds, by exposing ourselves to the right types of stimulation in the right amounts, by grasping *how* and *why* our physical and mental health are affected by certain lifestyle choices, and by partaking of nature's vast healing powers.

To be clear, the goal is *not* to stop feeling or to stop showing emotion. Feelings and emotions make us sentient beings and bring texture and richness to our lives. They bring valuable data that helps inform us about the choices we're making, the way we're living, and even what is healthy for us and could improve the state of our troubled and troubling world. It's not in our best interest to suppress any of this data. It's better to work with it and use it as motivation to take effective action, in one way or another.

With this book, we are popping the hood, so to speak, to see what's underneath, so we can address the changes that need to be made to keep the engine (our minds) running more smoothly. In part 1, you will learn more about the various forces that are making us feel fearful, powerless, or even at times despondent, and the physiological, psychological, social, and spiritual ripple effects of living with emotional inflammation. You'll be able to identify the form(s) of emotional inflammation that affects you most frequently. In part 2, what we call the "RESTORE plan" will help you figure out how you can reclaim your equilibrium and channel the distressing emotions you've been experiencing in constructive ways. As you'll see, the basis for calming emotional inflammation is rooted in psychology, neuroscience, and evolutionary biology, and it's designed to lead to a deep, sustainable improvement in the way you feel and function. The book is designed to help you foster the resolve, courage, and wisdom that can allow you to live with vitality, engagement, and joy.

This is a prime opportunity for you to pivot or shift gears, to transform the distressing feelings you have been wrestling with into steady calm by taking matters into your own hands to improve your well-being and that of the world around you. Instead of feeling vulnerable and bewildered, you can work to change conditions that fuel your worries by redirecting your energy toward upstream solutions, finding kindred spirits to be at your side along the way. The power lies in your hands and mind—let's put you in a position to wield that power effectually.

PART I

THE AGE OF HYPERREACTIVITY

CHAPTER 1

EMOTIONAL INFLAMMATION: THE NAME FOR HOW YOU'VE BEEN FEELING

There is no agony
like bearing an untold
story inside you.

ZORA NEALE HURSTON,
author of *Dust Tracks on a Road*

YOU WON'T FIND THE term *emotional inflammation* in the *Diagnostic and Statistical Manual of Mental Disorders* (DSM-5), the standard guide for the classification of mental health disorders. But it's a condition afflicting millions of women and men who are currently living in our noisy, chaotic, confusing, and often contentious world. The symptoms can include a maelstrom of anticipatory anxiety, nameless dread, an ongoing state of high alert, or new levels of hyperreactivity, agitation, or hypervigilance. Others experience post-traumatic or even what I have dubbed *pre*-traumatic stress symptoms.

It may come as no surprise that research suggests that soldiers facing deployment into combat situations often experience repeated disturbing thoughts, images, or dreams of traumatic experiences that could occur or have strong physical reactions when reminded of the possibility of such an event in the future. Perhaps it doesn't come as a surprise, either, to learn that individuals who are working on the front lines to prevent human rights abuses and racial injustices or battling the climate crisis have similar symptoms. But ordinary citizens can suffer symptoms like this too. They are increasingly asking their doctors for medications to help control symptoms that stem from the current, anticipated, and feared crises and disasters around us or to focus their scattered attention or help them sleep.

Basically, we're looking for ways to make the pervasive sense of *This sucks!* go away. For the more fortunate among us, the stream of apocalyptic messages comes through newsfeeds; however, we don't always have time to recover from one alarming piece of news before another follows. For some of us, it isn't just that these crises are in the news, but also that we're personally affected by climate issues, racial discrimination, sexual misconduct, and other social injustices. We are living in a world where bizarre is the new normal, where the unexpected has practically come to be expected. Disturbing political, environmental, and societal events—like the metaphorical version of Chicken Little's frantic warning, "The sky is falling!"—are playing, for many of us, in a repetitive loop in our minds.

Distrust in our institutions is rising as confidence in our leaders declines. The income gap continues to widen, and the economic vibrancy of the middle class, long the backbone of our economic system, is breaking down. Despite all the outrage and indescribable sorrow, mass shootings continue, and hate crimes, mistreatment of immigrants, nuclear missile testing, sexual misconduct scandals, and environmental threats—from the use of toxic chemicals and contaminants—are widespread and ongoing. As the planet continues to unravel from the increasingly frequent and intense impacts of the climate crisis, questions about the future of the human race are being asked. It's not surprising that millions of people are fearful about the state of the world and even the future of the human race. People want to know, *What the heck is going on?! How can I get rid of the sense of foreboding and this feeling of powerlessness? How can I protect myself and those I love?*

Compounding the problem, we have strayed from the natural conditions that are aligned with how we, as human beings, have evolved to live. Our internal body clocks (our circadian rhythms) have been thrown off course. Technology has stolen our hearts and captured our imaginations, and we are treating the natural world that nurtured us like a rejected ex. As we become increasingly disconnected from nature and oblivious to the many restorative benefits of living in harmony with it, our physical and emotional energy may be depleted, or we may stay revved in a state of high alert in case we need to fight or flee from danger. Meanwhile, this ever-present anxiety in our minds is like a dark and menacing black pool that has become the dumping ground for every new worry and fear that arises.

By way of example, consider forty-two-year-old Lauren, a high-achieving policymaker who on the surface seemed to be leading a charmed life. When she came to see me, her career was thriving, she was earning an impressive salary, and she was highly valued both at work and on the Washington, DC, social circuit. But inside, Lauren, who is smart, accomplished, charismatic, and attractive, was falling apart. She struggled with emotional lability, rapidly shifting moods that compromised her ability to do her work. The disturbing content of much of the news she tuned in to made her feel constantly on edge. She had a pattern of choosing emotionally distant boyfriends and erupting in bouts of neediness and anger that she'd later regret. Unable to comfort herself, Lauren would often end up eating or drinking too much or, worse, snorting a line or two of cocaine to escape from her distress. After a weekend of particularly troubling excesses, she decided she'd had enough and wanted to stop her destructive patterns. That's when she came in for help.

As we worked together, it became clear that the demands of Lauren's work and the pool of bad news she was swimming in (about political dysfunction, human rights violations, disasters, and ongoing threats related to the climate crisis) were making her feel like the world was going to pieces. What's more, it was driving her own sense of being out of control, which was intensified by memories of the chaotic atmosphere in which she had grown up. With regular therapy to uncover what was going on and a stint on medication to calm her symptoms, Lauren got control of her emotions and made some changes that were right for her newfound desire for stability and authenticity.

What about the rest of us? There's just no way around it; we're living in anxious times: "Collectively, the world is more stressed, worried, sad and in pain today than we've ever seen it," concluded the *Gallup 2018 Global Emotions Report*, which was based on 154,000 interviews with adults in 146 countries. The *2019 Global Emotions Report* did not provide better news. Around the world, worry and sadness, already at record highs, edged up even further, and anger increased even more. Meanwhile, according to the 2018 Looking Further with Ford Trends Report, 70 percent of adults in the US say they feel overwhelmed by all the suffering in the world today, and 50 percent of adults throughout the world say that following the daily news is stressful.

A WORLD OF WORRIES: GLOBAL TRIGGERS

Not surprisingly, individuals from different countries worry or feel stressed out about different issues. But a significant proportion of the world's population is distressed about the direction their nation is headed in, believing that it's on the wrong track. In a recent survey of people in twenty-five countries, unemployment was found to be the leading concern, followed by financial/political corruption, poverty, and social inequality. In Mexico, personal security is a leading source of stress. In Afghanistan and Yemen, war and humanitarian crises are at the top of the list. In the UK, the leading sources of stress are financial matters, work, and health concerns, whereas in Australia, the rising cost of living is the primary concern. While the triggers may be slightly different, this much is clear: in myriad ways, all around the globe, people are hurting.

"Deaths of despair"—from suicide and those linked to alcohol and drugs—are on the rise. From 1999 to 2016, according to the Centers for Disease Control and Prevention, suicide rates in the US increased by more than 25 percent, and 54 percent of those who died from suicide *had not* been diagnosed with a mental health condition. It's not just adults who are affected. From 1999 to 2014, suicide rates among kids and teens between the ages of ten and nineteen increased *33 percent*, and the latest data, from 2019, indicates that the gender gap in suicide is narrowing because more girls and young women are committing suicide than in the past, with the largest percentage increase in those aged ten to fourteen years.

The number of people diagnosed with major depression in the US increased by 33 percent from 2013 to 2018—and even more among young adults (an increase of 47 percent) and teens (a 47 percent jump for boys, and a 65 percent spike for girls). The percentage of high school students who had experienced periods of persistent feelings of sadness or hopelessness during the past year increased significantly from 2007 to 2017, according to the Centers for Disease Control and Prevention's Youth Risk Behavior Survey. (For the record, "persistent" in this survey was defined as almost every day for at least two consecutive weeks and sufficiently severe that the student stopped engaging in some of his or her usual activities.) Nearly one-third of the students surveyed experienced these persistent feelings of despair in 2017!

THE BODY, MIND, AND SPIRIT EFFECTS

Given these statistics, who would doubt that we are experiencing a rising state of emotional inflammation? Emotional inflammation takes a toll on your body, mind, and spirit in just about every conceivable way. For one thing, living in a continuous state of high anxiety causes your body's fight-or-flight response to basically get stuck in the "on" position: Your sympathetic nervous system stays revved up, releasing a flood of the stress hormones cortisol and adrenaline. Both of these stress hormones increase your heart rate, breathing, and blood pressure, straining your cardiovascular system, as well as your immune, endocrine, and neurological systems. These changes can amp up your pain response and—pay attention, here!—decrease fertility. Collectively, these physiological challenges contribute to allostatic load, a form of stress-induced wear and tear on the brain and body resulting from exposure to chronically or repeatedly elevated stress hormone levels, an effect that accelerates the aging process.

Unfortunately, that's not all. Feeling unsafe, hypervigilant, hyperreactive, and/or fearful about the future can lead to sleep troubles and changes in your behavior (with eating, drinking alcohol, or smoking). It can lead to feelings of helplessness, hopelessness, impotent rage, and despair. It can compromise your ability to function at your cognitive best by impairing your focus, as well as your ability to learn and remember new information. Anticipatory anxiety can hijack critical—and fragile—decision-making faculties by disrupting normal neural processes in your brain—reducing activity in the areas that play a role in the processing of risk and fear and areas involved in processing reward. These changes can alter how you make decisions by shifting the way you evaluate potential positive consequences and anticipated negative consequences of your options so that a greater emphasis is placed on the negative. Moreover, when we feel that we have lost our grounding or sense of stability, we can feel a sense of emptiness or feel adrift; or, we may feel alienated from ourselves or from others. Any of these sensations may lead to what feels like a spiritual crisis.

Any way you slice it, pervasive anxiety is a crippling way to live and work; it robs us not only of our well-being and quality of life but our ability to function. Some people try to get away from these uncomfortable feelings, distracting themselves by running from them, pushing themselves, consciously or not, to go faster, to cram their lives with more activities or more stimulation. Other people shut down or withdraw, while still others feel perpetually on edge or irritable.

As uncomfortable as these feelings are, it's essential to recognize their importance to us. They allow us, as a species, to evolve and survive, adapt, be resourceful, and creatively solve challenges. And they make us who we are as humans with the capacity for compassion, which is the foundation for empathy and altruism. Our feelings also drive our values. Caring deeply is a good thing, a source of strength and guidance; however, when it's untempered, the capacity to feel intensely can set you up to be triggered with emotions that can spin out of control. The upside is that embedded in these emotions is an enormous amount of energy—it's up to each of us to figure out how to harness and direct it toward effecting changes for the better. Once you understand and examine your feelings, you can grow; become more resilient, even courageous; address blind spots (things you haven't been able to see) in your life; and improve the ways in which you interact with other people. Try to look at this as an opportunity, rather than only a crisis.

Human beings have a tremendous capacity to rebound from hardship, to grow and learn from their experiences. Though it's a controversial concept in my field, *post-traumatic growth* can occur when people experience beneficial psychological, emotional, or social changes in the aftermath of a severe illness or injury, the death of a loved one, a natural disaster, or some other form of adversity. In a study of 3,157 US veterans, 50 percent reported at least *moderate* post-traumatic growth after their most traumatic event, and 72 percent of veterans who had previously screened positive for PTSD experienced some post-traumatic growth.

A WORLD OF HOPE

In late 2018, *Vice* asked 105 influential thinkers from around the world what gave them the most hope for the future. They were permitted to answer the question in any way they liked. Topping the list was young people and youth movements, which are reinventing activism and finding new ways to address mounting threats (such as climate change) and long-standing social injustices. After that, these thought-influencers mentioned technological and scientific innovations (including robotics and medical breakthroughs like genome editing and cancer immunotherapy), advances in equity and social justice (such as the Me Too Movement and the shifting of shame from victim to perpetrator), music, the creative imagination, human ingenuity, and human kindness and compassion. In other words, there's plenty to be hopeful about and inspired by, even in these challenging times.

As Daniel Szafir, PhD, an assistant professor of computer science, creative technologies, information science, and aerospace engineering at the University of Colorado Boulder, put it, "We have the recipe for success as a species: We are incredibly resilient and creative in the face of adversity, can build on the knowledge and developments of prior generations, and have a unique capacity for individual self-improvement over the course of a single lifetime. If you are reading this, you are amazingly lucky to be alive right now."

CHAOS AND CRISES IN OUR MIDST

Many of us are worrying about the crisis or catastrophe that could strike today or tomorrow—and the fear is both top of mind and deep in our hearts. As survey after survey has shown, stress, worry, and anger have intensified in recent years. In 2017, a survey of 1,019 adults throughout the US, on behalf of the American Psychiatric Association, found that nearly two-thirds indicated that they were "extremely" or "somewhat" anxious about keeping themselves and their loved ones safe and healthy and more than 50 percent were extremely or somewhat anxious about their finances or the impact of politics on their daily lives. In 2018, the American Psychiatric Association repeated the survey and found that 39 percent of respondents said they were more anxious than the previous year, particularly about their safety, health, finances, relationships, and the impact of politics on their daily lives.

Along with the dramatic increase in anxiety, the hierarchy of triggers for our collective case of emotional inflammation often reflects what's happening in the news. It can feel as though we're living in a horror-house hall of mirrors, where waves and spikes of disturbing, sometimes distorted, news assault us often out of nowhere. Fake news has permeated the culture, and worse, so has deep fake video, which is even more skewed and misleading; both are driving conspiracy theories that foster mistrust of each other as well as additional unease about who or what we can rely on for the truth. It is a time of moral vertigo, where the lists of disgraced former heroes, idols, and role models grow longer on a near-daily basis. Powerful, once-admired people in entertainment, politics, the media, the arts, and other influential domains have been taken down by accusations of sexual harassment, misconduct, or assault. Hearing that privilege allows some individuals to buy or bribe their kids' way into prestigious colleges and universities adds another layer to our collective outrage. Sometimes it feels like the world is undergoing an ethical free fall and we are experiencing drama overload.

Alexandra, a fifty-two-year-old writer in New York City, had always been somewhat anxious, but her anxiety stayed below the surface until she had kids. After a difficult divorce in 2010, her anxiety ramped up a bit more as she realized she'd been in a psychologically abusive marriage. It increased again in 2015 as she supported one of her twins, born female, as he transitioned to male. Then things really came to a head during the presidential election in 2016. Alexandra, who had been sexually assaulted when she was fourteen, said, "Seeing the way women were being treated across all aspects of life, and seeing the vitriol and abuse writ large on the news, was devastating to me. The public cruelty to women woke up all the trauma of what I'd been through." Besides feeling constantly on edge, she became hyper-vigilant: "I felt like if I took my eye off the ball for even five seconds, something worse would happen," she recalled.

When she began experiencing worrisome brain glitches, during which she'd have nonsensical thoughts or forget a point she was trying to make, she became truly alarmed. "It scared the crap out of me," she said. "The more scared I got, the more anxious I became and the worse I felt." In 2017, she was diagnosed with PTSD, brought on by an enormous amount of personal stress, as well as by the current political and social climate. In addition to going to therapy and increasing her antidepressant dosage, she now carries Ativan with her in case she feels on the verge of a panic attack.

Many of the issues that are contributing to our emotional inflammation are outside of our control. A 2019 Gallup poll, based on interviews with a random sample of 1,039 adults throughout the US, found that the top ten issues they worry about a great deal are as follows:

1. The availability and affordability of health care

2. Federal spending and the budget deficit

3. Hunger and homelessness

4. Drug use

5. Crime and violence

6. The state of the environment

7. The way income and wealth are distributed in the US

8. The availability of guns

9. The Social Security system

10. Race relations

The biggest concern among young people, ages thirteen to twenty-four, is gun violence in schools and elsewhere, with *53 percent* of those under eighteen saying it's a major worry for them, according to a March 2018 poll by *USA Today*. How many of these do *you* relate to?

With potential threats and concerns coming from multiple directions, often simultaneously, to many of us the world can feel like we are living in a house with both a faulty foundation and a leaky roof. Though the threats mount, some by the hour, those in a position to protect the public from these vulnerabilities are preoccupied with squabbling and looking out for their own (political) futures. The people who should be taking care of the proverbial house are behaving badly and shirking responsibility for cleaning up the messes that they or others created. Is it any wonder we don't feel safe?

The majority of adults in the US feel that we are living at the lowest point in US history, and the future of our nation is a significant source of stress, primarily because of the current political climate, the social divisiveness our country is experiencing, and concerns about health care and economic security, according to the American Psychological Association's 2017 *Stress in America* report. In a 2018 survey of adults in the US, researchers at the Yale Program on Climate Change Communication found that 69 percent are "somewhat worried" about global warming and 29 percent are "very worried"—the highest levels since the survey began in 2008.

A WORLD OF WORRY

Scientists, political scientists, futurists, attorneys, psychologists, security experts, entrepreneurs, business leaders, and other experts are worried. In 2018, *Vice* asked those same 105 influential thinkers from around the world (see "A World of Hope" box previously) what worried them most about the future, and again they were allowed to answer any way they liked, without direction or restrictions. Their lists were topped by concerns about digital technologies, automation, and artificial intelligence, especially biased algorithms, lack of transparency and accountability, ability to manipulate us, and potential to put human beings out of work; and climate and environmental change, including the loss of biodiversity and ecosystems, the degradation of the planet, the potential for human displacement and mass migration, and other impacts on society and the future of the human species. But they didn't stop there. Some of these highly respected thinkers also expressed concerns about the return of fascism as a global threat, the potential for global nuclear conflict, human apathy, guns in schools, growing social and economic disparities and inequities, an erosion of civil rights, public meanness and bullying, our ongoing struggle with differences, insufficient science literacy in society, the loss of connection to nature and each other, and world overpopulation. What an exhausting list of worries, indeed!

A perfect storm of influences has been driving this epidemic of emotional inflammation. Given how often these various fears and anxieties are voiced in the media or in our immediate social and professional circles, is it any wonder that so many of us have that *I can't look!* feeling the way we did while watching scary movies as children?

Rebecca, a sixty-one-year-old science policy analyst, has been working on climate and environmental issues for most of her career. Over time, she has learned how to manage her anxiety about climate change so that it's in the background for the most part. "It's kind of like having a family member who's slowly dying of cancer—you just have to accept it after a while and keep going," she says. These days, what really triggers her emotional inflammation and makes her feel angry, frustrated, and demoralized—especially since she has a son in his twenties—are news reports of high-placed elected officials who blatantly disregard the environmental legacy that's being passed on to future generations. "The ship is in very bad hands," she says, "and it's going to be a mean, ugly world because of all the stress multipliers we're creating for ourselves—climate instability, polluted water, food shortages, and vector-borne diseases."

Climate change is an existential threat to all of us, but the threat is particularly menacing for young people who will be at the center of the storm, literally, when conditions become more violent, the harm accumulates, and the inevitability of the destruction becomes more apparent. Many young people know well that they are in harm's way. Some say they will not have children because of the anticipated climate chaos and especially because of the carbon costs of putting another person on the planet. It should go without saying that at their age, they shouldn't even have to think about these issues. But they do.

THE SPREAD OF ANXIETY

Our concerns take up precious real estate in our minds. This can cause us to become preoccupied with the threats around us or to ruminate about the alarming scenarios that could come to pass if they play out the way we fear. "For many, anxiety is an ever-present uninvited guest . . ." an article in a September 2018 issue of *Medical News Today* noted. "It seems to be rampaging through society like a noncontagious cognitive plague, forming a low-level hum that hides in the corners of our collective minds."

continues

This description rings true, except that I would argue that anxiety, like emotions generally, is extremely contagious. In simple terms, emotions can be passed from one individual to another in a matter of milliseconds, often without the recipient being aware of it.

During any conversation or personal encounter, human beings naturally and unconsciously tend to mimic and synchronize our facial expressions, body language, speech rhythms, and tone of voice to match the other person's. When this happens, the muscle fibers in your face and body are activated at subtle levels. Those imperceptible muscle movements trigger the actual feeling in your brain by inducing the same neurons to fire that would if the emotion was generated internally, without any external influence.

What makes these particular brain cells, called "mirror neurons," so fascinating is that their activity can be initiated in response to your own feelings and desires or in response to what someone else is doing: That is, they become triggered when you make a certain expression or movement—such as smiling, frowning, or clenching your fists—and when you see another person performing that very same action. This is true at any age or stage of life.

Some individuals are especially susceptible to catching other people's feelings. In one study, researchers examined what happens neurologically when people who have sensory processing sensitivity—greater awareness and responsiveness to other people's emotions and cues in the environment—were shown digitized color photos of their romantic partners' or strangers' positive and negative facial expressions. Using functional magnetic resonance imaging (fMRI) to monitor the participants' neural reactivity, the researchers found that the highly sensitive folks had greater activation in brain regions that are involved with attention, action planning, integration of sensory information, and empathy than less sensitive people do.

Whether it happens at home, work, or other settings, this primitive emotional exchange—it's really a monkey-see-monkey-do phenomenon—is

continues

highly adaptive. After all, it allows you to sense danger, threat, excitement, or what people around you are feeling. This tacit knowledge allows you to take appropriate action to protect yourself, catch a welcome wave of enthusiasm, show compassion, or provide assistance to a family member, friend, or colleague. There's no question that compassion is a valuable quality in our mixed-up world.

But the contagious effect of emotions can, of course, go too far, especially when the people around you are ratcheted up with negative emotions like anxiety, dread, despair, and the like. In those instances, you may need to come to your own emotional rescue by physically disengaging from your companions (even if it's just to make a phone call or visit the restroom), by redirecting the conversation to a less distressing topic, or by using visualization techniques (such as envisioning yourself protected by a Lucite shield) so that you won't absorb or "catch" the other person's emotions.

THE ELEMENTS OF CONTROL

As difficult as it is to hear all the bad news about what's happening in the world, we should recognize that we have some control over what's triggering our emotional inflammation and that in some instances we've brought on the problems ourselves. Collectively, as human beings, we're essentially soiling our nests (our planet) by polluting our air, water, and land with the ever-increasing array of chemicals, toxins, metals, and other contaminants. We're exerting a perilously heavy carbon footprint with the mounting toll of emissions of greenhouse gases. The good news is that because *we* are causing many of the problems, *we* have the power to correct them. More of us need to do our part to make matters better.

Meanwhile, some of the factors contributing to our personal emotional inflammation *are* directly and individually within our control. Many of us are living in ways that are out of sync with our internal body clocks (the all-important circadian rhythms). Even though many people don't realize it, the master timekeepers inside us are thrown off by exposure to bright indoor light at times when the body expects and would benefit from darkness. We're spending so much time with technological devices that it is leading to a loss of downtime as well as musing time. As we increasingly use our bodies to function in ways that are inconsistent with their intended design, they are experiencing unnatural wear and tear, including chronic cases of social jet lag: a syndrome defined as a conflict between what our bodies need, based on our internal biological clocks, and what our lives require, based on our jobs, our family lives, and other factors. Social jet lag is more than just an annoyance or an inconvenience; it also can compromise your emotional equilibrium and your cognitive function.

As we become increasingly reliant on technology, based on the assumption that it makes our lives easier and makes us more efficient (which, of course, it often does), there is a cost: Studies show that the multitasking it permits, compared to doing one task at a time, can hinder productivity and performance. The volume of fragmented activities we try to perform can add to feelings of being overwhelmed. "When we wake up in the morning feeling like we don't have enough time to get it all done, the brain shifts to a state of chronic stress that hijacks our energy and attention," notes Heidi Hanna, PhD, fellow and Advisory Board Member of the American Institute of Stress. Technology also can be a perpetual source of distraction, thanks to the beeping, chiming, vibrating, or flashing notifications that divert our attention from what we were doing to check our phones or computers.

And what happens when the digital devices we depend on stop working properly? We're often at an utter loss, maybe even in a panic, about how to cope or function. Think about it: If your laptop crashes and you haven't backed up your files recently, weeks' worth of work could go down the drain. If you lose internet service and can't send emails or important documents, you may have a hard time continuing to communicate with colleagues or make progress on your work. When your mobile phone dies and you no longer have access to a navigation aid, how will you get to your intended destination? Who or how will you call for help? Do you even remember important phone numbers so you can call the right people from another phone to get directions? These forms of technostress can take an insidious toll on our well-being.

The exponential growth in the use of social media in recent years isn't doing our emotional equilibrium any favors, either. Staying in touch with people via Facebook, Snapchat, Instagram, and Twitter isn't a sufficient substitute for connecting with people in person. Research has found that adults aged nineteen to thirty-two, who have the highest use of social media, are twice as likely to feel socially isolated as those with the lowest use. This may be because people who spend so much time fixated on their digital devices have fewer opportunities for in-person interactions. Plus, seeing the real-life activities that others are (or appear to be) engaged in can give them a whopping case of FOMO (fear of missing out) or cause them to struggle with comparisons that leave them feeling as if they're not measuring up.

Either way, the results can be similar, leading to a profound sense of loneliness/inadequacy/alienation that feels like a dull emotional ache. Ironically, a 2018 online survey of 20,000 adults nationwide found that nearly 50 percent of people sometimes or always feel alone or left out, and 43 percent feel their relationships are not meaningful. Only 53 percent of the participants say they have meaningful face-to-face social interactions with friends or family members on a daily basis.

Then there are the hidden opportunity costs. Spending endless hours staring at digital devices has made us strangers in our own land— disconnected, even alienated, from the natural world. The collateral damage from this disconnect is that we lose our senses of awe and wonder along the way. Awe doesn't come easily when we're fighting our way through traffic, struggling to keep up with a burgeoning mountain of work, or reading about the latest national or international crisis.

But it's a singularly effective state that restores us emotionally, socially, and spiritually. In a series of studies, researchers at the University of California, Irvine, found that after having experiences that evoked awe, prosocial behavior increased among participants—that is, they were more likely to be generous and show concern for ethical behaviors. The experience of awe also decreases our sense of entitlement.

One way or another, we all can learn to put ourselves back in the driver's seat so we can guide our emotional well-being in the right direction. By unpacking your emotional pain and turmoil so you can see its component parts, you'll gain greater self-knowledge and awareness and be able to figure out the specific steps you should take to address *your* personal triggers. You can calm the emotional turmoil inside you by taming your thoughts and tension, engaging in regular physical exercise, promoting good gut health, and making more conscious choices about the ways you choose to live. These are straightforward, down-to-earth remedies for emotional inflammation, and while they're not necessarily easy to make habitual, they are simple to initiate. The unfortunate truth is this: We have been depriving ourselves of natural remedies that are readily available, and we don't even realize it.

But here's some more *good* news: A blend of cutting-edge research and aggregated lessons from various disciplines (including different forms of sensory therapy, nature therapy, and possibility therapy), featured in the RESTORE plan (see part 2), will help you design your own approach to reversing emotional inflammation. When you improve your state of mind, shift your body's internal balance in a healthier direction, and reconnect with positive forces in the world around you, it's a truly uplifting, revitalizing feeling. As Genevan philosopher Jean-Jacques Rousseau famously suggested, happiness and social harmony come with self-knowledge and self-mastery—and when you use this idea to regain your emotional equilibrium, you'll be able to grow and thrive in new ways that you didn't even know existed. But it's an inside job—because it needs to start with you.

CHAPTER 2

WHAT TYPE OF REACTOR ARE YOU?

Without
self-confidence
we are as babes
in the cradle.

VIRGINIA WOOLF,
English writer

J UST AS PEOPLE'S BODIES come in different shapes and sizes, emotional inflammation can take on varied forms or styles. So it's a mistake to assume that your own brand of emotional inflammation is the same as a friend's or loved one's. Each of us has our own personal responses to stress, alarming news, potential threats, and worries about the state of the world. These responses can vary physiologically, cognitively, psychologically, and spiritually, based on our inherent temperaments, past experiences, genetic predispositions, natural thought patterns, personalities, and lifestyles.

Even within the same family, styles of reactivity can vary considerably. As an example, Edward, a successful lobbyist, is usually creative, charismatic, and composed at work. But at home when he gets ratcheted up by his neighbor's conservative political signs or his rebellious teenage sons' behavior, he has a pattern of reacting in an almost histrionic fashion—becoming hotheaded, delivering character assassinations, and giving voice to worst-case scenarios that could (but probably wouldn't) happen. Meanwhile, his wife Stella, who is down to earth and measured by nature, often finds herself thrust into the role of referee or peacemaker during family conflicts, when what she really wants to do is withdraw and go for a walk in the woods. It wasn't until they went to couples' counseling that Edward realized how damaging his style was, and Stella recognized how this dance of reactivity was contributing to her own buried emotional inflammation.

It's crucial to understand the contours and contents of your own style of emotional inflammation before trying to take steps to relieve the emotional hyperreactivity or pervasive angst or dread you've been experiencing. Otherwise, it would be like trying to treat an injury or an illness without knowing what it is: you might end up applying heat to a sprained ankle when ice and compression would be more therapeutic (since heat could actually *exacerbate* the swelling), or you might take an antihistamine for nasal congestion due to a cold virus when a decongestant would be more effective. In other words, you need to know what you're dealing with (how to *name* it and *frame* it) before you can try to alleviate (or *tame*) how you're feeling. Once you identify and name your reactive style, you can start to gain control.

Let's pause for a little background: Social intelligence refers to our ability to pick up on the emotions of others—the dynamics in relationships, what we sense about others, and how we put that awareness to use. The higher our social intelligence, the more accurately and quickly we can identify not only what is happening emotionally in the world around us but how to engage in productive interactions and collaborations. Emotional intelligence is more about knowing our internal feeling states. The higher our emotional intelligence, the better we are able to accurately recognize and understand the nuances of our personal emotions moment to moment. Both of these forms of intelligence can influence the way you respond to triggers of emotional inflammation.

While you might have a prevailing reactor type, you might behave differently in different settings or with different people, depending on whether you're interacting with loved ones, friends, colleagues, or strangers. The most socially and emotionally intelligent people moderate their styles depending on whom they're dealing with and what the circumstances are. The goal is to understand what your impulses are so that you can help yourself better navigate sharp turns and potholes that appear on the road of life. Remember, too, that your primary identification with a particular form of reactivity can shift over time just like the manifestations of anxiety, depression, and grief can evolve with the passage of weeks, months, or years.

The quest is to identify the currently dominant form(s) of emotional inflammation you're experiencing so that you can begin to take effective steps to quell it and restore your emotional equilibrium. Understanding your unique triggers and reactions will help you find the most effective ways to relieve *your* emotional inflammation so that your body and mind can return to a more balanced state. The quiz that follows is designed to tease out which of four reactor types you have. Keep in mind that you might identify with more than one set of feelings or responses to triggers in each scenario that's presented—and that's perfectly fine. Many of us have hybrid forms of emotional inflammation based on our own unique blend of reactions to the chaos and crises in our midst, deeply held fears and worries, and thinking styles.

DISCOVERING YOUR TYPE

To embark on this self-discovery process, read the following questions and make a note of *all* the responses that resonate with you, including fleeting thoughts you might have about them. Even if there isn't a response that suits you perfectly, pick the one(s) that comes closest. This means you can choose more than one answer per question. Don't judge or censor your responses (no one is watching); instead, be fully transparent with yourself and answer as honestly as you can. (If no answer feels exactly right, pick the one that comes closest to resonating with you.)

1. When you're driving somewhere, commuting, walking the dog, taking a shower, or doing something else that doesn't require conscious thought, and your mind wanders, where might it go?

    a. I may imagine worst-case scenarios that could happen with issues I'm worried about in my personal life or the world at large.

b. I might start thinking about what I could or should do to try to exert more control in my life.

c. I tend to feel irritated with others or frustrated with the human race in general and want to express those feelings.

d. Usually I just think about getting through the day; if I go beyond that, I might fantasize about how I can protect myself from the conflict and hostility around me.

2. When you think about what worries or preoccupies you the most, what are you naturally inclined to do?

a. I'm likely to start to feel on edge or rattled and get overly anxious about even minor stressors.

b. I'd get busy thinking of ways to deal with the problem and get others to do the same, by getting involved in actions that address the issue.

c. I may become testy and lash out at others more easily over seemingly minor transgressions.

d. I would probably plan ways to comfort myself later by doing something that's easy like binge-watching favorite shows, hanging out with a pet, or engaging in another chill-out activity.

3. What are some of the most common themes in your dreams these days?

a. Apocalyptic themes or scenarios about getting lost or stuck in a dark or deep place or being surrounded by threatening or untrustworthy people.

b. Driving and the brakes stop working properly, or a sense that time is running out or things are falling on me.

    c. Being wronged, demeaned, or bullied, or getting back at others for the wrongs they've committed.

    d. Floating in a calm ocean and seeing land from afar but not wanting to approach it.

4. When you're stressed, what kinds of situations or activities tend to make you feel *worse*?

    a. Talking to people who have similar worries—hearing other people's fears and anxieties ratchets up my own.

    b. Being told to slow down and relax, especially by people who fail to see the urgency behind some of the issues I care about.

    c. Being around people who challenge my beliefs and values or my "take" on current events.

    d. Feeling judged as lazy or antisocial when I retreat or need personal time.

5. When you read the newspaper or online newsfeeds and find out about the latest scandal, crisis, or threat, how do you typically respond?

    a. I feel nervous and find it difficult to deal with events that disrupt my sometimes fragile equilibrium.

    b. I tend to feel revved up because I feel like I have to be hypervigilant in order to stay on top of what's going on; I'm likely to keep checking for updates.

    c. I get PO'd about what a dangerous circus the world has turned into and may become antagonistic toward people who challenge me.

    d. I vow to avoid news reports and find myself withdrawing from people and activities to conserve my energy.

6. When you first wake up in the morning, what thoughts and feelings typically go through your mind?

    a. I often have a vague sense of foreboding about what the day will bring and a fear that I don't have enough stamina to meet the demands I'll face.

    b. I need to pop out of bed and get started on my to-do list ASAP, so I can avoid the tsunami of issues that may amp me up.

    c. I often focus on the injustices and misbehavior from the day before that made me feel disrespected or even outraged.

    d. I usually want to roll over and go back to sleep.

7. When you think about the world ten years from now, what does it look like?

    a. It seems dark and frightening, with more storms, floods, and fires, an increasingly dysfunctional society, and troubled political leadership.

    b. It looks frantic and chaotic; people should be busy creating plans and stockpiling provisions for survival.

    c. It seems increasingly violent and mistrustful, because political institutions have abdicated their responsibility for protecting us and people are looking out for themselves.

    d. Honestly, I'd do just about anything to avoid thinking about it.

8. When you imagine hosting a large family dinner after a hectic week, what thoughts come to mind?

    a. I start stressing out about whether the food will be good enough and whether everyone will get along.

    b. Thoughts fly through my mind about cleaning up the house, setting the table, envisioning the menu, and completing other tasks—and I feel like I am on a runaway train.

    c. I might feel resentful that once again I'm going to be doing a disproportionate amount of the work, physically or emotionally.

    d. I start thinking about how to get out of various tasks that are required. I have a *What's the point?* feeling.

9. When you hear about bad things (such as a life-threatening illness or a serious accident) happening to people you care about, what feelings typically go through your mind?

    a. I often feel like danger is getting too close for comfort, and the protective layers in my life are wearing away.

    b. I tend to push my feelings aside and swing into what-needs-to-be-done mode.

    c. I often wrestle with feelings about how unfair life is.

    d. I tend to focus on the randomness of life, which makes me want to take cover to protect myself.

10. When you're in a social situation that's discordant with your (political, parental, or personal) values, how do you typically react?

    a. I want to change or neutralize the topic of conversation to avoid conflict.

    b. I might unleash a laundry list of injustices and other problems that disprove their assertions.

    c. I might get confrontational and question other people's judgment or morals.

    d. I might disengage in that moment and consider not spending time with these people in the future.

11. When you find out about a new highly destructive storm, horrifying crime against humanity, or other upsetting event, how do you generally feel physically?

    a. Vulnerable or afraid

    b. Jittery and amped up

    c. Hot and tense

    d. Depleted or exhausted

12. When you consider whether your inner aspirations and the realities of your external life reflect each other or are in sync, what are you inclined to feel?

    a. Uneasy and insecure

    b. Pressured and impatient

    c. Cheated and disillusioned

    d. Discouraged and wistful

Count up how many As, Bs, Cs, and Ds you selected, then read the corresponding analyses that describe you (remember: you can relate to more than one reactor type so read all the ones that apply to you).

- **If you chose mostly As, you're a *nervous* reactor.** It looks like you have the anxious, worried, or fearful form of emotional inflammation. These days, you may feel like you're swimming among ill-defined or unnamed threats and as though various hidden impediments are swirling around you. You may not know what's really bothering you or making you feel unsettled (and you may not *want* to know because it's too upsetting), but you do know that you don't feel good. You may even have multiple alarms going off in your head at various volumes, which may have a distracting effect and prevent specific unidentified fears from rising to the surface. Research has found that this heightened emotional reactivity may stem from adverse experiences (such as maltreatment, family instability, or financial hardship) during childhood; moving forward, it can also set the stage for the development of mood and anxiety disorders in adulthood.

We all have a sixth sense, and yours is indicating that something is not right. It's an important instinct that keeps you attuned to potential threats and evolving conditions. The upside is that if there's danger lurking, whether it's big, small, or in between, you are not going to be the person who misses the signs or falsely reassures everyone. The potential downside is that if you can't turn off your worries, or you don't make an attempt to better understand them, they can become a source of internal stress and friction. What you want to do is take your anxiety, saddle it up, and get some embedded energy out of it (which you'll learn how to do in later chapters).

- **If you chose mostly Bs, you're a *revved-up* reactor.** Your responses suggest that you have the frantic, hyperreactive form of emotional inflammation. Chances are, you have an endless list of things you feel that you could, should, or must do—and you're probably telling yourself that you should be moving or acting faster than you are to change the status quo in your own life or in the world at large. On the surface, this gotta-gotta-gotta style may seem proactive but deep down it may help you avoid thinking about what's really upsetting you. Your incessant activity can serve as white noise that drowns out the unsettling or dark feelings you may have. Researchers sometimes call this tendency "negative urgency," which is a propensity to act impulsively when you experience negative emotions or stress; the problem is, doing so can compromise your self-control.

Underneath the frantic behavior, you probably feel committed to righting the wrongs of the world, which means you have strong energy and goodwill. You recognize that people and the planet are hurting, and that there's a barrage of issues that need attention and it's important to act. The fact that you haven't organized your efforts efficiently or prioritized your actions shouldn't be held against you (so don't hold this against yourself!). Instead, consider this an opportunity to handle things better. To get there, it might help to ask yourself the following questions: *What's most important right now? Where or how can I be particularly effective in this situation?* The key is to figure out what you can do uniquely or especially well, then deliberately and consciously go about executing those actions.

- **If you chose mostly Cs, you're a *molten* reactor.** It appears that your emotional inflammation is largely marked by irritation, maybe even anger and/or indignation. You may feel embattled, shortchanged, frustrated, and/or fed up that "the world is a mess" because of other people's stupidity, greed, ineptitude, and/or selfishness. This ongoing state of aggravation can make you feel inclined to push back against people or situations that don't jibe with your values or playbook; or, you may feel like your annoyance needs to be expressed in order to get people to be more responsible in their behavior and accountable for their actions. As a result, you may find yourself susceptible to occasional bursts of outrage, sarcasm, or righteousness.

When bad stuff is happening in your immediate surroundings or the world at large, and good people are being hurt, getting mad is a natural and appropriate response to injustice. The goal isn't to suppress your anger or turn it inward. In fact, research has found that anger inhibition can increase your blood pressure during stressful tasks. What you want to do, instead, is acknowledge how angry you are and then take that moral outrage and indignation and turn it into something constructive. To do that, it helps to look for kinship with others who are equally outraged and determined to change things. You want to use your energy to fuel social change with constructive action—to channel it and direct it. Change occurs when people put their efforts together, not when one person rants and raves or busts up the place.

- **If you chose mostly Ds, you're a** *retreating* **reactor.** Your emotional inflammation is marked by a tendency to freeze, detach, withdraw, zone out, or numb yourself. Deep down inside, you may believe that what you feel or do doesn't make a difference, which can create a sense of powerlessness, depletion, despair, and/or resignation. This constellation of unfortunate feelings can make you feel physically and emotionally spent, unmotivated, and unfocused. It also can erode your belief in your personal ability to effect a meaningful degree of change or even humanity's ability to do so, which can make you inclined to retreat farther into yourself.

Consider the possibility that you may be among the gentle souls in an aggressive and competitive world. Perhaps you feel pain when you see unkindness toward others—or maybe it withers you spiritually, which can fuel your instinct to withdraw. Given the harshness of our culture, especially right now, it's understandable that you'd want to retreat to a place where peace, solitude, and/or coexistence are more attainable. This is a coping mechanism. But it doesn't end up helping you or anyone else. Instead, research suggests that it can lead to emotional inertia, causing you to get stuck in negative states of mind, which can increase your vulnerability to depression. Remind yourself to slow down and reflect on some of the more abstract issues you're struggling with on an emotional level. Remember that you're a part of nature and the fabric of humanity; you don't exist in isolation. Whether you realize it or not, you're seeking a harmonious connection with your surroundings. It's time to start taking steps in the right direction, rather than retreating inside yourself.

COOLING THE REACTOR INSIDE YOU

Now that you've identified your primary inflammatory feelings and reactive tendencies, you can begin to become more aware of how and when they flare up. This will allow you to be more conscious of the ways in which emotional inflammation affects you on a regular basis. This is the first step toward putting yourself in a better position to quiet the emotional storms you're weathering. Given the unpredictable atmosphere that we're currently living in—especially when it comes to political dissent, economic instability, human rights violations, gun violence, war and terrorism, environmental threats, and the unspooling havoc of ongoing climate change—it would be a mistake to count on the external world to calm down anytime soon. It's unlikely to happen.

It's up to each of us to grab the reins on our emotional reactivity and begin to cultivate a state of steadier calm inside us. The goal is not to change your inherent personality or your natural inclinations—those are part of what make you uniquely and distinctively *you*. Rather, the idea is to help you learn to navigate and manage your emotions more adeptly by gaining greater awareness and insights into yourself and greater versatility in terms of how you view and deal with the world.

It's a good idea to read about all the different reactor types because you may have loved ones or close friends with different styles; getting them to take the quiz can help you better understand each other. It's not your responsibility to manage other people's emotions, but understanding their reactive styles can help you figure out how to deal with them or communicate with them more effectively, especially in times of tension or conflict. Plus, we can all learn from each other's styles, because each of these reactor types represents a survival strategy that has helped us thrive in one situation or another. In and of themselves, these reactor types are not inherently unhealthy or healthy, maladaptive or adaptive; it's how you express them that matters. It's the elasticity, awareness, and management skills of the individual that render these styles useful or not. So try to cultivate self-acceptance and self-compassion as well as compassion for how other people react.

Not long ago, Marisa, a hedge-fund manager, was having difficulty understanding and connecting with her twenty-three-year-old daughter, Angie. There was frequent low-level friction between them that exasperated them both. Marisa is a go-getter by nature, while Angie, a writer, is sensitive and introspective. When Angie felt rattled by her mother, or she just needed to recharge, she would withdraw. By contrast, Marisa would try to address the strain between them head-on by asking questions and seeking clarification. Her efforts routinely backfired and stirred up more tension between them, along with feelings of rejection.

When Marisa talked to a therapist friend about the situation, the friend suggested that it may be due, at least in part, to stylistic differences in the ways they attempted to cope with stress. She recommended that Marisa try to bridge the gulf between them just by being kind and more accepting. When Marisa adjusted her style along these lines, the temperature between mother and daughter came down immediately. Over time, Marisa took a consistently gentler approach in relating to Angie, which gradually built up the trust between them and smoothed the turbulent waters. Marisa also gained some insight into the sense of calm that she didn't realize she was missing.

The challenge in managing your own reactivity style is a bit like trying to become a better driver. The reality is, you won't ever be able to control the weather, the driving conditions, or the behavior of other drivers around you. But you can practice and hone smart, safe skills that will allow you to steer and adjust your speed, be aware of the potholes and blind spots, maintain control in the face of the unexpected, and change lanes when you need to. In the context of your emotional well-being, developing these skills can help you avert or get out of a psychological or behavioral rut in which you're consistently responding to triggers in a certain way. It can help you avoid using tunnel vision where you can no longer see important issues clearly. It can help you sidestep friction with people who have different values or emotional styles. And it can help you dodge the emotional whiplash or repetitive emotional strain you might experience if you were to continuously react to every alarming news bulletin that comes along.

Developing a more nuanced appreciation of your psychological landscape and the triggers that frequently rile you will put you more firmly in the driver's seat of your emotional life. This is where you belong and where you need to be if you're going to be able to steer yourself toward greater emotional equilibrium. But first, you'll need to become highly attuned to the hazards and vicissitudes you might encounter along the way. As former professional racecar driver Jeff Gordon once said, "I don't think what makes a good race car driver is a fearless person. I think it's somebody that is comfortable being behind the wheel of something that's somewhat out of control." That pretty well sums up the challenges of navigating our turbulent world.

CHAPTER 3

THE

INFLAMMATORY

CASCADE

Inflammation has
always been a medical
mystery, but now it
has become an enemy
of long-term health.

DEEPAK CHOPRA, MD, and RUDOLPH E. TANZI, PhD,
coauthors of *The Healing Self*

T'S HARD TO FATHOM the possibility that an internal defense mechanism that could save your life also could turn against you and threaten your health and well-being. It sounds like a fictional form of biological mutiny, but it can happen, and it does with inflammation. Normally, inflammation, which is triggered by the immune system, is beneficial because it helps your body fight off disease-causing germs and repair injured tissue. When the battle has been won, inflammation is supposed to cease and desist. When it doesn't, chronic, low-grade inflammation, which is invisible to the naked eye, can occur and have a harmful effect on your organs, blood vessels, and cells. Chronic systemic inflammation corrodes the body's tissues, creating a degenerative spiral such that the more inflammation you have, the more at risk you are for developing chronic diseases such as heart disease, diabetes, and certain forms of cancer. In addition, systemic physical inflammation can impair your cognitive processes, impeding your ability to think and reason clearly, exercise good judgment, and access your memory bank. Over the long term, it has even been linked to dementia, while in the short term, it can affect your mood states. Indeed, inflammation in the brain is closely associated with a number of emotional conditions, including depression, anxiety disorders, bipolar disorder, PTSD, and others. Although depression is not an inflammatory disorder per se, a substantial body of literature shows the two are related. Mounting evidence suggests that the two conditions are not only closely connected, but they also may actually fuel each other. That's the story with hidden physical inflammation.

As I've seen in my practice, a similar downward spiral can happen with emotional inflammation. No matter what kind of reactor type you are, exposure to your personal triggers and the emotional inflammation that results can incite a flood of ill effects that can eat away at your well-being. Life in the modern world is challenging enough, so when people hear about the latest political scandal, human rights violation, environmental threat to human health, or metastatic climate issues that are threatening already fragile world states, they start to wonder, *How and where can we be safe? Who is going to take care of us? What kind of legacy are we leaving our children?* The images and thoughts that come to mind as you try to answer these questions can trigger a cascade of negative thoughts and emotions that may ricochet off each other. Or they can lead to anger, despair, or a state of behavioral or mental paralysis where you might feel unable to take action to improve matters.

Emotional inflammation stems from responses that are physiological and psychological. Physiologically, the sympathetic nervous system (SNS) and parasympathetic nervous system (PSNS) are like a teeter-totter—each is weighted according to the body's needs at any given time. In times of threat, the SNS dominates because it prepares us to fight or flee. In contrast, the PSNS takes over when the effort to restore or maintain calm is called for. Their interplay contributes to our internal equilibrium. When this particular system of checks and balances between the SNS and the PSNS works well, you're likely to feel good, physically and emotionally. In times of acute peril—if you were to encounter a potential threat, say, a rattlesnake ready to strike in the woods, a menacing driver on the highway, or someone following you on a dark street—your body is designed to optimize your chances of survival, thanks to its inherent stress response. This is the commonly referred to fight-or-flight response where your heart and respiration rates shoot up, your blood flow and blood pressure increase, and your muscles contract so that you can fight or run for your life.

Optimal energy is delivered to the parts of the body that need it most, while bodily functions that aren't critical in the fight for survival are put on hold.

Meanwhile, key areas of the brain, including the amygdala (which assesses and reacts to threats), are activated to appraise the severity of the threat you're facing and race to throw a plan into action. In life-threatening (or what may feel like life-threatening) instances, the prefrontal cortex—which is usually in the driver's seat as the brain's chief command center, keeping our impulses and snap judgments in check—starts to go dark, as the fired-up amygdala gets the upper hand and takes the wheel. The brain's neural circuitry is hijacked, greatly ratcheting up your fear, anxiety, and aggression, making it even harder to think clearly. Careful planning and measured thoughts are sacrificed in this time of urgency. Decisions are neither carefully weighed nor reviewed. When this happens, responses are primal. These physiological changes are part of the inherent survival mechanisms that allow us to react to emergencies, stand up to threats, and defend ourselves and our loved ones with swift action.

But what about situations that simply *feel* threatening? Threats that trigger our survival mechanisms come in a variety of sizes and shapes, and few are as dramatic as those just described. That sort of stress response would be way over the top if, for example, you got into another political argument at work, received a sky-high bill you can't cover, or witnessed some repugnant or disrespectful behavior. With everyday sources of upset such as these, your body's stress response can overreact; it can jump the gun to deliver an over-the-top response. The more often this happens, the more damaging it is to your health and well-being. In his book *The End of Stress as We Know It*, Bruce McEwen, PhD, notes, "The human mind is so powerful, the connections between perception and physiological response so strong, that we can set off the fight-or-flight response by just imagining ourselves in a threatening situation."

The body is *not designed* to handle chronic emotional stress. Living in a persistent or frequently triggered state of high anxiety, fear, or dread causes your body's fight-or-flight response to get stuck in the "on" position. When this happens, your sympathetic nervous system stays revved up, flooding your mind and body with the stress hormones cortisol and adrenaline. Your heart rate, breathing, blood flow, and blood pressure may stay elevated, and white blood cells go on a search-and-destroy mission that can end up attacking your own tissues and organs—which accounts for widespread inflammation. Chronic stress also pulls resources away from needs that become relegated to second tier status, such as digestive and reproductive functions. (This is why fertility and sex drive often drop when someone is under chronic stress.)

In addition to straining your cardiovascular system and disrupting your immune, endocrine, neural, and metabolic functions, chronic stress can even amp up your pain response. That's how the very system that was evolutionarily designed to protect you from harm can become a threat in itself. As molecular biologist John Medina notes in *Brain Rules*, "Our stress responses were shaped to solve problems that lasted not for years, but for seconds . . . when moderate amounts of stress hormones build up to large amounts, or hang around too long, they become quite harmful."

THE POTENTIAL PHYSICAL FALLOUT

As described earlier, the term *allostatic load* refers to the stress-induced wear and tear on the brain and body that can accelerate the aging process and lead to a range of health problems. Allostatic load can occur in a number of ways: when psychological stress continues unabated, when your mind or body doesn't adjust to an ongoing source of stress, or when the stressful event has ended but your body and mind haven't calmed down. In circumstances where the stress response is unable to shut down, your brain and body are subjected to continuous waves of alarming messages, including surges of stress hormones.

People who suffer substantial accumulations of psychological, social, or environmental stress are at risk for having the regulation of their physiological stress response disrupted. Some people seem to be more vulnerable to a heightened reactivity to stress than others are. This may be because of their genetic makeup or their experiences with previous traumas. Some lifestyle factors such as insufficient sleep and taking certain medications can increase stress. Stimulants, steroids, antiseizure drugs, and certain antidepressants can all magnify angry or aggressive feelings. Exposure to certain chemicals such as PBDEs (polybrominated diphenyl ethers), flame retardants that are in many consumer products, can amplify the activation of the sympathetic nervous system during stress. On the other end of the spectrum, beta-blockers, other antihypertensives, and Parkinson's drugs can make you feel more depressed or fatigued. The point is, it's wise to be aware that, on a regular basis, unknown and unexpected exposure to many substances can heighten your reactivity to stress.

The upshot of all this is that walking around with a swirling case of emotional inflammation—anxiety, a sense of foreboding, or a state of hyperarousal—can take a toll on your body and mind in just about every conceivable way. It can have enduring ripple effects—physically, mentally, emotionally, behaviorally, socially, and spiritually.

GENDER DIFFERENCES IN THE STRESS RESPONSE

Given the gender gap in many areas of health, it's not surprising that note-worthy differences exist in the ways men and women respond to stress physiologically. Research has found, for example, that when men and

continues

women experience acute stress, the right side of the amygdala gets fired up in men's brains, and the left side of the amygdala lights up in women's. This is worth noting because the right side tends to remember the *gist of the experience* while the left side tends to recall the *details of the emotional components*. This may help explain why men recall the basic facts of a stressful event, while women remember the emotional feelings and implications that were elicited, notes Larry Cahill, PhD, a professor of neurobiology at the University of California, Irvine. Incredibly, Cahill explains, these "sex-related hemispheric disparities in how the brain processes emotional images begin within 300 milliseconds — long before people have had much, if any, chance to consciously interpret what they have seen."

There are other differences as well. When men and women are faced with a challenging task, such as engaging in public speaking or doing a tricky math problem, both sexes report high levels of subjective stress; however, men have a significantly more robust cortisol response to both tasks than women do.

Also, men and women appear to use different neural resources while experiencing stress-induced anxiety. Using functional magnetic resonance imaging to examine the participants' brain responses, researchers at Yale University had ninety-six healthy men and women engage in a guided imagery exercise designed to induce stress or relaxation. During the stress-inducing imagery, men displayed greater responses in the areas of the brain (the caudate, midbrain, anterior cingulate cortex, and thalamus) that are involved in doing something after considering the possible costs and consequences, known as "instrumental action," and in motor functions. By contrast, women showed greater responses in brain areas associated with emotional experiences, verbal expression, and visual processing — namely, the posterior insula, temporal gyrus, and occipital lobe.

The message here is that it's a mistake to assume that men and women who are exposed to the same stressors are reacting to them or processing them the same way on a physiological level, let alone on an emotional one. *Remember this the next time you have a conflict with a member of the opposite sex!*

MENTAL AND EMOTIONAL STRAIN

Feeling unsafe, hyperreactive, and fearful about the future can lead to a continuous loop of peril that plays in your head, cognitively and physiologically. These feelings are not only symptoms of chronic stress, they can be drivers of it by perpetuating the stress response. After all, prolonged surges of cortisol and other stress hormones can increase feelings of anxiety and depression. This continuous stress reaction can trigger an array of emotions including anger, grief, sadness, or worry, that can turn into impotent rage, fear, or despair. It can lead to disturbing intrusive thoughts or sleep troubles and nightmares. For some, it leads to burnout and withdrawal. It can compromise your ability to focus or concentrate, learn or remember essential information, and function at your cognitive best in other ways.

It also can throw you into a state of rumination, where you brood, mull, or obsess over an issue so that these thoughts play like a broken record in your mind. Or it can lead to anticipatory anxiety, where you worry about something that could, but might not, happen in the future, or to emotional drift, whereby one anxiety ignites another. It can also cause you to catastrophize, where you imagine worst-case scenarios that could happen. Any way you slice it, this is a crippling way to live and work.

This nonstop stress reaction is also associated with a state of learned helplessness and feelings of powerlessness that can throw you into a state of behavioral paralysis. It can lead you to try to avoid situations or activities that remind you of what you've come to fear, or it can cause you to feel unable to take constructive action to improve matters. On the other hand, some people have a tendency to push themselves to go faster—to cram their lives with more activities or to seek more stimulation—in an effort to distract themselves or get away from the angst. It's almost as if they believe subconsciously that rushing through life will help them avoid the discomfort of fully processing or existing in these frantic, unstable times.

Whichever reaction styles resonate with you, the effects are similar. When your brain's prefrontal cortex takes a backseat to the amygdala during ongoing sensations of stress, the neurotransmitters that would normally keep your emotions in check are not sufficiently available, and you can end up, instead, experiencing an overwhelming tide of uncomfortable emotions.

In his compelling book *The Body Keeps the Score*, Bessel van der Kolk, MD, refers to the "emotional brain," whose primary task is to protect your welfare. That sounds helpful enough, but the emotional brain assesses information in a very general way and often "jumps to conclusions based on rough similarities." Within the emotional brain, he notes, "these reactions are automatic, set in motion without any thought or planning on our part, leaving our conscious, rational capacities to catch up later." His book is about the effects of serious psychological trauma (from, say, engaging in combat or being the victim of violence or abuse), but these effects also occur with more mundane but persistent sources of anguish or distress. It's just a matter of degree.

A priming effect can occur such that when you're in the throes of emotional inflammation, you become much more sensitive to the next crisis or stressor that comes along, both physiologically and psychologically. What this means is that a less intense stimulus or stressor can elicit a stronger physical and/or emotional response than it would normally. In a study in Switzerland, healthy participants were shown microsecond bursts of images of a fearful face or an emotionally neutral face while they looked at color words. The exposures were so brief that they were "subliminal stimuli"; that is, the participants were not consciously aware of the images. After viewing the color words and the faces, the participants performed a stressful task. Those who were shown the fearful face experienced a significant increase in cortisol levels after the stressful task, while those who saw the neutral face did not! In essence, a form of fear priming, below the level of conscious awareness, *increased* the participants' responses to subsequent stressful stimuli.

Similarly, researchers from the University of Utah did an experiment to gauge whether subliminally activating people's thoughts of their personal relationships—including supportive, indifferent, aversive, and ambivalent ones—would influence their stress responses to challenging math and speech tasks. The answer turned out to be a resounding *yes*. Those who were primed with random, forty-three-millisecond flashes of the names of people with whom they had negative relationships exhibited greater feelings of threat, lower feelings of control, and higher diastolic blood pressure reactivity during the stressful task. Those who were primed with the names of people they felt ambivalent about had the highest heart rate reactivity during the stressful task. These effects were true for both men and women.

When you're experiencing emotional inflammation, a similar phenomenon can occur: you can become more sensitive and/or react more strongly to the next threat or piece of bad news that comes along, or you might react to something that you wouldn't normally react to at all. In these instances, the subconscious mind takes the wheel, and more often than not we don't even realize that we've been primed to become upset. Once you're on the nervous edge, if you lose your footing, you can fall into the "stress abyss." Over time, swimming in a pool of toxic emotions can shrink the prefrontal cortex (the command post for self-awareness, self-control, foresight, and planning) and increase the size of the amygdala (the brain's fear and aggression center), changes that can make the brain even more reactive to stress.

Andrea, a forty-nine-year-old strategy and operations manager for a national nonprofit based in New York, became personally familiar with the priming effect, though she didn't know the name for it at the time. It started after the 9/11 terrorist attacks. She'd often start the day with the unsettling thought, *Is this the morning it happens again?* But her level of distress increased dramatically after the 2016 presidential election. "I felt so depressed by the whole dialogue, the vile nature of political discourse, the climate of intolerance and divisiveness we're living with," she said. "It's had a negative cascade effect on me: I'm tripped up by things like navigating technology or having difficult conversations at work that didn't used to give me anxiety. I'm not an obsessor by nature, but I often end up anxiously ruminating these days."

Andrea also said that since the election she had been drinking wine "twice as much, twice as often" as she used to, to try to numb her anxiety. She's hardly alone: alcohol consumption has increased dramatically in the US in recent years, with high-risk drinking (defined as four or more drinks in a day for women, five or more in a day for men) rising by 30 percent.

In addition to consuming alcohol, some people end up trying to numb their distressed feelings with medications, food, and other substances, or empty activities like endlessly shopping or playing video games. They seek instant relief or gratification with these behaviors in an instinctive effort to try to tamp down, mask, or undo their emotional distress. But seeking immediate relief compromises the sophistication of the choices you make. Behavioral myopia—taking action based on what feels good right now without considering the possible consequences—can keep people in denial about what's really going on with them. This is true with alcohol consumption, for example. Because having a glass of wine or two (or three) impairs someone's perception and thought processes to some degree, drinking can reduce anxiety by making it harder for the individual to focus on the thoughts and issues that provoke that angst; instead, the person's thoughts become narrowed.

Sometimes, too, pervasive fear and anxiety might cause you to avoid going to public places that had brought pleasure in the past, such as concerts, museums, or even shopping malls or nightclubs, or engaging in experiences such as demonstrations or marches. The hidden agenda might be to encapsulate yourself in a protective bubble or to avoid stimulation that might set you off emotionally. Or, if you continue to go to these venues, you might find yourself engaging in compulsive checking behaviors.

Recently, Stephen, a fifty-nine-year-old lawyer in Washington, DC, realized that he had adopted a habit of immediately looking for the exits when he enters museums, airports, theaters, department stores, conference halls, and other public places. He also mentally rehearses reacting to a threat if one were to occur and thinks about ways to try to mitigate the perpetrator's ability to harm people. "It has become automatic for me to do this—I don't consciously think about it," he says, "but it impedes my ability to fully enjoy what I'm seeing or doing." He added that these changes in behavior were a response to the increased gun violence and mass shootings in the US.

Whether you're in hypervigilance mode or denial, or you're acknowledging how you're really feeling, the insidious effects of emotional inflammation can harm your physical and emotional well-being in ways that sneak up on you. Your lifestyle practices, including what you eat and drink, whether you smoke, how often you exercise, and whether you get enough good quality sleep, also can stimulate the production of adrenaline, cortisol, and other elements of the stress response (the hypothalamic-pituitary-adrenal, or HPA, pathway axis). These dynamics contribute to a round-robin of distressing thoughts and feelings that can alter your behavior and damage your health, which in turn upsets your emotional equilibrium. And the effects don't stop there.

SOCIAL AND SPIRITUAL STRESS

By nature, human beings are social creatures, although some of us are more so than others. We have the capacity to relate to and care for each other, and to cooperate and support each other. And we benefit from these connections. Indeed, numerous studies have demonstrated the positive effects of social support on physical health and emotional well-being, including resilience to stress.

Unfortunately, emotional inflammation can take a toll on this aspect of our lives too. The harm from living in a state of high alert, helplessness, restlessness, or emptiness can seep down to our unconscious, unsettling our social proclivities and even our very souls. When there are big problems—as there are with the significant issues that are upsetting people these days—and no easy answers, the inclination to take action may become blunted. This can manifest in what social psychologists call the "bystander effect," in which a throng of people may witness something dreadful and instead of taking action, they just stand around or at most simply wring their hands. On a greater scale, the bystander effect is in play when large segments of the population observe social, political, and environmental wrongdoing but take little or no action. This anxiety-laced inaction, denial about the gravity of the situation, and relinquishing of responsibility can become the social norm—the expected, accepted behavior. But this paralysis ends up making us feel even more traumatized, as it stands in the way of behaviors that, driven by empowering actions, can reduce anxiety.

Living in a time of disgraced heroes—where professional athletes and coaches, politicians, military leaders, actors and producers, writers, and other people we once admired are taking a spectacular fall from grace due to their personal misconduct—adds to a feeling of bewilderment, cynicism, and loss. For young and old alike, having mentors, role models, heroes, or people we look up to can be uplifting and inspiring, encouraging us to dig deeper to find our best selves and aspire to greatness. So it's understandable that wondering how to reconcile admiring someone professionally while disapproving of his or her personal conduct can lead to the mental discomfort of cognitive dissonance (a term you may remember from Psych 101). These stressors can have destabilizing effects and can rob us of our *joie de vivre*—with unsettling ramifications both in our personal lives and in our deeper spiritual selves.

People often experience spiritual distress when they're battling life-threatening illnesses or facing end-of-life decisions. Military combat veterans who have seen or participated in morally injurious events suffer more from anxiety, depression, and PTSD than most people do; they also have higher-than-average levels of spiritual or religious turmoil. These connections are not surprising. What's more startling and more concerning is that increasing numbers of people who *haven't* experienced objectively traumatic events are also grappling with spiritual distress, existential dread or angst, or *weltschmerz*, which means "world pain" in German. (It describes a world weariness that stems from the discrepancy between how one wants the world to be and how it really is.)

I am seeing these struggles of the soul increasingly in my practice. In addition, it's becoming more common to encounter climate activists, media professionals, political types, office workers, and others who feel disengaged or want to escape the turmoil of the modern world. In my work with Our Children's Trust, I became sensitized to and started working more broadly with young people who are grappling with deeply traumatizing issues related to the climate crisis and the future they will be inheriting. Many young people do not want to have children because of the cost to the planet of adding another person and the fear of bringing a child into a chaotic world. Our government's unwillingness to protect our planet, despite the scientific consensus on the dangers, has unleashed a profound sense of cynicism. A feeling of futility is seeping into the lives of some young people during what should be an uplifting time of idealism and discovery and dreams for the future. Many lament the irresponsibility of adults and feel angry about the mounting responsibilities that are being heaped on them. Is it any wonder research suggests a correlation between problematic alcohol consumption and spiritual struggles among college students?

To be clear, I do not view these struggles of the soul as crises of religious faith but as struggles to maintain hope, empathy, compassion, and a sense of meaning and purpose in a world that feels to many like it is falling apart or going to hell. Having the feeling that life has no inherent value or significance or that your personal actions really don't matter can be either a driver or an amplifier of emotional inflammation. It can also be the *result* of emotional inflammation. When all three of these dynamics occur simultaneously, it's easy to become more fearful, angry, withdrawn, or agitated.

If anyone knows this, it's Catherine, a fifty-eight-year-old lawyer who has spent her entire career fighting for social and restorative justice, particularly for women, immigrants, and other disenfranchised people. A mother of four and a former foster parent in Chicago, she became a lawyer to try to make the world a better place, but in recent years she has increasingly questioned her ability to do so. "I spend a lot of time on social media because I'm afraid I'll miss something critical about what's happening in the world," she says. In particular, the discordant political climate and rampant human rights violations that have been grabbing headlines have ramped up her anxiety about the state of the world. Besides leading her to question her chosen life path, she has begun to lose hope for the future: "Many days, I'm not sure there will be a world that I'd want my grandchildren to live in," she says.

This kind of bleak outlook can penetrate the deepest parts of a person's psyche, affecting his or her thought patterns and actions, often unconsciously. When people lose a sense of meaning or purpose in their lives, they frequently stop looking for opportunities to expand their engagement with the world or to solve problems in their own lives and the world at large. They might stop taking care of their health or planning for the future because they don't want to (or can't) imagine it. Instead, they become focused on just getting through the day, handling challenges that arise in life as if they were playing a continuous Whac-a-Mole game.

Religion is becoming less important in the US and in other countries. In a 2017 survey of more than 5,000 adults in the US, 27 percent said they think of themselves as "spiritual" but not "religious," a *42 percent increase* from 2012; in 2017, an additional 18 percent indicated they are neither religious nor spiritual. These changes have occurred among people from all walks of life—men and women, Republicans and Democrats, and those of different races, ages, and education levels. *Is this an era characterized by a crisis of faith and hope?* The doubts and losses are there; whether this reflects the chaos and turmoil in the world, a deep-down cynicism, or other factors, we can't know for certain.

By any moniker—*spiritual emptiness, existential angst, weltschmerz,* or another term—it's clear that more and more people feel they're missing a connection to something important, to something larger than themselves. This spiritual void can be disorienting, perhaps making you feel aimless or rudderless in the world. But you don't have to accept this as the inescapable status quo, nor do you need to be at the mercy of the physiological and psychological stress processes inside you. In the chapters that follow, you'll discover myriad ways to dial down your hyperreactivity, calm your body and mind, and reclaim a sense of purpose, hope, and connection to others—despite living in a turbulent world. By using the right strategies and techniques, you'll be able to slow the emotional inflammation cascade and work your way instead toward a state of steady calm.

PART II

THE RESTORE PLAN: THE SCIENCE AND SOLUTIONS BEHIND COOLING DOWN

CHAPTER 4

RECOGNIZE

YOUR FEELINGS

Your intellect may
be confused, but
your emotions will
never lie to you.

ROGER EBERT,
the late Pulitzer-prize-winning film critic

T'S IN EVERYONE'S BEST interest to learn to remove the emotional blinders and identify emotions accurately, both the uncomfortable and the upbeat ones. After all, unpleasant emotions are normal and natural, a fundamental part of being human. Emotions fluctuate on a daily basis, often several times in a given day. If you didn't experience negative feelings now and then, the positive ones wouldn't be as noteworthy or joyful; your emotional life would likely be unnaturally narrow. You would also be deprived of the opportunity to glean important insights into yourself. Feelings, both the good and the bad, are silent messages, alerting you to pay attention to something in your personal or professional life, in your behavior, or in the world around you.

Instead of separating emotions into categories such as good or bad, positive or negative, happy or sad, it's better to view all your emotions as useful information, as "evolutionarily evolved responses that are uniquely *appropriate* to specific situations," says Karla McLaren, MEd, author of *The Language of Emotions.* "When you stop valencing, you'll learn to empathically respond to what's actually going on—and you'll learn how to observe emotions without demonizing them or glorifying them."

Being able to recognize and express what you're feeling helps you better understand yourself (leading to greater self-knowledge); validate your emotions and tend to your own emotional needs; and take steps to address those feelings directly by communicating and responding to them effectively. Having emotional self-awareness can motivate you to make healthy changes in your life, take action to improve the world around you, and become more psychologically resilient—that is, better able to cope with crises and rebound from setbacks.

FUN FACTS

Over the years, researchers have counted human emotions and come up with different numbers at different times. The latest research identifies twenty-seven discrete categories of emotion ranging from admiration and adoration to sympathy and triumph, with many different shades of meaning within each category. On average, people experience at least one emotion *90 percent* of the time they're awake—with an overall ratio of two-and-a-half times more positive ones than negative ones. Here's an eye-opener: People simultaneously experience mixed emotions—upbeat and uncomfortable ones (say, excitement and fear)—during one-third of their waking moments.

Some of these emotion-awareness benefits may seem counterintuitive because at first blush, trying to ignore unpleasant feelings of outrage, fear, despair, or [fill in the blank] may seem like a smart survival strategy in this chaotic world. It may feel like a promising way to stay poised and presentable, to safeguard your energy, and to prevent yourself from getting derailed by negative emotions. *After all, who wants to be at the mercy of their mood swings, hour after hour or day after day?* But this avoidance tactic can come back to haunt you in numerous ways. For one thing, people who aren't able to understand and put their distressing feelings into words may resort to maladaptive coping strategies such as overeating, binge drinking, smoking, compulsive shopping, gambling, or engaging in aggressive or self-injurious behavior. They may be more susceptible to chronic pain and have a higher risk of developing depression and anxiety. The tendency to squelch unpleasant emotions has even been found to impede executive functioning (your ability to plan, reason, and multitask), strain your heart during stressful tasks, and take a toll on your physical and emotional well-being in many other ways.

As an example, consider forty-five-year-old Joanna, a stay-at-home mother of two who worked hard to maintain a cheerful, energetic demeanor. She had a habit of keeping herself so busy with volunteer commitments, home-improvement projects, social activities, and exercise classes that she barely had time to think or register her emotions, much less recognize what they were trying to tell her. As a result, she often felt blindsided when something unexpected happened.

By contrast, thirty-year-old Nancy, a smart, successful media strategist, decided to enter therapy because she hoped that getting in touch with her feelings would help her become more successful with romantic relationships. When Nancy, whose arms were covered in scabs (under the long sleeves she wore, even during the summer), was asked how she was feeling about work, family issues, or other situations in her life, she would often draw a blank and become tongue-tied. She had excoriation disorder, a skin-picking condition that's related to obsessive-compulsive disorder. In her case, it was as if she were picking away at her feelings instead of acknowledging or examining them; she simply didn't know what she was feeling on any meaningful level.

Where do these kinds of emotional disconnect come from? For some people, it's a matter of not having the right vocabulary to specifically name their feelings, perhaps because our culture doesn't offer formal education to help people develop emotional awareness and a language that reflects emotional intelligence. Some people may have been raised with the notion that they shouldn't focus on their emotions, that it's more effective to try to be strong and stoic. Still others may naturally lack the basic self-awareness to be able to tell how they feel, other than perhaps unsettled or "off." Like Miss Clavel in Ludwig Bemelmans's Madeline series, they may sense that *something is not right*, but they're unable to discern what exactly is wrong in terms of their feelings. There's a phenomenon called "alexithymia," which is characterized by a person's inability to identify and describe his or her emotions; it's as if these folks can see emotions only in black and white, rather than in a kaleidoscope of vivid hues. It's a lackluster and perilous way of living and moving through the world, to be sure.

Sometimes simply being able to attach a name to an uncomfortable feeling can help ease it. Research shows that being able to accept your negative emotions without judging them—a process some psychologists refer to as "habitual acceptance"—can help you feel less stress during and after challenging everyday situations, which improves overall psychological health. This isn't surprising, considering that these traits are part of emotional competence (a.k.a. emotional intelligence), which encompasses the ability to identify, understand, express, regulate, and use your emotions wisely. Besides making it easier to navigate life smoothly, emotional competence is associated with better mental health, more satisfying relationships, greater occupational success, and greater overall happiness.

The conundrum is this: *How do you identify your feelings if you've been in the habit of trying to ignore them, suppress them, or otherwise avoid them?* It's not an easy switch to make. To get to the essential truth behind your feelings, it helps to try to unpack them, bit by bit, so that you can differentiate between closely related emotions such as anger, irritation, or outrage. Being able to really home in on how or what you're feeling is essential to cultivate emotional clarity and emotional granularity, which means the ability to distinguish between feelings with a high degree of precision, nuance, and specificity. It's about being able to accurately read and label your own emotional states.

TAKE YOUR EMOTIONAL PULSE

Periodically during the day, stop what you're doing for a moment and check in with yourself by asking, *How am I feeling? What specific word(s) describe my current mood? Overall, does my state of mind reside on the positive, negative, or neutral part of the spectrum?* If you want to go the extra mile, you could even chart the ups and downs of your daily feelings on a graph, which could help reveal patterns related to time of day, lifestyle factors, or what you're doing, hearing, or seeing. After a week, look at your daily graphs: Are there regular peaks and valleys in your mood level? Can you detect any factors that consistently trigger positive or negative moods?

That's not to say it's always easy for us to recognize our emotions precisely. On the contrary, it can be quite difficult for several reasons. Sometimes it's hard to distinguish between emotions that are close cousins—say, guilt and shame—because the differences are fairly nuanced. At other times, we don't *want* to know what we're feeling, so we use defense mechanisms to help with the self-deception—perhaps repressing the feeling by burying it in our subconscious or consciously pushing the thoughts out of our minds, a process called "suppression." With another defense mechanism called "reaction formation," emotions that are uncomfortable or perceived to be unacceptable or forbidden can be massaged into another behavior or response that conceals the true feelings (think of Shakespeare's famous line from *Hamlet*: "The lady doth protest too much").

Deep down, conscious or not, these defense mechanisms are efforts at self-preservation. We may be trying to see ourselves in a good light, save face with others, or maintain some better frame of mind than we would otherwise be in. It's worth plumbing these depths because research suggests that being able to differentiate between distinct emotions (such as anger and sadness) as well as emotions that are more closely related (such as anger and irritation) is strongly associated with emotional well-being, including positive mood, self-esteem, and emotional clarity.

The reason for this is that having emotional granularity arms you with more precise tools for handling various challenges that may come your way, as well as reaping maximum pleasure from positive experiences in your life. As Lisa Feldman Barrett, PhD, a professor of psychology at Northeastern University, notes in her book *How Emotions Are Made: The Secret Life of the Brain*, people who cultivate finely grained emotional experiences are able to be "more flexible when regulating their emotions" and allow their brain the opportunity to calibrate a response to suit their physical and emotional needs in any given situation. In other words, specific emotions that are named are easier to manage, accept, or respond to than vague, free-floating ones. No wonder people with greater emotional granularity are less likely to act out when they're angry or drown their sadness in alcohol—and more likely to find positive lessons in difficult emotional experiences. People with higher levels of emotional granularity also show greater resilience in the face of stress than people with low granularity. This is partly because the more precisely you can identify your emotions, the more actionable they become and the less likely you are to become hypersensitive or hyperreactive to them.

A study at UCLA found that when people put their feelings into words during twenty-minute expressive writing sessions, the act of labeling their emotions increased neural activity in the area of the brain that helps integrate emotions with other functions and regulates motor activity (the right ventrolateral prefrontal cortex) and decreased neural activity in the amygdala (which is the command center for processing fear and anxiety) on fMRI scans. By contrast, those who wrote about nonemotional topics didn't experience these particular changes in their brain activity. The writing sessions lasted eight weeks, but the brain changes among the participants who performed expressive writing predicted improved satisfaction with life and reduced measures of anxiety and depression *three months after* the final writing session.

Another hidden perk of recognizing your feelings is that it enables you to reach out and connect emotionally to the right people to get a sense of kinship or solace so that you don't feel so alone in your frustrations or experience that feeling of *WTF!* A case in point: On a politically volatile day last summer, an educator in Washington, DC, who is highly attuned to her outrage and despair about the inhumane treatment of undocumented immigrants (especially children who've been separated from their parents) and not shy about expressing these feelings, posted this message on social media: *I need a mood transplant. STAT!* Within minutes she heard from many others who were feeling the same way, and they began to brainstorm ideas for how they could support detained immigrants or even accompany them to court. Recognizing and expressing their feelings helped them feel less isolated and allowed them to find new ways to help themselves feel better as they worked to improve the dire situations faced by those in their community.

These benefits certainly beat the alternative because people who have low emotional granularity, particularly for difficult feelings, tend to be more reactive to their own bad moods. This heightened reactivity can lead them to hold on to their negative feelings with a death grip or to ruminate, mulling over a stressful situation or problem from every conceivable angle. Both practices can leave them susceptible to falling down a rabbit hole into feelings of gloom and dysfunctional coping mechanisms.

Let's say that you've been walking around, telling yourself (and others) that you feel stressed to the nth degree. If you were to dwell on how frazzled and tense you feel both mentally and physically, chances are you'd end up feeling worse; you might even end up trying to numb those bad feelings with a few cocktails or glasses of wine or a comfort-food fest, neither of which would make you feel better. But if you were to drill down into the bedrock of your emotions and realize that what you really feel is anxious or overwhelmed, you could try to pin-point the exact source of that feeling (perhaps an upcoming event or too many assignments at work) and think about what you could do to address the situation directly or what you could do to better process or defuse your unpleasant emotions.

LEARNING TO UNPACK YOUR EMOTIONS

For some people, engaging in free association can clear the cobwebs from their minds, almost like opening the cellar door to a musty base-ment and letting in light and fresh air. To do this, you might take a break and consider how you're feeling about what you're doing, read-ing, seeing, or thinking every few hours throughout the day. If a general word comes to mind—such as *stressed, anxious*, or *angry*—dig deeper and ask yourself what other emotions you might be feeling (maybe *fear* or *annoyance*) along with it. If you do this out loud in unedited, private moments, you might find yourself blurting out what you're really thinking or feeling, revealing the emotions that are taking a lot of energy to keep inside. This is really about unpacking your suit-case of feelings, or untangling the knot of emotions that is taking up space inside you.

When you think about this in the abstract, it can be hard to pin-point how you're feeling. You may just see a swirling mass of a feeling *quality* such as "dread" or "foreboding" rather than recognizing the specific emotions you feel. To get to the root of your feelings, spend five minutes looking at the word cloud below—no more than five so that you don't have time to filter your responses—and choose the emotions that resonate with your mood-state lately.

Optimistic

Fearful   Despondent

Regretful   Panicky   Shame   Disgust

Confusion   Positive   Determined   Outraged

Aggressive   Empathetic   Apathetic   Distrustful   Grief

Accepting   Sad   Annoyed   Shocked   Anguish

Resolved   Exuberant   Enthusiastic   Altruistic   Jittery

Isolated   Tolerant   Disappointed   Disrespected

Vulnerable   Self-critical   Hopeful   Moody   Upbeat

Joyful   Compassionate   Frustrated

Alienated   Helpless

If reviewing these words evokes other feelings for you or if words or phrases that apply to you were not on this word cloud, jot these down in the blank word cloud that follows. Give yourself another five minutes to think about your recent state of mind and jot down phrases, images, or words that occur to you. This is your opportunity to personalize it without any limits or restrictions. If you feel stymied or draw a blank initially, think about your recent responses to current events or situations in your personal life or on the world stage. Try to be as honest as you can by focusing on how you're really feeling when no one is watching—free-associate without judging, censoring, or revising what you write down.

Once you've finished your list, look at the order of the words you wrote down: *Did they progress from all negative to increasingly hopeful? Do they portray an internal tension or friction in going back and forth between various feelings?* If all the words are positive, consider the possibility that you may be in some degree of denial, focusing only on the window dressing rather than the emotions that lie beneath the surface. Also, consider this: *Is there a pattern of shallow, visceral reactions that came out initially, followed by more complex thoughts and feelings?* If so, think about whether you're giving yourself enough time in your life to reflect. If you came out with highly intellectualized words or phrases first, it might suggest that you put on a bit of a facade when engaging with the world, and you might benefit from striving for a deeper engagement or familiarity with your emotions.

Not long ago, I conducted a workshop at the Kripalu Center for Yoga & Health in Massachusetts on the psychological effects of climate change. To help the forty participants learn about the range of emotions people have about the current climate crisis, I asked each of them to write down whatever word or phrase came to mind when they hear the phrase *climate change*. They were instructed not to edit or judge their choices but to simply off-load their associations over the course of five minutes. After the exercise, I told them to pair up with another person and discuss their lists, while teasing out themes and ideas that emerged. Intrigued and excited by what they were learning about themselves, the participants became very invested in the exercise and were frustrated with me when I held them to the time limit for discussion.

It was like a collective epiphany as people realized how they were being affected and how many different emotions they were experiencing below the surface—emotions they had been suppressing or repressing. The process of self-discovery was exhilarating. And by doing this and sharing their word clouds with others, they were able to identify the types of people who would be their natural allies, people who had similar reactions to this issue. It was a revealing experience for everyone.

WRITE YOUR HEART OUT

Numerous studies have illustrated the benefits of expressive writing, especially when it comes to dealing with stress, trauma, anxiety, and loss. The practice also can help you become better at recognizing and processing your own emotions, as James Pennebaker, PhD, a distinguished professor at the University of Texas at Austin, has repeatedly shown. This is something you can do entirely on your own; no supervision required.

continues

Pennebaker's recommendation is to find a time of day and a place where you can write about a recent or still affecting emotional experience for at least fifteen minutes, without being disturbed. You can do this with pen and paper or on your computer.

If you need some prompts to get going, ask yourself the following: *What am I thinking about or worrying about excessively? What have I dreamt about that has stuck with me? What issue or feeling in my life have I been avoiding?* Don't worry about spelling, grammar, or punctuation and don't edit yourself; simply let your emotions flow through your fingertips. Do this for three or four consecutive days. After that, you can keep it or toss it or do whatever you like with it. This writing exercise is for your eyes only. It's a way for you to get a closer view of the secret life of your feelings.

AN EMOTIONAL PIGGYBACK EFFECT

Don't be surprised if unpacking emotions elicits another set of emotions. With a phenomenon called "meta-emotion," you might find yourself feeling angry about feeling fearful or you might feel sad about feeling anxious. It's a term you may not have heard, but a meta-emotion reflects how you feel about your feelings or how you react to them. A meta-emotion is a secondary emotion that occurs in response to a primary one, but it's a layered or superimposed emotion, rather than necessarily being a sequential one. In fact, a meta-emotion doesn't have to immediately follow the initial emotion; it can occur hours, even days, after the initial emotion that led to or triggered the second one.

For example, you might feel ashamed of feeling envious of a colleague's promotion. Or you could feel guilty about getting angry at your partner during a minor misunderstanding. Or you could feel annoyed at yourself for repeatedly checking newsfeeds throughout the day, a habit that makes you feel anxious and agitated. The trouble is, when you feel annoyed or guilty about feeling anxious or angry, it ratchets up the primary feeling and your emotional inflammation. Now, you've got three problems that end up compounding each other.

However and whenever it happens, the phenomenon of meta-emotion is actually quite common. When researchers from Washington University in St. Louis had seventy-nine adults from the community track their emotions and their emotional responses to their feelings for seven days, they found that 53 percent of the participants reported meta-emotional experiences, about twice per week, with negative feelings toward negative emotional experiences (such as depressive symptoms) being the most common. Interestingly, distress tolerance is considered a meta-emotion because it reflects a person's ability to tolerate or accept his or her own negative emotions. People with a low tolerance for distress often have trouble handling feeling upset or anxious, which is why their ability to function can be temporarily impaired by their negative emotions.

As with many issues in life, your parents' beliefs and behavior toward emotions can have a profound effect on the degree to which you can identify and tolerate your own feelings, particularly the uncomfortable ones. Some parents tend to be more accepting and supportive of their kids' difficult emotions and take a "coaching" approach to them by discussing and validating their feelings toward distressing events and using these as opportunities to foster intimacy and learning about emotions. In contrast, others have "emotion-dismissing" styles, whereby they don't view emotions as important, and they tend to ignore, deny, or dismiss their children's feelings. Research suggests that children of parents who have an emotion-coaching style are less vulnerable to emotional problems and have stronger emotion-regulation skills and a better overall understanding of emotions than kids whose parents embrace an emotion-dismissing approach. These emotional styles may rightfully belong to the parents, but kids internalize them at a young age and often carry them into adulthood.

Forty-year-old Julie, an artist, grew up in a household where her parents were not emotionally attentive or available to their kids, partly because they were so focused on their adult lives. When Julie worried about going to a new elementary school or she was upset by her brother's hostile teasing or the mean-girl behavior at school, her parents would often dismiss her feelings by saying, "Don't be so sensitive!" or "Grow a thicker skin," and Julie would end up feeling ashamed of her emotional response. This was a script that she unwittingly internalized, and it played in her head as she encountered unsettling challenges in college and in her twenties. It wasn't until she went into therapy in her thirties that she realized that she was not overly sensitive, as her parents had suggested, but a deeply feeling person who was susceptible to occasional bouts of anxiety. Once she changed the label in her head, it became easier for her to recognize her deeper emotions without judging them or reacting negatively to them, which in turn improved her ability to cope with them.

This isn't surprising, considering that having harsh judgments about your own feelings and/or behavior can create a constricting feeling, causing you to resort to primitive ways of defending or protecting yourself even if they're misplaced. For example, feeling embarrassed about your anxiety while dealing with a conflict might lead you to hunker down and isolate yourself from someone you perceive to be a potential threat. Or if you feel ashamed of your history of being belittled by your parents or other authority figures and a colleague disagrees with something you said in a meeting, you might be primed to interpret the situation based on what happened in your past rather than asking for clarification, or you might suspect the person is out to sabotage you somehow. In the meantime, these negative judgments about your own feelings essentially shut down your thinking and creative problem-solving abilities, and they can send you into a downward spiral of worsening feelings, which is not what you want or need.

Here's the reality in these instances: *you're* actually fine—it's your reaction to yourself that's the problem. The solution is to stop judging your emotions so you can put an end to the emotional tailspin you've been sending yourself into. That way, you can become more open to and accepting of your feelings and entertain the notion that there are healthy, constructive avenues through which you can make sense of these emotions or put them to use.

Looking at this another way, if you *don't* know how you're feeling, it's like thinking you can fix, say, a broken appliance without unscrewing the housing and looking at the parts inside to see where the problem is. Examining how you're truly feeling, not just on the surface but deep down, can elicit ideas about how to address what's upsetting you. When you spill out or unpack your emotions, they often feel less overwhelming or daunting. On a conscious level, this is because often when you pinpoint what's really bothering you, you may realize that it's not as big or pervasive as you feared or that it's easier to address than you may have thought. Being able to label a blurry, dark, nameless threat removes some of its grip on you and lets it become a potentially manageable challenge or series of challenges if you engage in deliberate reflection.

On an unconscious level, the experience of affect labeling, which is really a fancy way of saying "putting feelings into words," diminishes the response of the amygdala (the brain's fear-processing center) to negative emotional stimuli, which in turn reduces your emotional reactivity. It also activates brain regions that are responsible for controlling impulses and emotional reactions (the prefrontal cortex), focusing attention (the prefrontal cortex and the parietal cortex), and engaging in planning, reasoning, and other high-level brain functions (the prefrontal cortex). In other words, you're essentially downshifting activity in the reactive, highly emotional part of the brain while allowing the calm, cool, and rational parts to have greater influence over the problem at hand—a win-win situation for emotion regulation. Plus, the act of labeling an emotion without judging it provides you with some distance from the emotion itself. By acknowledging your anxiety or anger for what it is, it becomes a thing that's slightly separate from you, rather than a feeling that could swallow you whole. This is in keeping with mindfulness practices. Then, when you can see the emotion objectively—with some space between the raw emotion and you, as a person—you can choose how to engage with or respond to the feeling; you don't have to embody it. This is also why it's important to label your emotions by saying "I feel anxious" or "I feel angry" rather than saying "I'm anxious" or "I'm angry." What you feel is not who you are. So choose your words wisely!

BROADEN YOUR EMOTIONAL VOCABULARY

To enhance your own emotional granularity, it helps to learn as many "feeling" words as possible. If you're in a "bad" mood, don't stop there. Dig deeper until you can find which of the "fifty shades of crappy," as Lisa Feldman Barrett puts it, you really feel, whether this means angry, aggravated, discouraged, fearful, irritable, gloomy, horrified, uneasy, resentful, envious, sorrowful, or something else.

To expand your emotional vocabulary, it also helps to pay attention to the feeling words that are used in books, movies, podcasts, and the like. If you're unclear about the differences between *jealousy* and *envy* or *depressed* and *dejected*, look up the words in the dictionary. Then, make an effort to use finely grained emotion-related adjectives accurately in your own life.

When it comes right down to it, the difference between avoiding your feelings or leaving them unexamined and unpacking them is like the contrast between trying to drive along a fog-enveloped road at night versus being able to navigate clearly in broad daylight. When you identify *what* or *how* you're really feeling, you'll gain perspective, knowledge, and insights that can help you figure out what to do about it, whether that leads you to try to remedy a problem or accept your current state of mind without feeling so much turmoil. In the latter case, the question becomes: *What else can I do to help myself better tolerate how I'm feeling or reclaim my emotional equilibrium?* It might help to sit quietly, breathe deeply, and visualize your anxiety or humiliation evaporating into thin air. Or you could go for a brisk walk outside or pour your feelings into a journal or illustrate them with a picture (no artistic talent required). There's no perfect outlet for every emotion, and different strategies may appeal more to some people than others.

Certainly, the ultimate goal is to figure out how to calibrate and manage your feelings, especially the distressing ones, for the long haul. But before you can do that, you'll want to be able to tune in to your emotions and learn to see them in their various hues, rather than just in black and white. The vast majority of people, even those with alexithymia, have the capacity to improve their ability to label their own emotional experiences. This is the first, crucial step in the process of calming emotional inflammation because unless you're able to honestly and accurately interpret your feelings, you can't possibly figure out how to address them constructively.

THE RESTORE TO-DO LIST

☐ Seize free moments during the day to check your emotional pulse; consider how you're feeling and name the emotion as specifically as you can.

☐ Expand your emotional vocabulary; distinguish between whether you're feeling sad or tired, anxious or fearful, angry or annoyed. Also, pay attention to the feeling words that are used in books, movies, TV shows, and podcasts.

☐ Recognize how you feel about your feelings — your meta-emotions — and consider the extent to which those secondary emotions are compounding the primary ones.

☐ Cultivate acceptance of your feelings without judging them. Often it's not your emotions that are the problem — it's the way you're reacting to them that is.

CHAPTER 5

EVALUATE

YOUR TRIGGERS

We are not a victim of our emotions or thoughts. We can understand our triggers and use them as tools to help us respond more objectively.

ELIZABETH THORNTON,
British-Canadian writer

AFTER GROWING UP IN a chaotic household with two alcoholic parents, one of whom had a nasty temper, Alice married a loving, supportive man with whom she raised two well-adjusted kids. She also developed a thriving business as a health-care consultant, a circle of positive, encouraging friends she adores, and a healthy, active lifestyle that helps her feel physically strong and vibrant. By her own admission, life is good. So she couldn't understand why she began feeling on edge during the day and was having trouble sleeping through the night for the first time at age forty-eight.

When asked what she was particularly worried about, she cited the country's dysfunctional political leadership, the possibility of war, gun violence, various threats to human rights—basically, a laundry list of current events. Alice admitted that she's so afraid of missing something that she regularly checks the newsfeeds on her computer or phone during the day. As a child, staying highly attuned to potential mood changes in her family helped her sidestep potential minefields. Now, this hypervigilance was setting her up for emotional turmoil, as she reacted to the vicissitudes of modern life that are constantly highlighted in the news cycle.

We all have emotional triggers that can lead us to an emotionally charged or uncomfortable state, and they can vary from one person to another. Sometimes we have triggers in common such as seeing a child or animal being hurt, being treated rudely by others, or being fed a steady diet of alarming news. Other times the triggers may be unique to you, based on your personal or family history, your temperament, culture, values, ideals, personal beliefs, and other factors that make you who *you* are. What emotional triggers have in common are the feelings they elicit, such as a strong sense of discomfort or being destabilized in some way, and perhaps an unusually rapid acceleration of emotions.

When emotional triggers occur in your personal life, they're often easier to recognize than more global or abstract ones are because with the personal you might see the traces of an overly critical parent or a harsh teacher in the voice and behavior of another family member, colleague, or neighbor, for instance. Personal triggers often contain messages about what's important to you or what frustrates or maddens you. They're often a holdover (maybe even an emotional hangover) from past traumas, forms of childhood neglect, or other forms of mistreatment. On a personal level, some common trigger themes include the following:

- Having someone disrespect, embarrass, or shame you in front of others

- Feeling rejected, forgotten, or abandoned by someone you trust

- Someone attempting to manipulate or control you in a blatant fashion

- Feeling helpless, powerless, unsafe, or lost in challenging situations

- Someone being physically or emotionally unavailable when you need help

- Being used or exploited for someone else's personal gain

- Feeling overlooked, unheard, dismissed, or excluded

- Being criticized, judged, or disapproved of by someone whose opinion you value

- Feeling trapped in a place or situation you can't tolerate

- Having your privacy invaded by someone you trust

- Feeling let down or unsupported by someone to whom you've been generous and giving

For example, the 2018 "Stress in America: Generation Z" survey performed by the American Psychological Association, which involved 3,458 respondents in the US, found that members of Generation Z (who, at the time of this writing, are between the ages of fifteen and twenty-one) report more stress than adults in general do about issues that are in the news. In particular, gun violence (including mass shootings and school shootings), immigration issues (including the separation and deportation of immigrant and migrant families), and sexual harassment are significant stressors for this generation.

Meanwhile for some of us, including me, reading the latest report about the dire effects of climate change is the overwhelming stressor, and it can trigger a profound case of "ecological grief"—deep sorrow about experienced or anticipated environmental losses or degradation, including destruction of or damage to species, ecosystems, and meaningful natural landscapes. You may be especially susceptible to ecological grief if you value time spent in nature or you go to considerable lengths to protect the environment and preserve natural resources. The 2017 "Mental Health and Our Changing Climate" report that I contributed to and that was produced by the American Psychological Association and Climate for Health noted, "In general, climate change can be considered an additional source of stress to our everyday concerns, which may be tolerable for someone with many sources of support but can be enough to serve as a tipping point for those who have fewer resources or who are already experiencing other stressors."

Singly or in combination, personal and shared triggers can fuel emotional inflammation without you even realizing it. It may not always be easy to discern what triggers a particularly unpleasant or distressed emotion for you, but the process of exploring the underpinnings of your feelings will bring you closer to yourself emotionally in ways that can help you gain strength, resilience, and better coping skills. As the Swiss psychiatrist Carl Jung, founder of analytical psychology, put it, "Until you make the unconscious conscious, it will direct your life and you will call it fate." *That's not what you want!* The goal is to deconstruct the ill-defined dread that's swirling around you by shining a light into the darker places in your mind. You'll be able to go there safely on this guided journey.

REVISITING YOUR HISTORY

When your mood or state of mind takes a sudden detour from the steady road you thought it was on and you want to find out why, it's time to unravel the mystery. Hit the rewind button on recent events and try to trace the way you're feeling to an inciting moment, whether it was something you witnessed, read, heard, or experienced. Ask yourself: *What just happened? Why am I suddenly feeling what I'm feeling? What was I doing or thinking about before I began to feel this way?* Try to think back to the last moment when you *didn't* feel this way (when you felt fine), then try to fan out from there to figure out when your mood or mindset headed south and what was happening at that pivotal point. By tracing mood changes back to what sparked them, you'll gradually become more adept at recognizing your triggers earlier, which gives you the opportunity to put your emotional flak jacket on.

Whether you can pinpoint the trigger or you come up empty in a given moment, it also helps to consider these questions: *When have I felt like this in the past? Is there a pattern to what leads to this feeling for me? What other situations in my life have evoked a similar emotional response from me?* We all have emotional hangovers from the past, many of which become buried in our consciousness. By asking yourself these questions, you might realize that the shaming takedown you just witnessed at work echoed the harsh voice of your critical mother or father or that the sound bite you heard on TV from a prejudiced politician was reminiscent of the ugliness you witnessed from a bigoted neighbor when you were a kid. Your mind may be trying to make sense of what's happening now by linking current events to recurring experiences or associations from your past. As uncomfortable as this may feel in the moment, this ability to draw emotional connections between past and present events is highly adaptive—part of the human survival mechanism, really. It's also the basis for feeling empathy and compassion toward others.

If a connection doesn't come to mind immediately, don't get frustrated. Instead, sit with the issue. A short while later, you might have an "aha" moment, and a connection between your past and present will occur to you. At other times, you may need to act like a detective and dig a little deeper because we all have a tendency to hide painful triggers from ourselves. It's a self-protective mechanism: we don't want to know exactly what these triggers are, or we don't want to acknowledge that particular issues stir us up. But being able to unearth and pinpoint the people, places, words, or situations that evoke unpleasant emotions will release some of the power those emotions have over you and help you figure out how to handle them constructively.

As Harvard psychologist Susan David, PhD, notes in her book *Emotional Agility*, "Emotions dredge up old business, confusing our perception of what's happening in the moment with painful past experiences." This is especially true when it comes to current traumas and past traumas. Just ask the many women who'd been sexually assaulted or coerced at some time in their lives and experienced a resurgence of their earlier trauma at the height of the Me Too scandals. Sometimes the connections aren't obvious or transparent, however. At times, you may find yourself in a particular psychological or emotional state and have no idea how you got there because you aren't aware of the chain of associations that have been going through your mind. Unbeknownst to you, it's as if a wire that you didn't know existed becomes hot and trips a circuit breaker or blows a fuse; you can't locate the origin of the problem, and you don't know where to even look for it, but your emotional reaction can light up, nonetheless.

In these instances, a situation that's currently upsetting you can activate bad memories from your childhood or even earlier in your adult life, and they can become superimposed or entangled with each other. If you were bullied at school or on the playground as a child and you've been experiencing bouts of what feels like hostile teasing or ridicule at work, the old trauma could be retriggered while you're experiencing the current one. The same thing can happen if you were held to unrealistic standards as a child and it feels like your boss is doing this to you now, causing you to feel doubly overwhelmed and unappreciated. Depending on your reactor type, this maelstrom of past and present feelings can magnify how you're feeling at this moment or even lead you to overreact to what's happening now; or, it can cause you to shut down emotionally and/or socially (so you can tend to your psychological wounds) or move in the wrong direction because your judgment is clouded.

Negative memories pack a powerful punch—and research suggests that we tend to remember them more vividly than positive memories, especially if they're rich in sensory details (striking sights, sounds, smells, etc.). Sure, bad memories get filed away for a while; they're not just hanging out in the forefront of your mind (at least we hope not). But when something bad happens and it reminds you of a previous event, you may feel as though you're on a runaway train that's traveling back in time to a dark place. If a current situation evokes negative emotions and this shade of negativity closely matches a signature from a troubling event from your past, your mind will locate the negative memory more easily than it would a positive memory. This is your mind's equivalent of scanning a QR code on your smartphone to immediately get information about a product you're looking at or pay for parking at a meter. When it comes to emotions and memories, your mind does this automatically, without any effort or awareness from you.

If you grew up in a home with an abusive or psychologically unstable parent, for example, the mercurial or mean-spirited behavior of your boss or our political leaders could trigger an especially personal sense of angst. If a partner cheated on you or stole from you, reports of lying, cheating, stealing, or engaging in other forms of misconduct among people who run financial institutions or who are in privileged positions may make you more susceptible to feelings of rage, outrage, disgust, or helplessness. If your parents had a pattern of drinking excessive amounts of alcohol and behaving irresponsibly, you might find yourself highly sensitized to how many drinks people around you consume at a social gathering, which can be highly unsettling as you wonder whether someone is going to act up, act out, or be unable to drive home. This is what happens with emotional triggers; the unconscious mind makes connections that we're unaware of.

By examining and unpacking your current emotional state and considering whether an event from your past could be fueling your reaction, you can gain insight into your feelings and better manage them by reframing what belongs in the here and now and what doesn't. (Sometimes hindsight really can be 20/20 when it comes to your emotional well-being.) Or, you can take steps to reason with yourself as you pass through the experience, instead of being buffeted by the emotional tailwinds. Bringing links between your past traumas and present triggers into your conscious awareness can help you understand and even anticipate the issues or situations that are likely to lead to emotional inflammation for you. That way, you won't be caught off guard.

PUTTING YOUR FINGER ON YOUR POTENTIAL TRIGGERS

It's time to start unraveling the mystery of *you* by exploring your current state of mind. Think of this as an adventure; a path toward greater self-understanding and self-compassion—and an expanded appreciation of the complexity of *you*. To get a sense of the modern-world issues that tend to rile or upset you, put on your imaginary miner's hat and head into the depths of your mind to see what lies below your conscious awareness. (You may want to do this with a trusted friend or partner.) Consider your true feelings about the following subjects, without letting preconceived ideas about the right or politically correct way to think or feel about these subjects guide you; simply let your real feelings flow out of you in a free-association style. As you read the following words and phrases, jot down the first three to five words or phrases that come to your mind in response (don't edit or change what occurs to you instinctively):

- Climate crises

- Me Too scandals

- Human rights abuses (on a grand scale)

- Political corruption

- Racial, religious, gender, or political discrimination

- Environmental threats (toxins in our midst)

- Volatile financial circumstances

- Natural disasters (wildfires, floods, storms)

- International threats

- Social divisiveness in this country

- Hate crimes

- Nuclear weapons threats

- Gun violence

If other current events are triggering emotional inflammation for you, write them down here:

_____

_____

_____

A SAMPLE TRIGGER RESPONSE

Don't worry if you feel put on the spot, thought-tied, and unable to come up with the right words to describe how you feel in response to the prompts listed above. Take a deep breath, exhale, and peruse this sample response. Rather than letting this person's examples sway or influence you, try to use them as inspiration to unlock the floodgates on *your* true feelings.

- Abuse of children—disgusting, sad, scary, outraged

- Ultranationalism—threatening, unnerving, depressing

- Political gridlock—disturbing, vulnerable, vague

Now it's your turn!

After you've completed your list, assign a value to each of these concerns in terms of their potency for you on a scale of 0 to 3 (with 0 being neutral and 3 being intense). Do this quickly so you don't have too much time to think about it or second-guess your instinctive responses. Once you've finished this, place these triggers into a hierarchical list from a potency of 3 to 0, based on how they affect or resonate with you. This will give you a sense of what is likely to get you riled up these days. It might be illuminating to go back to the lists of emotions you've been feeling lately (see chapter 4) and think about how they may be connected to your top triggers.

If you want to dig a bit deeper, think about the way you responded to the descriptions of certain triggers—that you felt disgusted, violated, sad, and threatened when you thought about Me Too scandals, for example—then consider whether any situations from your past have evoked similar feelings for you. As you've seen, emotional injuries or reverberations from the past can make you vulnerable to similar insults and assaults in the present. It's almost as if you have an emotional ember lying beneath your consciousness, and it's predisposed to flaring up from time to time. If you hear a single piece of distressing news and find yourself reacting surprisingly strongly to it, think about what else may be crashing around you or whether the news has somehow opened Pandora's box and exposed you to a deep abyss of other fears and worries. Or it may be that a more superficial emotional injury is on the way to healing but then the scab gets ripped off and the wound bleeds again when another upsetting event occurs.

As it happens, we often experience emotions in our bodies, and sometimes our bodies register those feelings before our minds do. So if you have trouble pinpointing how you're feeling with words, you may want to scan your body for clues. When researchers in Finland performed a series of cross-cultural studies with 701 people from West European and East Asian cultures, they had the participants view various words, stories, movies, or facial expressions then color specific regions on silhouettes of bodies where they felt activity increasing or decreasing while they viewed each stimulus. This exercise in mapping bodily sensations in response to emotions revealed that basic emotions—including anger, fear, disgust, happiness, sadness, and surprise—were associated with sensations of elevated activity in the upper chest, which likely reflects changes in breathing and heart rate. Increased sensations in the arms and torso were associated with anger. Decreased sensations in the arms and legs corresponded to sadness. And increased sensations in the gut (the digestive system) and throat were found primarily with disgust. The most fascinating revelation was that these effects rang true among people cross-culturally.

So if you have a mental block that makes it difficult to recognize your emotional triggers (which some people do, in a subconscious effort to protect themselves from emotional discomfort), paying attention to your bodily sensations can give you clues about what you're experiencing. Even if you are highly attuned to your emotional reactions, sometimes they can sneak up on you, and you might experience a particular bodily sensation before you are aware of the actual trigger or your response to it. That's because we all have blind spots to reflexive emotional states we're susceptible to experiencing.

Not long ago, Suzanne, an arts management consultant, experienced this phenomenon during a family get-together. When she was in her twenties, Suzanne survived the dramatic implosion of her family of origin following her parents' prosecution for fraud; their filing for bankruptcy and divorce; and her sister's addiction problems, which led to a prolonged stint in rehab. Though she had emotional scars from her family's considerable losses, she became an emotionally well-adjusted adult with a healthy marriage, three kids she adores, and a successful career. As time went on, she even cultivated solid relationships with her emotionally needy parents, both of whom had remarried but who often leaned on her as if she were the responsible adult in the family. To her credit, Suzanne was well aware of their faults and foibles and was quite adept at foreseeing potential drama and dodging or managing it.

But when her father and his second wife came to visit for Suzanne's forty-fifth birthday, she was blindsided during a conversation about the latest indictments for insider trading that were dominating the news cycle. In a sharp left turn, her father took the conversation down a surprising path in which he revised their family's history to make himself look like a victim, rather than the perpetrator of wrongdoing. Suddenly, Suzanne began to feel cold and shaky in her arms, legs, and torso, signs she recognized as a tip-off that she was on the verge of experiencing a huge surge of anxiety, agitation, and outrage. To head off a flare-up of the kind of emotional inflammation she'd experienced frequently in her twenties, she excused herself from the conversation to tend to things in the kitchen.

It was the best thing she could have done for herself. By physically disengaging from the triggering situation, she was able to short-circuit her emotional reaction before it got too revved up or entrenched. If she hadn't noticed the physical signs, she would have been caught completely unaware by the turn of events—until it resulted in a full-blown flare-up of emotional inflammation.

LESSONS FROM PAST TRAUMA

One of the ways you can better process trauma in a present situation is to think about a previous time (or two or three) when you were traumatized and may have felt rattled and at an impasse. Remember that with effort and time, you were able to process what happened and get beyond it. Instead of just waiting for time to pass now, think back and try to identify some of the key actions you took that helped you heal from the emotional wound and promote your recovery. This may be a really important roadmap in helping you figure out how you can handle trauma generally. If you can do it once, you can do it again. This is a resilience that is created or determined in part by your own conviction and confidence that you can do it. But if you're really struggling on your own, don't hesitate to seek professional help.

RECOGNIZING INTERNAL TRIGGERS

As you consider the various forces that could be contributing to *your* emotional inflammation, it's smart to consider your inner landscape, particularly your thoughts, in addition to what's happening around you. Sometimes your thoughts about what you're seeing or hearing, about what other people are doing, about things that happened in the past or that could happen in the future can ignite certain emotions or amplify them. Even a fleeting thought or an image that comes to mind in response to something you see, hear, smell, or taste can elicit a chain of thought associations that can send you down an emotional rabbit hole; yet, you may not be aware of that chain. A dream hangover also can send your next-day emotions for a ride: after a bad dream or nightmare, some people wake up and feel relieved that it's over, but for others, a heaviness or darkness can hover and skew the mood of the day in the direction of the emotional tenor they experienced in the dream.

In addition, the way you think about or judge how you're feeling can evoke a secondary set of emotions (or meta-emotions). If you tell yourself that you're selfish for turning down an invitation to an event because you're exhausted, the thought that you're selfish can make you feel guilty about bowing out and that can trigger other unpleasant emotions. Similarly, engaging in emotional reasoning, believing something to be true because of your emotional reaction, can reinforce the feeling you already have, increase its intensity, or summon a secondary set of emotions. Say you think to yourself that you're overwhelmed at work and can't handle it—that very thought can ratchet up your anxiety.

This is why rather than accepting your negative thoughts at face value (and allowing them to upset you), it's wise to get in the habit of questioning whether these thoughts are true or whether you should replace them with different thoughts that are perhaps more accurate. Most people tend to be harsh judges of themselves—their own worst critics, really—which is akin to death by a thousand cuts—a slow, torturous decline. The point is this: You don't have to believe everything you're thinking, and you don't have to let your thoughts manipulate your emotions. Sometimes your thoughts can be off-base, skewed, or just plain wrong (a.k.a. various forms of cognitive distortions, which you'll read more about in chapter 7), in which case you could be telling yourself falsehoods and upsetting yourself for no valid reason.

Also, consider the possibility that if something isn't right with your physiological equilibrium, it can disrupt your emotional equilibrium, which can make you particularly vulnerable to emotional triggers. (Your physiological and emotional equilibriums really do reside on a two-way street.) If you didn't sleep well last night, if you're feeling sick or run down, if you haven't eaten in more than four hours (in which case your blood sugar has likely taken a dramatic dip), or if you're overstimulated by bright lights, noise, or crowded conditions, your emotions can easily get hijacked and taken in an unpleasant direction, or your mood shift could be magnified by these factors. In fact, a 2017 study from the Johns Hopkins University School of Medicine in Baltimore found that a single night of sleep that's disturbed by forced awakenings every hour (for eight hours) can significantly reduce people's positive moods, leaving them more vulnerable to negative ones. Our emotional responses really are a product of many moving parts.

In addition, your biological age can affect your emotional reactivity in response to various triggers. When researchers at the University of California, Berkeley, had young, middle-aged, and older adults watch films that were designed to evoke either strong feelings of sadness or disgust or neutral emotions, there was a considerable age gap in their reactions to the sad stimuli but not to the neutral or disgust-eliciting films. People in their forties reacted more intensely physiologically (with increased blood pressure) and emotionally to the sad films than those in their twenties did, but those in their sixties had greater sadness reactivity than those in their forties or twenties did. The theory is that this may be because as people get older, they experience a greater number or intensity of personal or social losses in their lives, which can increase their reactivity to sad stimuli. Looked at another way, sad experiences or experiences of loss can sensitize us to future stimuli that are in a similar emotional vein.

Admittedly, bringing your emotional triggers to your consciousness can be unsettling, maybe even a bit painful. But there
are plenty of psychological, social, and emotional benefits to doing
so. For one thing, identifying your triggers can bring a modicum
of relief because once the triggers have names, shapes, contours,
colors, images, and perhaps even faces, they're less threatening than
undefined, unpredictable, sinister forces are. Once you recognize
who or what has been riling or unnerving you, these instigators and
agitators begin to lose some of their power or hold over you. You
may be able to see them coming from a distance, anticipate their
arrival ahead of time, or recognize them immediately as they're
striking—and find clever ways to accept, dodge, sidestep, or disarm
them to protect your emotional equilibrium. If you know that
looking at social media or online daily newsfeeds often stirs up distressing emotions for you, you can choose not to expose yourself
to them (at least not regularly). Moreover, by becoming aware of
the factors that arouse emotional inflammation for you and sharing
them with your partner (and vice versa), you can gain insights into
each other and take steps to avoid pushing each other's sensitive
buttons or pulling those upsetting triggers.

The idea isn't to bury your head in the sand in an effort to avoid all
unpleasantness or potential conflict but to be selective and judicious
about the potential triggers you subject yourself to so that you can conserve your emotional energy. This is especially important given that
there are plenty of people, situations, and world events that we can't
avoid facing. With triggers that are truly unavoidable, you'll want to
take responsibility for fortifying your emotional strength, maintaining clear boundaries with provocative influences, and dialing down
your own reactivity with your thoughts and actions (as you'll learn
to do in the chapters that follow). Think of these as vital acts of self-
preservation, an increasingly valuable instinct and behavior in a world
that feels utterly out of control.

THE RESTORE TO-DO LIST

☐ Make an effort to trace shifts in your mood back to an inciting moment—perhaps something you saw, read, heard, or experienced—that caused your mood to take a detour.

☐ Consider the possibility that emotional scars from the past could be affecting your reaction to a situation you're currently facing and exacerbating your emotional inflammation.

☐ Pay attention to bodily sensations such as changes in temperature or shakiness that may provide clues that you are or are about to be triggered in a particular situation.

☐ Stay attuned to disruptions in your physiological equilibrium—if you're tired, hungry, or overstimulated—that could magnify your emotional reactions. If you address the physiological issue, you might come to your emotional rescue, as well.

CHAPTER 6

STEADY YOUR

BODY'S NATURAL

RHYTHMS

Our body is a well-set
clock, which keeps
good time, but if it
be too much or indis-
creetly tampered with,
the alarm runs out
before the hour.

JOSEPH HALL,
English bishop, satirist, and moralist

THE HUMAN BODY IS a masterfully engineered machine, sublimely tuned by nature. An estimated 37.2 *trillion* cells must work together cooperatively day and night. Have you ever stopped to wonder, *How does this all work?* or *What keeps all these moving parts in order?* Thanks to groundbreaking research, we have recently learned that every cell has its own timekeeper that can be thought of as a local clock. Deep within the brain, in the hypothalamus, lies a master clock that regulates all the local clocks, making sure that each one is set to the same time. This complex, coordinated process is in sync with the alternating cycles of day and night and with all the degrees of changing light that occur in a twenty-four-hour period as Earth rotates on its axis. Called the "circadian rhythm"—from the Latin words *circa*, which means going around, and *diem*, meaning day—this internal process regulates the human body's sleep-wake cycle, among many other functions.

The master clock (think of it as circadian rhythm central) sends hormonal and nerve signals throughout the body, synchronizing the cells' clocks to the day-night, light-dark cycle of life. On a continuous basis, the master clock can determine what time it is based on messages from photoreceptor cells in the retina that register light conditions outside and report these to the brain via specialized pathways.

Meanwhile, the cellular clocks keep local time, making sure that various activities *locally* are timed right and are appropriately coordinated with other cells and organs. This is why, for example, key enzymes are produced at certain times, blood pressure and body temperature are controlled, hormones are secreted, the gut microbiome is populated with the right balance of bacteria, and gut motility is appropriate for the hour. Satchin Panda, PhD, a professor in the Regulatory Biology Laboratory at the Salk Institute for Biological Studies in La Jolla, California, and author of *The Circadian Code*, notes that these specialized circadian clocks help "every cell figure out when to use energy, when to rest, when to repair DNA or replicate DNA." Working in harmony, these internally synchronized pacemakers help maintain homeostasis, the body's physiological equilibrium, to ensure proper functioning and good health.

Occasional *interruptions* to your body's inherent time-keeping systems—from traveling through a few time zones, for instance—aren't a big deal. But as Dr. Panda explains, "Repeatedly disrupting your circadian clock can have adverse health consequences, as every system in your body starts to malfunction." The regulatory scheme of our innate circadian rhythm does the equivalent of "knocking" on every cellular door to communicate, at any given moment, what time it is and what it should be doing. Because it regulates the release of essential hormones, including cortisol (the primary stress hormone), melatonin (which sets the stage for sleep), and serotonin (a feel-good neurotransmitter), the body's circadian rhythm governs your sleep, blood pressure, pain response, allergic response, digestive function, immune response, mood, alertness, energy, and even the way you metabolize medications. If you're disturbing your circadian rhythms and their entrainment (or synchronization), it's tantamount to believing you can drive to an unknown place without using a GPS or even a map while having random obstacles thrown in your path and still expecting to arrive at your destination safely and in a timely fashion. *It's not gonna happen.*

If you don't travel often or stay out late on weekends, you might think you don't need to be concerned about this issue. But that's not true. Every day, many of us are living and working in ways that are at odds with our physiology, compromising the timing and functioning of our internal body clocks. Many of us are living with serious disruptions to our circadian rhythms, because we're exposed during the evening hours to too much bright, indoor light and excessive additional light from technological devices. These choices, made unwittingly, lead to the loss of precious downtime and in some cases to essential time to reset our psyches in thoughtful reflection or even the opportunity to experience awe or wonder (more on that later). What's more, these days, people often have inconsistent sleep habits—sometimes wildly inconsistent ones—that throw their body clocks further off course. As a result, we end up forcing our bodies and minds to work harder or less efficiently than they need to, which has ripple effects on our whole system.

Here's one way this can happen: On a typical weekend, people often stay up later than usual, then sleep in past their regular wake-up times, throwing their bodies' internal clocks off even more than they were during the week. Meanwhile, spending weekday evenings exposed to bright lights and to the intense blue light from digital devices resets their internal clocks because it fools the light-sensitive cells in the eye into believing that it's still daytime. This then suppresses the release of the sleep-inducing hormone melatonin, making it even harder to fall asleep. Whether it's because of this delay in melatonin release or the shortened night of sleep the person gets, melatonin (nicknamed the "hormone of darkness") can stay elevated for several hours in the morning—part of the reason people often feel groggy, foggy, and cranky during the day, especially during the week.

One of my patients, thirty-six-year-old Sean, is a social worker and an aspiring songwriter who lives with his girlfriend. Because he has a demanding day job, he often stays up late to work on his music. Once his creative juices start flowing, he's able to write lyrics and put melodies to them for hours at a time, as he enters a state of "flow," or complete immersion. Coined by the psychologist Mihály Csíkszentmihályi, the term *flow* describes an optimal state of complete absorption with what you're doing that can cause you to lose all sense of time and space. It's an incredibly gratifying experience while you're in it, as Sean well knows. But because he was getting so stimulated by his own creativity at night and skimping on sleep as a result, he would end up feeling agitated and on edge during the day. Needless to say, this is not a good state for a social worker to be in.

Besides being sleep-deprived and emotionally revved up, the real problem Sean was grappling with was a massive case of social jet lag. *Social jet lag* was coined in 2006 by Till Roenneberg, a professor of chronobiology at the Institute of Medical Psychology at Ludwig-Maximilian University in Munich, Germany, to describe the misalignment between a person's social and biological time-related needs—that is, the gap between how we are living and what our bodies call for at any given time. It has become an incredibly common hazard of modern life. Unlike the jet lag you might experience from traveling across various time zones, which is transient until your master clock recalibrates to the local time, social jet lag doesn't require you to leave home. Worse, it can become chronic: The phenomenon occurs when there's a conflict between what your body needs, based on your personal sleep quota and the timing of your internal biological clock—whether you're an early riser or a night owl, for instance—and what your life requires, based on your job, your family responsibilities, and other factors.

In an illuminating study, researchers from the University of Chicago conducted a two-year analysis of the activity patterns of 246,000 Twitter users throughout the US to reveal how technology and social pressures are taking a toll on our sleep habits and our daytime functionality. By monitoring and analyzing Twitter activity in fifteen-minute increments, the researchers discovered that continuous periods of low Twitter activity were linked with adequate sleep but the nighttime break in tweets shifted to later times on the weekends than on weekdays. They found that people in the US experience an average of seventy-five minutes of social jet lag from weekdays to weekends, with those in the Central and Eastern regions of the US having a greater amount than those in the West. The magnitude of social jet lag also varies by season, with less occurring in the summer.

Previously, in a large-scale, epidemiological study, researchers from Germany and the Netherlands analyzed the sleep duration, sleep timing, and social jet lag among 65,000 people living in Europe. It turns out that 69 percent of them suffered from social jet lag, experiencing at least a one-hour difference between how long they slept on weekdays versus weekends, and one-third experienced a two-hour discrepancy or more. This suggests that people's circadian rhythms are continuously being forced to adjust and readjust to shifting social pressures. The researchers also found that in recent years the amount of time people spend outside absorbing light has declined dramatically, and that those with social jet lag have a higher likelihood of being overweight.

This isn't surprising given that scientific research has found a correlation between insufficient sleep, levels of appetite-regulating hormones, and increased food consumption. Specifically, too little sleep leads to an increase in the hormone that makes us feel hungry (ghrelin); at the *same time*, too little sleep leads to a *decrease* in the hormone that signals when we've had enough to eat (leptin). It doesn't take a math whiz to run the equation: alterations in appetite-regulating hormones—particularly, elevated levels of ghrelin and decreased levels of leptin—add up to increased food consumption. In addition, social jet lag can have serious metabolic consequences, significantly increasing a person's risk of developing metabolic syndrome (a dangerous cluster of conditions that includes elevated blood pressure, high blood sugar, excess belly fat, and high cholesterol or triglyceride levels), prediabetes, or type 2 diabetes, especially in adults. Unseen by the naked eye, metabolic syndrome causes the *entire body* to be prone to inflammation, increasing the risk of heart disease, stroke, and type 2 diabetes.

FUN FACTS

Paris is often romantically referred to as the "City of Light," but it wasn't always this way. In the preelectric/pre-oil days of the late 1600s, the dark alleys were often infested with criminals, and the crime rate was off the charts. Fed up with these conditions, King Louis XVI ordered oil lights to be strung along roads and passages to make them safer. Paris became one of the first cities in the world to have light at night—hence, the nickname. A booming café society was spawned, and it became a status symbol to be out after dark because it suggested that you had the means to afford a personal oil lamp and to live in a desirable, illuminated area.

BEWARE THE HAZARDS OF UPSETTING YOUR BODY CLOCKS

Not surprisingly, social jet lag tends to go hand in hand with insufficient sleep, which is a problem on its own. But social jet lag also involves being active and awake when you should be sleeping, or snoozing when you should be alert and engaged, either of which can throw your body and mind into states of disorientation and disequilibrium. These circadian rhythm disruptions are a large part of the problematic dynamic linking shift work with an *increased risk* of developing multiple medical conditions, including breast and prostate cancer, gastrointestinal disorders, cardiovascular disease, and diabetes.

But even if you work a nine-to-five schedule, you can still set yourself up for social jet lag, and it can have a substantial spillover effect on the rest of your life. Indeed, the effects can be far-reaching, contributing to problems with excessive daytime sleepiness, compromised academic achievement, impaired cognitive function, and even challenges with controlling one's balance. Moreover, social jet lag can have a detrimental impact on your mood and state of mind, potentially leading to emotional distress, including anxiety, depression, and aggression, as well as unhealthy behaviors such as increased alcohol consumption, bad eating patterns, and decreased physical activity. A study from Maynooth University in Ireland even found that social jet lag in adults is associated with attention deficit symptoms and impulsivity. In other words, social jet lag can amplify many different forms of emotional inflammation, fueling agitation, depression, manic behavior, impulsivity, and other unwanted states of mind—without you even realizing it.

Jennifer, a forty-nine-year-old humanitarian aid worker who often traveled to war-torn countries and sites that had been ravaged by natural disasters, discovered this the painful way. Her work involved long hours, extensive air travel, occasional brushes with danger, and lots of time away from her husband and three teenagers. Calm, compassionate, and measured by nature, Jennifer made it all look easy, but the suffering she saw and the tragic stories she heard took a toll on her. By her own admission, she drank too much wine, didn't get enough sleep, and had developed an exercise addiction (to running, in particular, which she called "my form of Prozac").

After a three-day trip to Syria left her severely sleep-deprived, and her flight home was delayed by six hours, Jennifer arrived home feeling frayed at the edges. When her husband vocalized his resentment about her extensive work travel and her distractedness when she was home, she became uncharacteristically irritable with him. It had become an ongoing refrain in their marriage, and it didn't usually bother Jennifer. But after this trip she became more reactive toward him.

She hadn't recovered her equanimity before heading off on another work trip forty hours later. After that, the cycle of social jet lag (compounded by travel jet lag) began anew, and it persisted. Somehow Jennifer continued to manage the stress of dealing with the suffering she saw, and she remained poised and proficient at work. But when her mercurial schedule and extensive travel disrupted her internal equilibrium, she reached a tipping point and became alternately combative or withdrawn from her husband—reaction styles that felt foreign and quite uncomfortable for her and, of course, for her husband.

To try to counteract the undesirable symptoms of social jet lag and emotional inflammation, people are increasingly seeking medications—stimulants to pep them up and help them focus during the day and/or drugs to help them relieve anxiety or snooze better at night. Between 2006 and 2016, the use of prescription stimulants *doubled* in the US. The use of antidepressants has *increased 65 percent* since 2000. And from 2014 to 2018, the use of benzodiazepines (commonly known as "tranquilizers") *more than doubled* among adults in the US. These trends address the wrong issue because they are not getting to the source of the problem, and they bring on another set of problems because many of these drugs foster tolerance and dependence. Plus, their use creates an unhealthy feedback loop in which people take desperate measures to try to correct their own self-sabotaging behaviors, hoping for a better outcome, but they are really just hitting the repeat button on the harmful cycle.

What they should be doing instead is taking steps to restore their bodies' natural rhythms. A case in point: Researchers at the University of Colorado Boulder found that when healthy people went camping in nature for just *one weekend* during the summer, melatonin was released one-and-a-half hours earlier, and peak melatonin levels occurred an hour earlier during the night. These hormonal shifts help people fall asleep more easily, maintain sounder sleep throughout the night, and wake up more easily and naturally. In other words, going camping can counteract the negative effects of our modern lifestyle and essentially reset our bodies' circadian rhythms, thus preventing social jet lag.

City dwellers, take heart: You don't need to head into the woods to reap these benefits. These effects have nothing to do with sleeping in a tent and everything to do with the fact that while camping, you're not looking at brightly lit devices at night or going to bed at random times. Instead, you're going to bed shortly after it gets dark and you're waking up with the sun. Spending daytime hours in natural sunlight—which provides more than four times the illumination you'd experience inside during the summer—also contributes to better sleep patterns and daytime alertness. All of these beneficial patterns can be achieved wherever you are if you dim the lights when the sun goes down and wake up shortly after the sun rises and expose yourself to natural sunlight, whether you're sleeping in nature, the suburbs, or right in the middle of the city.

In a small study at the National Institute of Mental Health, a group of volunteers was followed to see the effects of artificial light on their sleep patterns. They were in complete darkness for fourteen hours at night (compared to their usual eight hours in the dark), with no exposure to artificial light. In just three weeks their sleep settled into different patterns—often segments of four to five hours at a time—but perhaps more significantly their nighttime secretion of melatonin increased, and they logged an additional hour of sleep during the night. In the debrief that followed, participants reported they had never felt so awake and spoke of experiencing "crystal clear consciousness." When I spoke to my friend and colleague Tom Wehr, MD, about his study, he asked, in a pain-tinged voice, *Is being fully awake something that most people in modern society will never know?*

POWER DOWN INTO DARKNESS

Research from the University of Geneva in Switzerland found that imposing a curfew on the use of electronic screen devices at 9:00 P.M. in the evening improves the early onset of sleep, increases sleep duration, and enhances daytime alertness. There's no mystery to the mechanism behind this effect: Using electronic devices (tablets, laptops, smartphones, and even TVs) before turning in for the night suppresses the release of the sleep-promoting hormone melatonin, thanks largely to the artificial blue light that is emitted by these screens. Normally, the pea-size pineal gland in the brain begins to release melatonin about two hours before your usual bedtime. Exposure to any bright light in the evenings can prevent the pineal gland from releasing melatonin, thus delaying sleepiness. But blue light is especially problematic, because it is *highly* activating. Even if you're not staring at a screen, if enough blue light strikes the eye, melatonin won't be released at the appropriate time, and it will be harder to get in the mood to snooze. And if you slip into bed with your laptop, phone, or tablet, as many people do these days, you're asking for trouble: the more electronic devices you use in the evening, the harder it becomes to fall asleep or sleep soundly.

Teens are particularly vulnerable to these effects because their circadian rhythms shift a bit later at night naturally during adolescence. So watching TV, FaceTiming with their friends, or playing video games will delay the release of the sleep-inducing hormone even later, which will make it more difficult for them to get up on time for school.

Let's face it: We live in a 24/7 world that rarely unplugs or turns off completely, where the pings, dings, buzzes, and ring tones that emanate from our digital devices have become the soundtrack of our lives. This can have an insidious effect on our minds and bodies, partly due to technostress—the vigilance of being on guard and having to respond to whatever request comes next—but also due to the stimulating effects light-emitting devices have on our brains.

And thanks to our cubicle culture, many of us are deprived of sufficient natural light during the day, which saps our vitality, interferes with our ability to focus, and compromises our productivity and our moods. Making matters worse, inconsistent sleep-wake patterns—alternating between sleeping too little and too much, along with bedtimes and awakening times that are all over the map—further disrupt our internal clocks. Like rowdy teenagers throwing a party when their parents are out of town, we are breaking the rules and failing to realize there will be consequences. But there are. Our bodies register the effects of stress and chaotic schedules, and they register the disregard for the harmonious rhythms our bodies have evolved to need.

FUN FACTS

Until the mid-1600s, humans had a very different sleep style compared to present times. Back then, we used to sleep in *segments*. Medical texts, court records, diaries, and literature—from Homer's ancient poem the *Iliad* to Chaucer's *The Canterbury Tales* to works by Charles Dickens—brim with references to sleep that was broken up into segments called the "first and second sleep." Before the world was exposed to artificial light at night (often referred to as ALAN, for short), when the rays of the sun began to diminish, humans and most of the plant and animal world began to shut down as well. Sleep then came on in response to a cascade of reactions that was shaped by millions of years of evolution. As darkness deepened, the "first sleep" took people into a slumbering state for four to five hours. This was followed by a period of one to two hours of semi-wakefulness when people might muse or relax—a time akin to a meditative state. The second sleep, consisting of another four to five hours, followed, and would end by yielding to the first rays of sunlight, announcing the new day. The point is this: *Despite being designed to sleep one way, we have deluded ourselves into thinking that we can disregard our evolutionary patterns without suffering consequences.*

RESTORE INTERNAL ORDER

We're not masters of the universe the way we may like to think we are. The advent of technology has given us this false sense of mastery, lulling us into thinking that we can work anytime, anywhere, or have the lights on at any time of night without suffering negative consequences, despite the fact that for millions of years, plants, animals, and other living things have been living in sync with the light-dark cycles of the universe. Until artificial lighting was developed, the sun was the primary source of illumination for human beings, and after sunset, people settled down into the fading light.

As a result, they usually got plenty of rest or sleep. Fortunately, you can flip the switch on these habits by respecting your circadian rhythms. Honoring your body's natural rhythms is a crucial first step toward maintaining your physical and emotional equilibrium. The body is a bit like a Rubik's Cube: When the parts (or systems) are in the proper alignment, changing one thing can send everything else off-kilter; the more things you change, the more difficult it is for your body to achieve alignment because of the cascade of effects on other systems. Some people are better at compensating for these disruptions to their body's equilibrium than others, but many of us are left struggling.

On the other hand, living in harmony with the way we have evolved brings physiological and emotional balance, creating a good fit between our bodies and minds, between what we're doing and how we're designed to function. Honoring our body's natural rhythms helps stabilize our mood, become more resistant to stress, feel less physical pain, and generally feel and function better physically and mentally. It's an essential step in cooling and calming emotional inflammation.

The following are some ways you can adjust your habits so that they support your body's inherent rhythms:

- **Put yourself on a sleep schedule.** Establish a regular sleep-wake schedule so that you go to bed at approximately the same time each night and wake up at the same time each morning. It's fine to vary your bedtime by an hour or two occasionally but don't sleep in more than an extra hour on the weekends (unless you're sick); otherwise, you will end up disrupting your sleep pattern for the next night.

- **Identify your slumber sweet spot.** Most adults need seven to nine hours of sleep per night to feel and function at their best. Once you figure out how much *you* need, determine what time you need to get up in the morning and work backward to set an appropriate bedtime; or, you can identify what time of night you typically feel sleepy and then set a wake-up time accordingly. If eight hours of sleep is the sweet spot for you, you could choose to turn in at 10:00 P.M. and wake up at 6:00 A.M. or go to bed at 11:00 and get up at 7:00 or hit the sack at 12:00 and sleep until 8:00 A.M. Choose a pattern that works for you based on whether you're more of a lark (a morning person) or an owl (a night lover) and what your work schedule requires. Whatever pattern you select, keep it consistent so that your cellular clocks continue to operate efficiently.

The question of how to go to bed earlier when you're not used to doing so is a bit of a conundrum. If your bedtime has been inconsistent and you want to start turning in at 10:00 P.M., you may not feel sleepy initially. One strategy that sleep experts sometimes recommend is to move your bedtime fifteen to thirty minutes earlier each week until you're consistently getting the amount of sleep that makes you feel and function at your best in a time frame that works for your life. That's what Sean, the social worker, did. At my suggestion, he gave himself a creative curfew of 11:00 P.M. for his songwriting and gradually worked himself into a consistent sleep schedule. Once he was getting enough sleep regularly and he had recovered from his social jet lag, his daytime moods became steadier, and he found it easier to handle the emotional vicissitudes he regularly encounters working with his clients.

- **Brighten your mornings.** When you get up in the morning, expose yourself to bright, natural light to stimulate alertness, enhance your mood, and help calibrate your circadian rhythms. Take a brisk walk outside or have breakfast in a sunny spot. If you struggle to reset your internal clock to the "awake" setting in the morning, consider buying a commercial light box that emits 10,000 lux, which mimics a bright, sunny day. Sitting in front of such a light box for thirty minutes in the morning, perhaps while you have breakfast or read the newspaper or newsfeeds, has been found to stimulate alertness and improve mood. Alternatively, you could opt for a desk-lamp style light box for your desk at work.

- **Adjust your indoor lighting.** Fascinating research has found that office workers who are exposed to greater amounts of light in the morning fall asleep more quickly at night. They also have better sleep quality and better moods, including less depression and stress, than those who are exposed to low light in the morning. In the "old days," that is how human beings lived. We absorbed the light of the day because we were mostly outside. In the modern era, this has changed dramatically, and the consequences are likely much greater than we bargained for or even know how to assess. Most people's work lives aren't compatible with spending hours outside during the day, so it's important to catch those rays of light however you can—by working near sun-drenched windows or walking outside at lunchtime or during a break. Not only will you be more productive and more focused, but you'll also feel mentally revitalized and less reactive to stress.

Consider talking to the powers that be at work about the quality of the artificial lighting in your office because it will affect how you feel and function, too. If you crave the warm, cozy glow of incandescent light bulbs, a "soft white" LED bulb labeled "2700K" is soothing. In commercial spaces where bright light is called for, "bright white" or "cool white" bulbs (3500K–4100K) or "daylight" bulbs (5000K–6500K) are used because they are associated with increased productivity and alertness and are generally energizing. The highest numbers include blue tones, which are especially activating and can enhance vigilance, reaction times, and faster cognitive function. Fluorescent lights, by contrast, can have a negative impact on mood and lead to eyestrain and dizziness in some people, whereas some studies show that exposure to red light can increase alertness and performance in the afternoon. So consider the quality and type of your artificial indoor lighting carefully.

- **Establish a bedtime for electronic devices.** To avoid giving yourself social jet lag in the evening, give yourself a digital curfew at least ninety minutes before you plan to go to bed. At the appointed time, shut down all your digital devices and turn to a quiet, relaxing activity by dim amber light from a clamp-on reading light or a nearby bedside lamp. After all, it's not just the light that's generated by digital devices that's problematic; all the light around you can be, too. In fact, exposure to overhead light before bedtime can suppress melatonin release for about ninety minutes.

- **Darken your evenings.** There is another good reason to make sure that your bedroom (or wherever you sleep) is dark: When people are exposed to light during the night, their total daily melatonin production is suppressed dramatically, by as much as 50 percent. In other words, that nighttime light exposure throws the body's twenty-four-hour hormone-production schedule off-kilter. It's also wise to install a dimmer switch on the overhead light in the bathroom—or use a dim night-light—so that bright vanity lights don't stimulate your senses and alertness while you're taking care of bathroom business before hitting the sack or if you get up during the night.

- **Set the stage for sound sleep.** If you have trouble moving your bedtime earlier on your own, you could try taking a small dose of melatonin—the National Sleep Foundation recommends 1 to 3 mg—two hours before you want to go to sleep to reset your internal clock. This should be a short-term strategy, however, not one you want to become dependent upon. Be sure to talk to your doctor before taking melatonin supplements because they can interact with many different medications—such as anticoagulants, diabetes drugs, and sedatives, among others—and they may be contraindicated for people with certain medical conditions (such as an autoimmune disorder or seizure disorders). Melatonin also shouldn't be used during pregnancy or while breastfeeding.

Keep in mind that a wide array of prescription and over-the-counter medications, including certain antidepressants, decongestants, anticonvulsants, bronchodilators, corticosteroids, beta-blockers, and anticholinergic drugs, can contribute to sleep problems. Even ibuprofen and aspirin have been found to disrupt sleep in some people, increasing the number of awakenings and decreasing their sleep efficiency. If you suspect a particular medication is making it difficult for you to fall asleep or is causing middle-of-the-night awakenings, talk to your doctor to see if perhaps you can change the time of day when you take it or find a substitute drug.

Similarly, eating heavy, fatty, or spicy foods in the evening can cause sleep problems for some people. Pay attention to your caffeine intake as well, not just from coffee but also from tea, chocolate, and coffee-flavored foods (such as ice cream or yogurt). In some people, caffeine is metabolized very slowly, and it can take their bodies as long as nine to twelve hours to completely remove it from their systems. If this describes you, having a pick-me-up latte at 3:00 P.M. could end up leaving you wide awake at 10:00 P.M. when you want to turn in for the night.

✦ ✦ ✦

Ultimately, honoring your body's natural rhythms requires taking back control of your nights and days. It's about putting time on your side and making conscious choices about the way you want to live so that you can restore your internal equilibrium, physiologically and psychologically.

Yes, changing your behavior requires giving up the patterns you chose, consciously or not, in the past, and making the switch does take some effort and resolve. But if you make it a priority to stop upsetting your body's internal rhythms and start living in sync with your body's inherent needs, the payoffs will be well worth the effort. Your mood is likely to end up on a more even keel, and your energy will increase. Your physical health will probably improve and your emotional equilibrium will, too. Think of it this way: By respecting your body's rhythms and doing whatever you can to maintain their regularity, you'll be resetting your internal emotional thermostat, which will improve the way you react to and deal with the stresses and strains that are unavoidable in our modern world.

LIVING IN SYNC

You've probably noticed that the way you feel and function fluctuates throughout the day. These ups and downs are due to your body's circadian rhythms, which include twenty-four-hour hormonal and temperature changes, among other oscillations. If you stick with a fairly consistent schedule, day and night, many daily rhythms are somewhat predictable from day to day. Establishing this physiological consistency, which is what the body craves naturally, sets us up for greater emotional stability and resilience. Here's a look at some of the fascinating scientific findings on this subject:

- **Morning:** Research shows that people are significantly less sensitive to pain in the morning than in the afternoon. So consider scheduling a dental or medical procedure for 7:00 to 10:00 A.M.

- **Midmorning:** For most people, alertness, reasoning skills, and short-term memory are at their prime mid-morning. Complex decision-making skills are high from mid-to-late morning, too, which may be why firefighters tend to have one of their fastest response rates at this time.

- **Early afternoon:** Alertness declines and sleepiness sets in, and it has very little to do with what you ate for lunch. There's a physiological reason this is considered siesta time in many parts of the world.

- **Late afternoon:** Many exercise abilities peak. From 4:00 to 7:00 P.M., you're likely to have your best performance in physical activities involving strength, speed, and power.

While these peak windows apply to many people, they may be slightly off if you're a true morning person or a night owl. In some instances, there can be as much as a four-hour difference in these peak times, according to Michael Smolensky, PhD, a chronobiologist at the University of Texas at Austin and coauthor of *The Body Clock Guide to Better Health*. To personalize these patterns, your best bet is to track your own physical and cognitive performance throughout the day, gauge how it varies in different areas, then try to schedule key activities for when you're at your personal best.

THE RESTORE TO-DO LIST

☐ Establish a regular bedtime and awakening time that takes into account your optimal amount of sleep each night; keep it consistent during the week and on the weekends.

☐ Give yourself a digital curfew at least ninety minutes before bedtime. Turn off all electronic devices, dim the lights, and engage in an activity that helps you downshift from the day.

☐ Expose yourself to bright, natural light when you get up in the morning to stimulate alertness and reset your body's master clock.

☐ Identify sneaky disruptors to your sleep rhythms—medications you might be taking or foods you may be eating—and see if you can alter the time you take or eat them. (Check with your doctor before doing so with drugs.)

☐ Try to schedule key tasks—such as those requiring strong reasoning or decision-making skills or physical strength and power—to coincide with your peak performance times during the day.

CHAPTER 7

THINK YOURSELF

INTO A SAFE

SPACE

Negative thoughts
stick around because
we believe them, not
because we want
them or choose them.

ANDREW J. BERNSTEIN,
American author and executive consultant

N TROUBLING TIMES, YOUR mind can be your best friend or your worst foe, depending on how you use it. Take thirty-year-old James, for example. If a human rights violation or horrifying abuse of power came to light, James would glom onto it and be unable to let it go. If stress in his personal life ramped up, he would perseverate about it, which would ratchet up his agitation and anxiety. A successful lawyer who had a volatile relationship with his life partner, James had become dependent on the drama in his personal life and his habit of ruminating about world calamities to drown out his own existential crises (about his identity, purpose, and place in the world).

To tamp down the emotional fires in his life, he often used recreational drugs or drank excessively, which made him feel more out of control. It wasn't until he broke up with his partner and met a calmer, more stable man that James began to tune in to his thoughts instead of running away from them. He began practicing meditation and engaging in creative writing about his tumultuous childhood and romantic life, which helped him better process these experiences. In addition, the combination helped him appreciate the positive things in his life that he'd been overlooking; this had a mood-stabilizing effect and made James feel stronger and more resilient.

We may not be able to control the morass of distressing events that is occurring on the world stage, but each of us can wield some control over how we think about them or respond to them. When you become hyperreactive to something you see or hear, your body tries to figure out if you should fight or flee, and your sympathetic nervous system sends stress hormones racing through your body. Your coping mechanisms will get called into action, and depending on whether your coping style is healthy or not, the same will be true of your response to the upsetting news or event. If your response is problematic, you could end up ruminating or perseverating about it, shutting down emotionally, swinging into a frenzy, or getting testy with those around you.

In other words, many of us are contributing to our own anxiety, trauma, and sense of depletion with our habits, which are hidden triggers for emotional inflammation. Being constantly bombarded by negative news and up-to-the-minute newsfeeds can put us in a state of hyperarousal. According to research from Stanford University, when people use social media to call attention to racist, sexist, abusive, or unpatriotic behavior that's occurring on the national or international stage, comments provoke moral outrage that goes viral but they also trigger a complex array of emotions that can contribute to what feels like bullying and be difficult for viewers to handle. Given the immediacy of social media, it becomes hard for us to distance ourselves from these messages in terms of time and space. It doesn't have to play out this way.

Harnessing the power of your mind can help restore your emotional equilibrium—and there are many ways to do this. To level your own emotional playing field, start by removing or reducing negative influences on your thinking patterns and moods. That alone will help put you in a calmer, more balanced state of mind. It also helps to develop positive cognitive (thinking) habits so that you can come to your own emotional rescue when you're facing alarming news, threats to your well-being, and other sources of everyday stress.

To be clear, the goal is *not* to start walking through life like some Pollyanna who pretends that all is sweetness and light. That's not a realistic or sustainable approach to life. To survive and thrive in this world, you need to be able to view things clearly, take responsibility for dealing with challenges, learn from disappointments, and rebound from setbacks, while also treating your emotional distress. All of these actions require cognitive and emotional skills. The mind-shifting plan that follows will help you get to that package of prizes.

CONTROL THE FLOW OF INFORMATION IN YOUR LIFE

We're living in a world where information overload is rampant. When too much information comes at you all day long, your ability to process or digest it all and to make effective decisions is impeded; this in turn can stop you from taking action, leaving you stuck in a state of behavioral paralysis. The cognitive flood also can rev up anxiety about how to respond and cope with what seems like an endless stream of disturbing information. As neuroscientist Daniel J. Levitin, PhD, writes in *The Organized Mind: Thinking Straight in the Age of Information Overload*, "Our brains do have the ability to process the information we take in, but at a cost: We can have trouble separating the trivial from the important, and all this information processing makes us tired." When the emotional valence of some of that excess information is alarming, anxiety provoking, or disturbing in other ways, it can lead to a form of emotional overload that upsets your equilibrium.

Limit Your Exposure

Part of the solution is to control the flow of inflammatory information in your life by closing the gates when appropriate. For one thing, you can moderate the amount of alarming news you're exposed to, perhaps by putting yourself on a media diet: setting limits on how frequently you check newsfeeds, resolving to read the news only in the morning and then avoiding it for the rest of the day, or giving yourself entirely news-free days. Whichever strategy you choose, think of this as a healthy form of self-care that can foster self-preservation.

Andrea, the nonprofit strategy and operations manager introduced in chapter 3, lives with her boyfriend, who works in television news.

Even when he's not working, he enjoys watching the news and feels energized by it. Andrea, on the other hand, finds it painful and frustrating to tune in to. "Watching the news makes me feel depressed and helpless," she says. "I want to be able to form my own opinions about what's happening, and I feel like that's been taken away in the current climate." So the couple has struck a bargain: He'll watch; she won't. Instead, she'll read the morning paper to stay abreast of current events and spend the rest of her day and evening focusing on her own regularly scheduled life.

Develop a Questioning Mind

To filter the information that affects you emotionally, it also helps to improve your critical thinking skills, including your ability to view an issue from multiple angles. According to the Foundation for Critical Thinking, "critical thinking is the art of analyzing and evaluating thinking with a view to improving it." There are many different ways to improve your critical thinking skills. Like calling a time-out when the other team goes on a scoring streak, you can interrupt your emotional tear by asking some key questions such as, *What is the source of this information? Is it reliable or biased? What evidence is presented to support the claims that are being made?* (It's especially important to ask these questions about posts on social media, where fake news is rampant.) Try to keep an open mind as you listen to other people's ideas, positions, and arguments without thinking of your response; then, analyze the information you've just heard, breaking it down into various components and examining the issues from all sides.

Let's say a controversial initiative is being presented in your community or workplace. Before you speak up, it's wise to consider the following: *Why does this person/committee believe this is the best approach moving forward? What are the potential upsides and downsides? How does this reflect and address changing needs in the community? Is the logic behind the proposal supported by evidence, facts, or data? Are there other ways to address this issue that might be as effective and less controversial?* By asking questions that begin with *how* and *why*, you'll be able to gain deeper insights into a particular issue. Honing these skills will help you become more adept at thinking for yourself and less likely to accept upsetting information at face value.

To exercise critical thinking skills in relation to what you're seeing or hearing in the media, avoid the knee-jerk reaction. Instead, hit the pause button and ask *how* and *why* questions about the information that's being presented, as well as, *What are we not being told about this?* Remember: The media often focuses on the sensational, inflammatory, or aberrational news based on the mantra "If it bleeds, it leads" to grab people's attention and hence boost their audience. Good news tends to get buried.

Reframe Your Own Thoughts

Similarly, it's wise to use critical thinking skills when evaluating your own thoughts, rather than blindly accepting them, because you could be inadvertently fueling your emotional inflammation with the way you're thinking. There are two components to sources of stress in life: the news, events, or challenges that happen, and the way you think about them. As far as the latter component goes, your thinking style can ratchet up your stress level or help dial it down. For example, if you discover that you'll be getting a new work supervisor who has a tough reputation, you could look at this change as a "threat," which would amp up your stress level, or reframe it as a "challenge," which would make it feel less daunting and more manageable.

Strategies like this have been proven to work. In one study, researchers randomly assigned participants to appraise their anxiety as *beneficial* before they engaged in a mock salary negotiation or gave them no specific instructions about how to appraise the situation. Before and after the negotiation, the participants' cortisol levels were measured, and this is where things get interesting: Those who were instructed to appraise their anxiety as *beneficial* had higher cortisol responses, but this was associated with a positive effect because they performed better in the negotiation and emerged with higher salaries. In other words, framing the anxiety as *beneficial* made the effects of stress strengthening, rather than debilitating.

In another study, researchers manipulated people's mindsets by showing them film clips with either a "stress-is-enhancing" or a "stress-is-debilitating" message before putting them through a social stress test. Here, again, those in the stress-is-enhancing group thrived, experiencing sharper increases in growth hormones and positive mood and greater cognitive flexibility than those with the stress-is-debilitating mindset did.

These are just a few examples of what's called "cognitive reframing." It is a cornerstone of cognitive behavioral therapy, or CBT, which helps people change the way they think and behave in order to change the way they *feel*. The underlying premise is that your thoughts affect your emotions. But the converse is true as well: moods can affect the content and emotional valence of your thoughts—through what's called "mood-congruent" cognitions. The gist of this pathway is that positive (or good) moods produce positive thoughts, while negative moods produce negative thoughts. The combination of these effects means that moods and thoughts reside on a two-way street, with both affecting each other, which is why making a conscious effort to take steps to push both in a positive (or at least away from a negative) direction is smart. A hidden perk in this is that consciously putting yourself in a good mood also puts you in a better position to take action on or fend off the triggers that are getting to you.

Remember, too, that a variety of cognitive distortions (a.k.a. twisted thoughts) can *magnify* the effects of your triggers and hijack your moods, taking them more deeply into negative territory. The following are among the most common distortions:

- **All-or-nothing thinking:** viewing a situation in extreme or absolute terms, without appreciating its nuances

- **Catastrophizing:** making a situation seem more dire or threatening than it is by envisioning worst-case scenarios

- **Jumping to conclusions:** believing something is true when there's no evidence to support your assumption

- **Magnification:** blowing an upsetting situation way out of proportion, which adds to your frustration and distress

- **Overgeneralizing:** viewing a single upsetting event as part of an ongoing pattern

Each of these thought patterns has the potential to worsen emotional inflammation. That's why it's important to learn to question or talk back to these twisted thoughts (in your head). Or, consider the possibility of a sampling error in your judgments. If you tune in to the style and emotional valence of your thoughts, you can correct or redirect them when appropriate—perhaps by asking yourself how likely it is that your worst fears will actually happen, by considering whether there's any evidence that what you're saying to yourself is true and by banishing words like *always* or *never* from your self-directed vocabulary. These are all effective ways to silence the negative chatter inside your head.

When faced with a challenging or upsetting situation at work or in her personal life, twenty-four-year-old Tara, a marketing assistant in Oregon, says she has a tendency to "take a fear to an extreme level." Sometimes she'll imagine worst-case scenarios that could happen; other times, she becomes fixated on all the different ways a financial issue or a work situation could harm her. "Situations that are ambiguous or where someone clearly has a hidden agenda can send me into end-of-the-world mode," she admits. That's when her thoughts can spiral into patterns about all the things that could go wrong, that the situation is hopeless, or that she was a fool to expect things to work out differently—any of which further ratchet up her anxiety.

To stop herself from getting lost in these negative thinking patterns, she'll often seek a reality check from her partner or a mentor about how dire a situation really is. She also has been trying to shift her perspective to consider the upside of what she can learn or gain from navigating her way through a particular challenge. And she recently quit Twitter, which "exposed me to a lot less negative thinking," she says. "When I have the urge to vent negatively, I want to tweet and without the app I can't, so the feeling de-escalates."

FUN FACTS

Human beings have an estimated 60,000 to 80,000 thoughts each day. Interestingly, many of these are repetitive, meaning we had the same (or similar) thoughts the day before, the week before, and so on. "The mind tends to get stuck in repetitive thought loops that squeeze out the possibility for new ideas and inspiration," notes Deepak Chopra, MD, cofounder of the Chopra Center for Wellbeing and a world-renowned pioneer in integrative medicine and personal transformation. Because they help you expand your awareness and/or consciousness, different forms of meditation can help you break out of these thought ruts, gaining new insights, ideas, and sources of inspiration.

BEWARE THE HAZARDS OF OVERTHINKING IT

Believe it or not, there's a danger in thinking too much—that is, in *overthinking* a problem or upsetting situation. Rumination, as you may know, is the tendency to cogitate or dwell on distressing situations so much that these thoughts end up playing repetitively in our heads like a broken record. You might think you're being proactive by thinking about the many facets of a problem. But as you go over and over the same thoughts and ideas, you can end up with binocular vision, becoming so fixated on a particular aspect that you often aren't able to see the bigger picture. Meanwhile, you can end up feeling worse and worse about the situation and perhaps life in general.

Rumination is not only self-defeating; it's associated with adverse health consequences, including an increase in anxiety, sleep disturbances, cardiovascular effects (e.g., high blood pressure), overeating, or drinking too much alcohol. As Sonja Lyubomirsky, PhD, explains in *The How of Happiness*, rumination "sustains or worsens sadness, fosters negatively biased thinking, impairs a person's ability to solve problems, saps motivation, and interferes with concentration and initiative." While you may think you're gaining insights into yourself or traction with your problems, with rumination you're more likely to gain "a distorted, pessimistic perspective" on your life. Besides draining your mental resources, rumination can send your mood into a downward spiral because it causes you to think about situations with increasing negativity. When you're in a distressed state, negative thoughts and memories are more readily accessible so you're likely to use *them* to interpret what's happening now. The skewed picture you get can interfere with your ability to take effective action, which can lead to more worry and stress. *Not what you're looking for!*

Fortunately, you can learn to break the rumination habit. The trick is to catch yourself in the act, then to distract yourself with an absorbing activity such as reading or watching something engrossing, listening to enjoyable music or playing a musical instrument, taking a brisk walk, or tending to pets. Or you could consciously shift your focus to someone else by doing a small act of kindness, such as offering to bring dinner to a friend who is sick. Taking actions like these will essentially short-circuit the rumination impulse. If you need to, you can use thought-stopping techniques to keep yourself out of thought-spinning mode: Visualize a stop sign or tell yourself *I'm on a thought vacation; I don't need to think about this now*, while breathing deeply and exhaling slowly to consciously choose to redirect your attention.

Meanwhile, make an appointment with yourself to confront the issue, either later in the day or even the following day because the goal is not to avoid your problems but to handle them when you feel more in control of your emotions. At the appointed time, give yourself ten to fifteen minutes to consider what's bothering you or how the situation needs to change and what you can do about it. Identify the most feasible, worthwhile steps you can take and formulate a plan of action. If you've been ruminating, say, about the tension between you and your partner, find a mutually agreeable time to talk to him or her and if little progress is made and the issues are important, suggest going to a counselor together. To get the issue out of your head and translate it into something you can do something about, it can help to put your thoughts and ideas into words by writing them down on paper or your computer. Besides unburdening yourself, the act of putting your feelings into words helps you organize and make sense of them; you may even discover that what was bothering you isn't actually as overwhelming or threatening as you initially thought.

If it turns out that you can't do anything to change a situation you've been obsessing about—such as a serious illness in your family or a politician's betrayal of public trust—try to accept the reality, painful as it is, and consciously decide to stop mulling it over. Acknowledge your feelings honestly and try to find some insight or wisdom that you can take into the future. Or channel your anger or frustration into a constructive activity to improve another aspect of your world (see chapter 10).

FUN FACTS

Ever wonder why you gain savvy insights or have creative breakthroughs while you're taking a shower? It's not a fluke. The theory is that this happens because when you're doing something routine, like showering, your brain essentially goes on autopilot, allowing your prefrontal cortex (PFC) to relax and turning on your brain's default mode network (DMN), an interconnected group of brain regions that appear to be less active when you're engaged in a task that requires paying attention. With your PFC relaxed and your DMN switched on, your mind can make new, creative connections or solve problems that your conscious mind would have overlooked. Plus, when you're relaxing in the shower, your brain may release dopamine, the motivating, pleasurable neurotransmitter, and more alpha waves will ripple through your brain, just like when you're meditating; both effects can ignite creative sparks.

MEDITATE TO CALM YOUR MIND

In addition to striving for mindfulness in everyday life, the practice of Transcendental Meditation (TM) or mindfulness meditation is extremely effective in creating a buffer zone between ourselves and the upsetting nature of world events and conditions. TM, which involves silently repeating a mantra, usually a word or sound, while sitting with your eyes closed, liberates the practitioner from the moment, allowing the person to enter a unique kind of silence that brings a deep feeling of inner peace. Studies have illustrated the many benefits of practicing TM, including reducing stress and anxiety and improving sleep, memory, and mental clarity. The American Heart Association has gone so far as to encourage clinicians to recommend it to help patients reduce high blood pressure, and the US military endorses it as a form of treatment for PTSD.

In contrast, mindfulness meditation centers on being present in the here and now by focusing on your breath; when your attention wanders, you bring it back to your breath. Mindfulness practices have been found to reduce anxiety and improve pain management, while also enhancing emotional regulation and cognitive functions like working memory. It doesn't require a major time investment: When inexperienced meditators engaged in brief, thirteen-minute guided meditation sessions daily for eight weeks, they experienced a dramatic decrease in their bad moods and anxiety and improvements in their attention, working memory, and emotional regulation, according to a study from New York University.

Both forms of meditation have their proponents, and depending upon your personal needs, you may prefer one practice over the other. I suggest trying one or both to see which works for you.

DEVELOP A TOLERANCE FOR DISCOMFORT

Given the current state of the world and the myriad pressures we're all facing on a regular basis, discomfort and uncertainty are bound to be facts of modern life. We might as well get used to these feelings. I'm not suggesting taking a defeatist attitude or simply accepting the status quo but rather learning to tolerate a modicum of discomfort or uncertainty without letting it penetrate or dominate your mind and spirit.

This line of thinking is a feature of acceptance and commitment therapy, or ACT, a hot topic in psychology that encourages people to mindfully accept their feelings and reactions and then choose to behave and live in ways that are consistent with their personal values. It's an approach

continues

that allows you to move forward without struggling with your inner feelings.

Rather than fighting flashes of frustration, anxiety, or anger, sometimes it's better just to sit with those feelings and accept them. Notice that they're present without judging or latching on to them. Instead, view them as if they were leaves floating on a stream, and they'll likely pass naturally. When someone has an emotional reaction to something in his or her environment, a chemical process in the body is activated that puts it on alert, but it lasts for only ninety seconds, according to neuroscientist Jill Bolte Taylor, PhD. After those ninety seconds have passed, any remaining emotional response stems from the person choosing, consciously or not, to stay in that emotional cycle.

Since I learned about the ninety-second effect, I have become a big fan. Often when I start getting ratcheted up by an issue, I can quickly lapse into a ruminative state, grinding back and forth over the same material, which makes me feel even more frustrated and agitated. Now, when I become aware of what I'm doing, I firmly and repeatedly say, *Ninety-second rule! Ninety-second rule!* to remind myself that the hold the emotional chemical alert has on me is short-lived. I also remind myself that *it is my choice* whether to hold on to these emotions. It doesn't work instantly (*What does?!*), but the strategy becomes more effective each time I use it, and as the grip of strong emotions gives way to reason, I feel an empowering sense of relief.

If you simply notice that swell of emotions and don't hold on to it, you can feel it fade away, too. The key is not to engage, not to judge or ruminate about your feelings or what triggered them. Acknowledge and name how you're feeling, as if it were an object outside of you. Let yourself feel what you feel but then be willing to let go of it. As Taylor writes in her book *My Stroke of Insight*, "My favorite definition of fear is 'False Expectations Appearing Real,' and when I allow myself to remember that all of my thoughts are fleeting physiology, I feel less moved when my story-teller goes haywire and my circuitry is triggered."

CHANGE THE CHANNEL IN YOUR HEAD

After evicting unnecessary negativity from your mind (or at least putting it into an appropriate perspective), it's time to steer your attitude into a more constructive, upbeat direction. As far as our minds are concerned, research has found that it takes three times more positive than negative stimuli for us to maintain a healthy equilibrium that allows us to lead upwardly spiraling lives. The point is, people need more positive experiences than negative ones to allow them to thrive. "Positivity doesn't just change the contents of your mind, trading bad thoughts for good ones; it also changes the scope or boundaries of your mind. It widens the span of possibilities that you see," Barbara Fredrickson, PhD, explains in *Positivity*.

Creating and reaching this critical tipping point can mean the difference between suffering and thriving, between feeling upbeat and downbeat. To find *your* ratio, you can pause to take your emotional pulse at regular intervals throughout the day. You can also take steps to tilt the balance in your favor by consciously buffering yourself from negative stimuli (including people and newsfeeds), talking back to your own negative thoughts when they arise, becoming more mindful, and focusing on what's going right in your life.

In the spring of 2018, forty-three-year-old Matt, an entrepreneur and marketing expert in Wisconsin, felt demoralized by all the negativity on his social media feeds, so he decided to start writing a daily gratitude journal and posting it. At first, his goal was to find at least one thing he was grateful for each day, but he soon found it easy to identify multiple things to appreciate on a daily basis. Actively thinking about how to capture a series of positive moments—whether it's cooking a delicious gourmet meal, spending time in nature, or exploring a place he's never been—and sharing them has made him feel more upbeat and optimistic, he says, and it has had a positive effect on the people who read his posts. Matt's experience is hardly unusual. Numerous studies have found that expressing gratitude—whether it's by listing specific or general things you're grateful for or communicating your appreciation to other people—is associated with greater emotional well-being and life satisfaction.

In a cohort of people with anxiety or depression, researchers in California examined the effects of intentionally targeting the "positive affect system," which is characterized by upbeat emotions such as joy or excitement and guides people toward potentially rewarding situations. The participants completed ten one-hour weekly sessions in a positive activity intervention protocol with multiple components, including activities such as expressing gratitude (by writing about up to five things for which they feel grateful), performing up to five acts of kindness for others in a day, identifying their personal values (and writing about why they're important and how they use them in their everyday life), and practicing optimism (by imagining their "best possible future" in a chosen area of their lives and considering how they could make it happen). The goal was to generate "upward spirals of positive thinking, emotions, and behaviors" to help people overcome anxiety and depression—and it worked! After the ten-week intervention, as well as at the three- and six-month follow-ups, the participants, who had the freedom to choose which activities they incorporated into their daily lives, showed significant increases in their positive emotions and psychological well-being, as well as decreases in their negative mood symptoms.

As this study suggests, many of us can train ourselves to focus our attention differently, as a way to enhance our emotional health. Using the right strategies to shift your attention and attitude can help restore your emotional equilibrium for the long haul. You also can use them to come to your own emotional rescue when you need immediate relief in any given moment or if you're suffering from an emotional hangover after, say, an intense argument with your partner or a friend. In other words, these strategies can break a negative emotional spell. Here are some ways to put these tactics into practice:

- **Alter your vocabulary.** When anxiety rears its nerve-racking head, take a closer look at the situation at hand and try to reframe it—perhaps as excitement or eagerness if you're preparing to give a presentation, for example. As social psychologist Amy Cuddy, PhD, writes in *Presence: Bringing Your Boldest Self to Your Biggest Challenges*, "By simply reframing the meaning of the emotion we're experiencing—by nudging ourselves from anxiety to excitement—we shift our psychological orientation, harnessing the cognitive and physiological resources we need to succeed under pressure."

- **Put your feelings into words.** Using expressive writing to pour your heart out about emotionally charged issues in your life can be beneficial for your health and emotional well-being in numerous ways—and it can help you gain a new perspective on what happened. Whether it's because describing your feelings with words feels somewhat cathartic, helps you organize disorganized thoughts into more cohesive ones, or enables you to learn to better regulate your emotions, the results are often similar: the act of writing can help you get through or gain a sense of control over upsetting experiences.

- **Consider the long view.** When something upsetting happens, ask yourself: *Will this matter next week? Next month? Next year? How important is this, really?* Getting some perspective by giving the situation's likely impact a reality check can take some of the punch out of a trigger.

- **Count your blessings.** Think about and jot down what you most appreciate in your life. Besides improving your emotional well-being and social relationships, feeling and expressing gratitude increases your neural sensitivity (in the brain's prefrontal cortex) to experiencing gratitude in the future.

- **Take a pleasant trip down memory lane.** Consciously recalling positive memories or good times when you're in a bad state of mind not only improves your mood in a given moment but also activates the prefrontal cortex, which helps with emotional and cognitive regulation. The preponderance of research supporting this effect has given rise to what's known as "reminiscence therapy," which is being used to great effect with people of many different ages.

- **Practice self-affirmations.** Whether you choose to write about them in a journal or simply take time for reflection, focusing on your personal core values, attributes, and actions, and why they're important to you, can give you a strong sense of being competent, good, and effective as you face challenges in life. It also can bolster your sense of self-control, your self-image, and your overall emotional well-being.

- **Show yourself compassion.** The aim is to cultivate kindness, understanding, and empathy toward yourself, to recognize that your negative emotions and thoughts are harming you, and to cut yourself some slack by changing the conversation in your head. Remind yourself that none of us is perfect and that we all have occasional lapses in judgment or make mistakes.

- **Give yourself permission to let loose.** After a deeply upsetting conflict with someone who disrespected or hurt you, think about what you'd really like to say or do. Then, go ahead and *imagine* (in your head) cursing that person out or showing your anger or frustration in another way—try not to hold back! These are clearly unpleasant actions to feel that you have to take but acting this out in your head often feels cathartic. Just like conjuring up a peaceful scene can calm you, visualizing something like this can release the toxic emotions you may be feeling. And once you have chilled out, your brain's prefrontal cortex can weigh in to see if there's anything you can learn from what transpired. Remember: there is no reason to feel bad about negative feelings you have toward someone if you don't act on them.

- **Put color on your side.** Exposing yourself to serene colors, such as green or blue, has calming, restorative effects on the mind and body, whereas red and yellow can be more arousing, according to color psychology research. Of course, color saturation and brightness play a role in the effects so pay attention to these qualities as you try to surround yourself with hues that have the power to influence your mood and energy in the right ways.

- **Tune in to appealing music.** Listening to relaxing or happy music that is personally selected can improve a person's mood after dealing with a stressful situation, according to research from the Netherlands. It also can enhance blood pressure recovery after a stressful experience and distract you from the urge to ruminate about what just happened. So grab your phone and earbuds or pick up that musical instrument so you can tune in to music that nourishes your mind and soul.

- **Do something nice for someone else.** Contrary to the common assumption that the key to happiness is to focus on yourself, research has found that performing acts of kindness for others or for the world at large leads to greater psychological flourishing by leading to an increase in positive emotions and a decrease in negative ones. So consider bringing a meal to someone in need or volunteering for a cause you believe in. Practicing prosociality (behaviors that are intended to benefit others) on a regular basis even has a contagious effect, inspiring other people to pay kindness and generosity forward.

✦ ✦ ✦

All of these thought exercises really involve engaging in deliberate emotional regulation, not letting the brain's amygdala (the mass of gray matter that's involved with fear and aggression, in particular) hijack your feelings and run away with them. With all of these thought maneuvers, you're basically turning the dial in your brain from negative thought processes that can send your mood and attitude into a nosedive toward positive ones that can heal and energize you. This way, your mind is reset to a more balanced perspective, allowing you to shape your thoughts or question them in smart, constructive ways. Besides helping you reclaim your emotional equilibrium, these healthy forms of mind control will help you move forward and improve matters in your own life and in the world around you.

In the seventeenth century, the French philosopher and mathematician René Descartes's proposition, "I think, therefore I am," was intended to provide a stable foundation for knowledge in the face of radical doubt. In the centuries since then, the world has certainly changed, but our basic human insecurities persist. With all due respect to Descartes, perhaps it's time for an updated proposition: "I think well, therefore I *am* well." Creating a foundation for emotional equilibrium in a tumultuous world is no small thing. Putting the power of your mind to good use by improving your critical thinking skills, correcting cognitive distortions, and consciously steering your thoughts in healthy directions not only buffers the effects of emotional triggers, it also engages the reward circuitry in your brain.

THE RESTORE TO-DO LIST

☐ Catch your negative thoughts, give them a reality check, then correct any distorted thinking, throughout the day.

☐ Control the flow of information in your life by setting limits on how and when you tune in to various sources of media, including social media.

☐ Get in the habit of questioning your stress. What might it be telling you? Could it be an opportunity in disguise? Find the hidden message and you may be able to deactivate the threat element.

☐ Banish words like *always* or *never* or *should* from your self-directed vocabulary, just as if you were speaking to a dear friend.

☐ Remember that physiological reactions to emotional issues naturally last for a maximum of ninety seconds; what happens after that is up to you.

☐ Practice gratitude by making a habit of naming three to five things you're grateful for on a regular basis.

CHAPTER 8

OBEY

YOUR BODY

With every act of self-care

your authentic self gets

stronger, and the critical,

fearful mind gets weaker.

Every act of self-care is a

powerful declaration:

I am on my side.

SUSAN WEISS BERRY,
American mindfulness coach, writer, and painter

T HE BASICS OF TAKING good care of your body are well-known—eat well, exercise regularly, get enough sleep, don't smoke, and manage stress. When it comes to calming emotional inflammation, all of these good-for-you measures still apply, but several interesting nuances come into play in terms of the specific elements that matter and why. Yes, you should still stick with a healthy, largely plant-based diet, do regular cardio and strength training workouts, get seven to nine hours of shut-eye per night, avoid smoking, and take time to decompress from stress. But that's just the starting point. Especially during times of emotional inflammation, taking the extra steps to quiet your hyperreactivity, agitation, angst, or other uncomfortable emotions—from the inside out as well as the outside in—is more necessary than ever. When people are stressed to the nth degree, they often take the path of least resistance or let their healthy intentions slide, which certainly doesn't help them feel better and may actually make them feel worse.

Let's start with the issue of diet, a subject that's often mired in confusion given the various claims that are associated with different eating plans. Food is such a loaded topic in its own right. People often have strong opinions about what's good to eat and what's not, when and where it's acceptable to eat (or not), sometimes even attaching moral virtue to the way they eat. With a phenomenon that's been dubbed "orthorexia," people become so obsessed with eating healthy foods that they eliminate many ingredients, sometimes even entire food groups, and their rigid rules guide what they will or won't do socially (for them, exercising with friends is okay, for instance, but going out for lunch isn't). Environmental concerns often come into play as well, as some people make a concerted effort to buy local (to reduce their carbon footprint), go vegan (for compassionate reasons), or reduce food waste and packaging (for the sake of the planet). In other words, deciding what or how to eat can trigger a variety of emotions, some of which are difficult.

The truth is, food is still a basic human need, essential to our physical health, cognitive function, and emotional well-being. Just as loading up on junk food or sugary foods can send your blood sugar and mood on a roller-coaster ride, skipping meals or eating infrequently can leave you feeling depleted, physically and emotionally. While there isn't a perfect diet for treating emotional inflammation, what does matter *significantly* is how your body responds to the foods you eat, and that depends in large measure on a rising star in the field of medicine: the gut microbiome. The gut microbiome consists of a community of more than one hundred *trillion* microorganisms, including bacteria, fungi, and viruses, that reside, albeit to varying degrees, throughout your gastrointestinal tract. *There are ten times more microbes than there are cells in the human body!* The idea of having so many "bugs" moving around in our intestines may feel off-putting at first, but the latest research suggests that the presence and function of these microorganisms are as critical to human health as, say, a properly beating heart.

Under optimal conditions the beneficial microbes far outnumber the harmful ones and coexist peacefully and symbiotically, playing key roles in the human body's daily operations. The human gut microbiome is like a miniature factory, with an array of highly skilled workers delivering a volume and variety of products that boggle the mind. The hardworking microbes break down foods into small component parts that the body uses for various functions. They produce amino acids, the building blocks of protein, which are involved in nearly every process in the body. They help modulate the immune system, protecting the body against disease-causing microbes and other intruders. They produce vitamins needed for nerve function (B vitamins) and others that are critical to blood clotting (vitamin K). They are even involved in creating conditions in the brain that affect memory function, our ability to think and perform complex tasks, and even how we feel and behave. (That's a lot of work for such tiny creatures!)

A burgeoning area of research shows that the gut microbiome is in constant communication with the brain. Like chatty teenagers, the gut and the brain send messages back and forth using the body's neurons (via the enteric nervous system) and bloodstream (in the gut's case). These messages influence your mood, your response to stress, your circadian rhythms, and even your sleep patterns. The gut microbiome, often dubbed the "second brain," plays such a prominent role in conditions that affect our well-being that new research suggests the connection between the gut microbiome and the brain is at the forefront of a "new approach to mental health." Indeed, the composition of the gut microbiome and the way your gut communicates with your brain may affect your risk of developing depression, anxiety, and other mood disorders. (Studies in Sweden and the Netherlands have identified what researchers say may be "melancholic microbes.")

Here's another shocker: It is estimated that 90 percent of serotonin, the well-known neurotransmitter involved in mood regulation, is manufactured in the digestive tract from . . . (drum roll, please) . . . the work of *microbes*! Gut bacteria have also been found to increase or decrease levels of other neurotransmitters including dopamine, which stimulates the reward, motivation, and attention centers in the brain; norepinephrine, which stimulates the "take action" functions in times of stress; and gamma-aminobutyric acid (GABA), which lowers anxiety and generally quiets the nervous system down.

Your microbiome, like your fingerprints, may be quite different from your friends' and family members' microbiomes. Each of us has a unique network of these microorganisms inside us. Initially the network is determined by genetic factors, then it is influenced by conditions at birth as we pass through the birth canal and drink our mother's breast milk. As time goes on, where we reside and how we live—including the air we breathe, the water we drink, the foods we eat, and the chemicals we are exposed to, including the medications we take—can change our microbiome. This is where we can make choices, take charge of our health, and tip the bacteria balance in our microbiome in either a positive or a negative direction.

MIND YOUR MEDICATIONS

For your microbiome's sake, it's wise to pay attention to the medications you take. As you may know, antibiotics can disrupt the balance of bacteria in your gut, which is one reason doctors recommend taking them only when they're truly necessary, but other drug-related factors can affect it, too. Animals raised on industrial farms are routinely given antibiotics to promote their growth and stave off infection. When they are slaughtered and enter our food supply, they become a major source of unwanted exposure to antibiotics and can alter our microbiomes when we eat them and contribute to antibiotic resistance.

But that's not all. A 2018 study from Germany found that more than 200 *nonantibiotic* drugs—including antivirals, antipsychotics, proton pump inhibitors, chemotherapy drugs, and some blood-pressure medications—can upset the growth of different species of human gut bacteria. This does *not* mean you should stop taking these drugs (unless, of course, your physician says it's okay), but it does mean that you should take extra steps to protect your gut bacteria if you are taking them.

FOODS FOR THOUGHT AND STEADY CALM

Let's start with broad principles about eating patterns that can profoundly affect the microbiome. First, the sobering news: A high intake of starchy carbohydrates, simple sugars, saturated fats, animal protein, highly processed foods, and artificial sweeteners promotes the proliferation of *bad actor microbes* in the gut. Among many different harmful actions, these bad actors can promote inflammation and skew the ratio of health-promoting to health-threatening bacteria in the gut. Now, some good news: If you consume foods with the right types of bacteria and/or anti-inflammatory properties, you'll help the good actors in your gut flourish and reduce inflammation throughout your body *and* mind.

In recent years, advances in nutrition research have identified specific components of foods that can improve the health of our guts. Probiotics, the beneficial bacteria or yeasts found in certain foods, and prebiotics, nondigestible components in certain foods, are high on the list—forming a dynamic duo for your gut. When you eat foods that are high in probiotics, they contribute to increasing the population of good bacteria in your gut. When you consume foods that are rich in prebiotics, these natural food components promote the growth of good gut bacteria (probiotics).

To make this less abstract and help you better understand their different roles, return to the image of your body as a factory that requires expertise and excellent teamwork to get the job done. Probiotics are the workers that help you thrive mentally and physically and deliver the product: optimal functioning of various bodily systems. They work night and day but need to be *fed* well to continue to *function* well. That's where prebiotics come in. These highly nutritious foods keep the workers going. If you feed those workers a steady diet of fast foods or processed foods instead, their output drops and their chief product—your physical and emotional health—goes down with it.

Good sources of *probiotics* include yogurt, kefir, kimchi, sauerkraut, miso, tempeh, and kombucha—foods that naturally contain beneficial bacteria in the form of live cultures or that have developed good-for-you bacteria through the fermentation process. (Those who don't consume dairy products can rest assured that many nondairy products, such as coconut-, cashew-, and soy-based milks and yogurts also contain these beneficial bacteria.) *Prebiotics* are plentiful in lentils, chickpeas, red kidney beans, garlic, onions (including shallots, spring onions, and leeks), asparagus, bananas, apples, chicory, Jerusalem artichokes, and savoy cabbage. Grains such as oats, bran, and barley are also solid sources of prebiotics. For a powerful impact, you can incorporate foods with probiotics *and* prebiotics in the same meal. Try sliced bananas in a cup of yogurt and sprinkle chia seeds on top or create a stir-fry with garlic, onions, asparagus, and tempeh.

Probiotics occur naturally in food and consuming them in their original form is preferable to taking them as supplements (meaning pills). This is mostly because the Food and Drug Administration does not require dietary or probiotic supplement manufacturers to prove safety, efficacy (whether or not the product does what it claims to), purity, or potency as it does for drugs, so you don't always know what you're getting with these products. Besides, there isn't one type of probiotic that's right for everyone. In a perfect world, you'd be able to undergo testing and get a probiotic prescription that's personalized for you and your microbiome, and then you'd be able to consume the specific form of bacteria that would help you. Even in our *im*perfect world, a personalized prescription for your microbiomes may someday become routine—but we're not there yet. In the meantime, the advice provided here falls into the *won't-hurt-could-help* category for your physical and mental health, and since these food suggestions are inherently nutritious, there's really nothing to lose by adding them to your diet.

Of course, the good gut diet also includes eating anti-inflammatory foods. To make it simple to choose the right foods, Andrew Weil, MD, a pioneer in the field of integrative medicine, created an Anti-Inflammatory Food Pyramid that's loaded with nutritious vegetables and fruits, whole and cracked grains, beans and legumes (including lentils and peas), healthy fats found in nuts and extra virgin olive oil, fish and shellfish, whole soy foods, cooked Asian mushrooms, tea (white, green, and oolong), herbs and spices (such as garlic, ginger, oregano, cinnamon, and turmeric), and moderate amounts of red wine. ("Moderate" here means up to one glass per day for women, two per day for men.) When it comes to dietary fats, omega-3 fatty acids (found in flax-seeds, chia seeds, walnuts, and canola oil, as well as cold-water fatty fish like salmon, tuna, halibut, anchovies, and sardines) tend to have the most potent anti-inflammatory properties.

FUN FACTS

If you have a sweet tooth, treat yourself to a guilt-free 1.5-ounce square of dark chocolate with a minimum content of 70 percent cacao. It has anti-inflammatory effects, and as an added perk, the polyphenols (plant-based nutrients) in dark chocolate can help the body form more nitric oxide, a compound that causes blood vessels to dilate, enhances blood flow, and reduces blood pressure. What's more, new research found that consuming dark chocolate that has at least 70 percent cacao has positive effects on stress levels, mood, and memory in humans. *Sweet news, indeed.*

If your moods are all over the map, it's wise to moderate your caffeine intake and alcohol consumption to avoid revving yourself up excessively or inadvertently depressing your mood. To keep your blood sugar (and hence your mood) on a relatively even keel, plan your meals and (healthy) snacks ahead of time so that you're eating something every three to five hours. That way, you won't get jittery or "hangry." Also, include some protein in every meal and snack because protein takes longer to digest than carbs or fats do, so you'll end up with a slower, more sustained rise in blood sugar, which will help keep your mood and energy steadier.

Ultimately, if you feed your gut bacteria well—with live and active cultures, fermented foods, plenty of fiber, and anti-inflammatory foods—and limit your intake of saturated fats, added sugars, and highly processed items, you can take charge of promoting a diversity of bacteria in your gut, which can in turn help you calm inflammation throughout your body and mind. Want some proof? A study at the College of William and Mary found that people (especially those with preexisting anxieties) who consume more fermented foods are less susceptible to social anxiety than others. Similarly, research has found that consuming yogurt or fermented milk—both available in nondairy options—on a daily basis can reduce people's reactivity to stressful situations.

Don't forget to drink plenty of water and other noncaffeinated fluids (caffeine has a diuretic effect) throughout the day, too. It may surprise you to hear that dehydration, even in a mild form, can affect your mood and mental function. Research shows that when healthy young women developed mild dehydration (on the order of losing 1.4 percent of their body weight) while exercising, it triggered a substantial downturn in mood. This included increased tension-anxiety, depression-dejection, and anger-hostility, as well as reduced concentration and a significant increase in fatigue or inertia. In healthy men who have been exercising, mild dehydration (from losing 1 percent of their body weight during a workout) brings on a similar response.

Here's the hitch: Don't count on thirst to warn you that you are becoming dehydrated; by the time you feel thirsty you may have already lost 1 to 2 percent of your body's water content. Furthermore, some people are less sensitive to thirst and have little idea that they are dangerously dehydrated. Here's some advice: Sip water frequently during the day. The current recommendations from the National Academy of Sciences suggest that women should consume approximately 91 ounces and men about 125 ounces of water per day from a combination of beverages and water-rich foods. If this sounds daunting, consider this: about 20 percent of your fluid intake comes from consuming water-rich foods.

To be clear: None of these dietary approaches provides an immediate or complete remedy for the angst, despair, agitation, or other ill-at-ease feelings you may be experiencing. There is no such remedy. But their cumulative impact over time can certainly help. Addressing these feelings effectively is a long-term proposition, an investment in gently calming the internal flames that can stoke your emotional inflammation over time. The goal is really to quiet the physiological turbulence inside you, which will raise the bar or threshold for what elicits *your* emotional reactivity.

THE TRUTH ABOUT STRESS-RELIEVING SUPPLEMENTS

These days, people seem to be perpetually searching for a panacea that will protect their bodies and minds from the harmful effects of stress and exhaustion. Solid evidence shows that some herbal remedies such as rhodiola, ginseng, or ashwagandha can help. And while swallowing nutritional supplements like B-complex vitamins or fish oil or seaweed supplements is appealing because it's such an easy thing to do, they are not always appropriate for everyone. They can interact with different medications you may be taking or foods you may be eating, or you may be particularly sensitive to their effects because of your age, underlying health status, or other factors. The consequence could be that you end up with an additive effect or that the concentration of a medication is altered,

continues

or you experience another unpleasant or worrisome side effect. Plus, some of them contain impurities. This is why I am reluctant to make a blanket recommendation for taking nutrients or supplements or to blindly endorse them without knowing the whole health picture for a given individual.

That said, Western medicine can learn a lot from Eastern medicine, especially when it comes to the growing body of information about incorporating natural remedies and good nutrition into everyday health. If you're interested in trying one of these remedies to see if it helps you calm down from the inside out, talk to your doctor—but don't be surprised if your physician doesn't know much about nutritional or herbal remedies. Many Western physicians have not been trained in this area. If your doctor says he or she isn't knowledgeable about nutritional or herbal treatments, consider consulting a functional or integrative physician or a naturopath who *is* knowledgeable and can provide an approach that is personalized to your situation or condition.

MOVE YOUR MOODS THE RIGHT WAY

These days, we are more sedentary in our personal lives and our work lives than our preindustrial brethren were. We're living in an increasingly automated world. Instead of going shopping, we can order our clothing, books, groceries, furniture, and other household items online and have them delivered. We can have our dry cleaning picked up and delivered. We can do our banking from home and rely on direct deposit for our paychecks. We don't even need to walk down the hall to communicate with a colleague; we can simply send an email or make a phone call. Sometimes we don't even need to show up at work; we can telecommute, instead.

We, as a society, have eliminated many opportunities for movement from our everyday lives. And we are paying for it, because human beings were *made* to move and our brains have been set up to *reward* us for doing it. If we were meant to live like statues, we'd be fixed on pedestals, and we wouldn't have arms and legs that can move in multiple directions. Regular exercise is critical not only for our physical health but for our mental health, too. It improves just about every aspect of our health, from head to toe, reducing blood pressure and heart rate, improving digestion, regulating blood sugars, and enhancing the quality of sleep.

A less apparent benefit of regular exercise is that it can improve your health and well-being by augmenting the number and diversity of beneficial microbial species in the gut. While no two people's microbiomes will have the same response to regular exercise, most people will have an increase in microbes that reduce inflammation throughout the body, among other positive health effects. But—and this is a very big *but*, so pay attention here—when people *stop* exercising, the positive effects will disappear, and the microbiome will go back to the way it was before the exercise regimen began.

In addition to being energizing to your body and mind, exercise is also immensely effective in helping you manage emotions and sharpen mental functioning. Aerobic exercise, in particular, induces the release of brain-derived neurotrophic factor, or BDNF, a protein that occupies the receptor sites for cortisol so that the stress hormone can't "land" and activate those sites. The result is that instead of getting a jolt of anxiety, you get a dose of brain nourishment. In other words, exercising, especially during stressful times, is like wearing a waterproof raincoat in a downpour: the moisture (stress) will sit on the surface but won't penetrate and soak you with anxiety, fear, despair, and the like. This means that when stress causes an increase in cortisol levels, people who get plenty of exercise will deactivate the stress hormone more quickly than those who don't. Aerobic exercise also raises the concentration of serotonin in the brain by increasing the transport of the amino acid tryptophan, a precursor to serotonin, across the blood-brain barrier.

In one study, researchers from Harvard University examined the effects of aerobic exercise (cycling, in this case) on people's ability to regulate their emotions after a stressful task and concluded that regular exercise strengthens our emotional resilience to the prolonged effects of stress. In another study, researchers at the University of Mississippi had healthy adults engage in stretching, walking, or jogging for fifteen minutes, then showed them a film clip intended to elicit a negative emotional response. Those in the walking and jogging groups experienced lower levels of anxiousness and anger in response to the film, whereas those in the stretching group had higher anger scores afterward. Their negative emotions were triggered, in other words, simply because they didn't get the emotional-regulation perks of aerobic exercise, as their peers did.

You may have had this experience yourself: after tying yourself into knots over a stressful issue, you go for a brisk walk or a jog and find that afterward, while the issue has hardly been forgotten, it no longer has the grip on you that it did earlier. Regular physical activity also reduces the impulse to ruminate about stressful events, which in turn can reduce your reactivity to stress and decrease your chances of experiencing a priming effect whereby your response to one stressor can influence, and often magnify, the way you respond to a subsequent stressor.

What's more, in both men and women exercise can reduce depression and anxiety. In some cases, regular aerobic exercise works *just as well* as an antidepressant in treating major depression, and it may even be superior at reducing the risk of a *recurrence* of depressive symptoms. The factors are complex, the neurotransmitters are varied, and people are different. But if you net it out, it's indisputable that exercise really is good therapy for mood management, which is why more and more mental health professionals are prescribing it.

So the million-dollar question is, *What type of exercise is most effective at relieving emotional inflammation?* The answer is that it depends on *you*—the forms of emotional inflammation you have, how your brain is wired and your body designed, and of course the types of activities that naturally appeal to you. That said, certain generalities may hold true: If you are feeling amped up, anxious, or overstimulated, a long walk *in nature*, a soothing swim, with its rhythmic qualities and the calming sensation of water running over your body, or a gentle yoga class, may be the special sauce to help you settle down, physically and emotionally, and feel more grounded and centered. If you feel the need to blow off steam (as in, you're feeling frustration, irritation, or anger), you might benefit from an empowering cardio session, such as jogging, spinning, or kickboxing. If you've been feeling depressed or isolated, engaging in activities that get you out of yourself and involve others like dancing, playing a team sport, or joining a running or cycling club may provide a mood-refreshing way to reconnect, defuse tension, and help you forget about yourself or put your problems in perspective. Whatever your personal preferences or emotional needs may be, there's some form of physical activity that will do your mind and body a world of good. Don't miss out!

WHAT'S OXYTOCIN GOT TO DO WITH IT?

Produced primarily in the hypothalamus and released into the bloodstream through the pituitary gland, oxytocin is often called "the love hormone" or "the bonding hormone" for good reason. It surges when mothers give birth, snuggle with their newborns, or breastfeed, or when we fall in love, cuddle, or simply connect, even with our pets. But it's not just a matter of activating pleasure receptors. Because it fosters an overall sense of trust between people or between people and animals, oxytocin reduces symptoms of anxiety and depression and even quiets down the often

continues

irrepressible amygdala. In short, through various pathways, oxytocin soothes emotional inflammation.

When oxytocin is released, it not only affects the brain, calming our mood and softening our behavior; its impacts also trickle down to other body systems, lowering stress hormones like cortisol and norepinephrine and decreasing heart rate and blood pressure, for example. In one study involving women who recently had babies, researchers at the University of North Carolina School of Medicine in Chapel Hill directly linked higher circulating oxytocin levels with lower cardiovascular and sympathetic nervous system reactivity to a stressful task, which, in this case, was public speaking.

Recent research on oxytocin is yielding truly fascinating findings. Administering intranasal oxytocin to individuals diagnosed with autism or schizophrenia can improve their comfort and ability to interact socially. Higher levels of oxytocin may help us remember what we learn in positive situations and forget what was felt in stressful ones. Other studies show that individuals with low empathy may have low concentrations of oxytocin; these individuals score poorly on tests that evaluate the ability to read emotions from facial expressions.

The take-home message is this: Getting a firm, feel-good hug before going into a stressful situation (whether it's giving a presentation at work or going for a worrisome medical examination) could help you stay calm, cool, and collected during the event because your oxytocin levels are likely to stay elevated not just for minutes but for hours. When oxytocin is administered in a nasal spray, its levels in the saliva stay high for about two-and-a-quarter hours. To get that "shot" of oxytocin from a hug, it can't be a flimsy, one-sided hug; it has to be a firm, authentic one.

GET A GRIP ON STRESS — BEFORE IT GETS ONE ON YOU

Some sources of stress are unavoidable and can take a toll on your peace of mind, but there is also a positive form of stress called "eustress" that is actually good for you. Sources of this "good" kind of stress—for instance, getting a promotion at work or having a stellar athletic performance—can motivate you, improve your performance, and help you grow. So the goal isn't to eliminate all forms of stress but to manage the negative forms (the ones that cause *distress*) so that they don't trigger anxiety, irritation, or withdrawn or frantic behavior—or harm your health.

Over time, chronic negative stress can set the stage for the development or exacerbation of many different medical conditions, from digestive distress and reproductive disorders to heart disease and other chronic diseases, and deeply compromise your emotional health. Stress overload can even harm your gut microbiome: When high cortisol levels continuously course through your body, the bacterial balance in your gut can be disrupted, triggering inflammation. Adding insult to injury, this bacterial imbalance in the gut—known as "dysbiosis"—can send us into a feedback loop that contributes to more stress, anxiety, and depression.

This is yet another reason to get the upper hand on stress in your life, in whatever healthy ways work for you. As you've seen, consuming healthy, anti-inflammatory foods and exercising regularly can keep your physiological equilibrium, including your gut microbiome, in a balanced state. Though this helps control your emotional response to stress, it's not enough on its own. It's also essential to develop strong coping skills, including problem-solving techniques or tools that help you handle the challenges in your life more efficiently and flexibly. These include a clear, effective communication style, time management skills, the wherewithal to know when to delegate, and the ability to create and maintain healthy boundaries between you and other people and unnecessarily upsetting situations. Being able to perform healthy mind-shifting practices (as you saw in chapter 7) also can help mitigate some of the effects of stress—or at least help you avoid magnifying them.

Alexandra, the New York City writer (see chapter 1) whose anxiety spiraled out of control in 2017, has always been an avid exerciser. But her mounting anxiety inspired her to make some radical changes in her life to reduce her stress level and her exposure to triggers. She took up meditation and yoga, disengaged from social media, stopped watching cable news, and cut back on going out socially as often as she used to. "I became very self-protective—I trained myself not to chase my anxiety or do things that were ramping up my anxiety," she explains. "Things are much better now—I'm wearing my anxiety a lot more lightly."

Indeed, it's wise to cultivate and hone ways to use your personal decompression valve so you can unwind, relax, and restore your emotional equilibrium regularly, as Alexandra does. Here, too, there's no one-size-fits-all approach that works for everyone. To cultivate and fortify inner calm, it behooves you to try several techniques until you find the one that is most effective for you. Some good ones to start with include yoga or other forms of exercise, guided imagery (conjuring up soothing scenes or experiences in your mind, using as many senses as possible), progressive muscle relaxation exercises (which involve systematically and slowly tensing then relaxing muscle groups from head to toe), and meditation. Various apps and resources for many of these methods can be found online.

As with any skill, these techniques require practice for us to be able to derive the desired effects. So commit to engaging in your technique of choice for an agreed upon time—say, twenty minutes per day. Even if it ends up being only a five-minute decompression session, it's better than nothing. But in general the longer and more often you practice these techniques, the more stress will be released from your body and mind.

One simple practice that I recommend everyone master and use regularly is deep breathing. This activates your parasympathetic nervous system, which induces the relaxation response. Breathing is such an automatic body function that many of us don't give it much thought. But the way you do it can have a *profound* effect on the way you feel and function. People who are particularly susceptible to anxiety, for example, tend to have a faster, shallower breathing pattern that leads to a higher heart rate and increased levels of carbon dioxide in the blood—both of which add to the overall stew of anxiety, fatigue, depression, a feeling of being unfocused, and general malaise.

Many different breathing patterns have been recommended for various purposes, such as relaxing or energizing yourself. The approach that I like for an easy and quick dose of calm to lower stress is the five-six-seven pattern. To do it, close your mouth and slowly inhale through your nose to a count of five seconds, hold your breath for six seconds, then, ever so slowly exhale through your mouth, making a whooshing sound, for seven seconds. With the slow exhale, you may experience an instant sense of relief, your shoulders letting go, and your blood pressure perhaps dropping, too. Repeat the pattern for a total of five to ten complete breaths. Do it two to four times per day—not just when you desperately need to calm down—and you'll lower your stress reactivity all day long.

Of course, making it a priority to get plenty of good-quality sleep and maintain a consistent sleep-wake pattern (as you saw in chapter 7) are also important steps for dialing down your emotional reactivity. People who experience partial sleep deprivation or insomnia are susceptible to increased emotional reactivity, particularly increased activation of the amygdala (the brain's fear center) during exposure to emotionally stimulating images or situations. What's more, rapid eye movement, or REM, sleep, which is most closely associated with dreaming, is important for emotional processing. So if you don't get enough deep sleep, you may find yourself even more emotionally reactive than usual.

To set the stage for sounder slumber, do some aerobic exercise during the day but not too close to bedtime since vigorous activity may rev you up. Avoid exposure to bright light in the evenings, including TVs and other electronic devices. Dim the lights and engage in activities—reading a not-too-stimulating book, listening to calming music, taking a warm bath, or inhaling soothing scents (see "Fun Facts" in the following box)—that help you unwind from the stresses of the day and shift into a more relaxed state. Make sure your bedroom is quiet, dark, relaxing, and at a comfortable temperature (ideally, between 60°F and 67°F, according to the National Sleep Foundation). If unwanted light streams into your bedroom, consider installing blackout shades or curtains. If outside noise disrupts your sleep, consider using a white noise machine or an app with soothing sounds from nature (such as wind or waves) to mask it.

If anxiety or stress makes it difficult for you to fall asleep or stay asleep, consider investing in a weighted blanket, which can make you feel grounded, safe, and supported, thus helping you sleep better. It's a similar principle to swaddling an infant before putting the little one in a crib to sleep. Because a weighted blanket mimics the feeling of being enveloped in a gentle hug, it triggers the release of oxytocin, which, as you have seen, can make you feel calm and relaxed. If you want to try one, look for a weighted blanked that's appropriate for your body size (about 10 percent of your weight) and that is made of a material that feels good to you. Also, make sure the weight is evenly distributed throughout the blanket to provide firm, constant tactile stimulation across your body.

FUN FACTS

Dating back to ancient times, essential oils have been used to promote better health and well-being, particularly in early Chinese and Egyptian cultures. More recently, a robust body of research has shown that harnessing the power of aromatherapy—by inhaling the scent of lavender essential oil, in particular—reduces anxiety and improves the quality of sleep in healthy people, as well as in those with various medical conditions. Similarly, inhaling vetiver oil or the aroma of vanilla has been found to have sleep-supportive effects. All of these scents work their soporific magic by altering brain waves in ways that enhance the amount of time spent in deep, slow-wave (delta) sleep.

Whether it's through diet, exercise, sleep, or stress management, the proper care and feeding of your body can have a significantly positive ripple effect on the way your mind feels and functions. The right dietary patterns, regular physical activity, good quality sleep, and stress-easing strategies can help calm the physical and emotional fires inside you, as long as you're consistent with these salubrious approaches. It may take some time and effort to fine-tune your life-style habits so that they better cater to your body's needs. And it will, of course, take time for the therapeutic effects to kick in. But it's worth the wait: Not only will these healthy strategies essentially reset your body's internal stress meter, but they also are beneficial for your mind, body, and spirit in many other ways. You have nothing to lose with these approaches—and so much to gain.

THE RESTORE TO-DO LIST

☐ Take care of your gut microbiome—it needs you!—by putting anti-inflammatory and probiotic-rich foods on your plate each day.

☐ Get in the habit of moving briskly for at least ten minutes every day. Your body was designed to move; besides enhancing your mood, aerobic exercise will help stress roll off you.

☐ Give yourself a shot of oxytocin: ask for a firm hug (or two) from someone you trust.

☐ Manage your oxygen–carbon dioxide flow and ratio using the five-six-seven breathing rhythm to decompress regularly.

☐ Get good scents on your side to calm yourself. Your nose will get them to the right place—your brain.

CHAPTER 9

RECLAIM

THE GIFTS

OF NATURE

One touch of nature
makes the whole
world kin.

WILLIAM SHAKESPEARE,
Troilus and Cressida, act 3, sc. 3

THINK ABOUT THE LAST time you went for a languid walk in the woods, meandered through a garden, or strolled along a tranquil beach. It undoubtedly felt like a gift to yourself, a privilege to be soaking up nature's sublimely restorative effects. Chances are, you weren't worrying about twenty things you didn't get done at work yesterday, your kids sassing you, or what was happening with the political circus in Washington, the refugee crisis, the latest sexual-misconduct scandal, or other incendiary issues. In all likelihood, you were attuned to the kaleidoscope of colors in the landscape, the sound of birds chirping, the feel of the breeze as it wafted across your skin—and you probably allowed your mind to wander along with your feet. Even if you started the stroll dwelling on what's wrong with the world, those thoughts probably faded from your mind as you began to reconnect with the awe-inspiring effects of the natural world around you. You probably returned feeling refreshed and rejuvenated from the time you spent outdoors (assuming you didn't have your phone in your hand the whole time). The experience likely transported you out of your own world of worries and helped you feel part of something larger than yourself through the power of awe.

There's no mystery behind these effects, and there's even a word for this underlying connection: *biophilia*. It means love of living things (*bio* meaning "life," and *philia* meaning "love for") or nature-relatedness. Social psychologist Erich Fromm is credited with creating the term, while biologist Edward O. Wilson popularized it in his book *Biophilia*, where he offered the hypothesis that humans' affinity for nature is innate. With a mounting body of exciting, insightful studies, research continues to deftly illustrate the restorative power of spending time in nature. It reduces depression, symptoms of attention deficit disorder, and even PTSD. A dose of nature can calm us down, boost our spirits, reduce our stress levels, and enhance our creativity. It also reduces blood pressure and improves immune function, including decreasing the markers of inflammation, such as proinflammatory cytokines and interleukin 6. In addition, it increases vitality and energy, as well as generosity and altruism, making people more caring.

Yet many of us are living in ways that alienate us from nature, amplifying our angst and robbing us of the wonder we get from seeing the complexity and beauty of the ecosystems around us. We are immersed in the business of our day-to-day home, commuting, and work lives, and have become, essentially, an indoor society. In this current era of confinement and technology-driven sensory deprivation, we live by artificial light and are separated from the smells, sounds, and sights of the natural world in which we evolved. A recent survey of 12,000 adults and children in the US found that 56 percent report spending *five hours or fewer per week* outside in nature.

To one degree or another, most of us are experiencing "nature-deficit disorder." Richard Louv, the author of *Last Child in the Woods*, coined this term to describe "the human costs of alienation from nature, among them: diminished use of the senses, attention difficulties, and higher rates of physical and emotional illnesses." With nature-deficit disorder, we are depriving ourselves of exposure to fresh air, the radiant power of the sun, the infinite beauty and complexity of plant life, the intriguing sight of animals in their natural habitat, and the sounds and smells that emanate from a healthy ecosystem.

And yet many of us are not even aware of this deficiency. As Florence Williams writes in her book *The Nature Fix*, "We don't experience natural environments enough to realize how restored they can make us feel, nor are we aware that studies also show they make us healthier, more creative, more empathetic and more apt to engage with the world and each other." Every day we are learning more about how being in nature and hearing its special sounds of brooks gurgling or the wind rustling through the trees, watching the enchanting behavior of animals, or witnessing broad expanses of trees, plants, and varied terrain has physiologically and psychologically calming effects on human beings. And it's not just because it's a shift from your regularly scheduled (indoor) program; it's also because of the way our brains respond to nature.

When children spend free time or recess in natural environments, such as green spaces or grassy fields, they show an increase in their ability to concentrate, to stay focused and attentive, compared to similar time spent in built environments such as blacktops, playgrounds, or basketball courts. The kids might be playing with their friends in both settings and enjoying themselves, but the effects are different. Natural environments create a greater sense of feeling restored. The benefits of being in green spaces have been touted since ancient times. Increasingly, we have research that explains the reasons. One has to do with Attention Restoration Theory (ART), a concept developed by Rachel and Stephen Kaplan, PhD, professors of psychology at the University of Michigan. According to ART, people can concentrate and direct their attention more effectively after spending time in nature because interacting with environments that are inherently intriguing, that capture our imagination with natural stimuli—leaves rustling in a breeze or water flowing over rocks in a stream—make a play for our attention in appealing ways that don't demand *too much* of our attention or effort. This gives us a break from the effort of *directed* attention, a conscious, intentional focus on specific information and the cognitive process that accompanies it. This allows our minds to have a chance to rest and replenish.

By contrast, spending time in urban settings creates intense, jarring stimulation from blasting horns and sirens and background din, as well as the chaotic randomness of crowds and traffic. The urban setting is a frenzied jungle—its lack of order and predictability demands our directed attention to cope with so much uncertainty and overstimulation. Urban settings may be exciting but few feel restorative. Being able to softly or gently attend to fascinating stimuli—what researchers call "soft fascination"—is a key part of ART because it "requires little effort but also leaves mental space for reflection." This is important because mental fatigue can trigger mood changes and psychological distress. "Irritability is a hallmark of a person who cannot draw on directed attention," as Stephen Kaplan put it in 1995. Regularly feeling cranky or as though your brain is fried are sure signs of emotional inflammation.

TLC FOR THE SPIRIT

Let's take a closer look at how and why time spent in nature is soothing to the anxious mind, body, and soul. On a primitive level, green environments provide human beings with a sense of safety because they suggest sufficient biodiversity, water, and enough raw material to have and make a place of refuge (whether it's made from leaves or sticks). Exposure to sunlight is essential for a multitude of body functions, including the synthesis of vitamins, hormones, and neurotransmitters—and to wake us up, give us energy, and keep our internal clocks running on time and our moods upbeat.

And then there is the restorative power of the ocean. Water has an amazing capacity to bring feelings of calm, pleasure, and joy because it offers a bounty of sensual experiences. Looking at natural bodies of water is captivating; their simplicity is soothing. Viewing an expansive vista of water actually can change our brain waves, as seen on an electroencephalogram (EEG), which records brain wave patterns. During these experiences, brain waves settle into a slow and more harmonious pattern, similar to what happens when we're in a meditative state, explains Richard Shuster, a clinical psychologist and host of *The Daily Helping* podcast. In addition, oceans, in particular, feature waves of water that are mesmerizing with their rhythmic predictability and comforting pitch; gazing at their shimmering surfaces ignites the brain's reward centers. Hearing the sound of the waves quiets our amygdala and connects with opioid receptors that make us feel peaceful.

From an evolutionary or vestigial perspective, the appeal of natural bodies of water is understandable. Our amphibian ancestors came from the sea, so our profound attraction to it may stem in part from the fact that it was once essential for our predecessors' survival. Even today, our own bodies consist largely of salt and water—at birth, a baby's body is approximately 78 percent water, whereas an adult man's is 60 percent water—so a symbiotic attraction to oceans cannot be discounted.

There's no question that being in a variety of natural environments stimulates our senses of sight, sound, smell, touch, and possibly even taste. In a 2017 study involving 128 adults, researchers in Taiwan found that after the participants engaged in a two-hour forest bathing (or *shinrin-yoku*) experience—which included visual stimulation (viewing the scenery), auditory sensations (the sound of birds singing and running streams), olfactory input (the scents of plants), and tactile stimulation (touching the surfaces of leaves and trees)—their autonomic nervous system activity (based on pulse rate and blood pressure) decreased and their mood states improved considerably. Specifically, their scores on measures of tension-anxiety, anger-hostility, fatigue-inertia, depression-dejection, and confusion-bewilderment were significantly lower, and their scores on a measure of vigor were much higher. (In scientific literature, *vigor* refers to the presence of energy, enthusiasm, and liveliness, as well as the absence of fatigue, weariness, and exhaustion.) By engaging our senses of sight, hearing, smell, and touch, forest bathing serves as a bridge that joins human beings harmoniously with the natural world.

Humans are multisensory creatures, long evolved to depend on our senses for safety and survival. When we spend time in nature, our senses may be engaged in ways that we may not even be aware of. As researchers from Australia noted in a review in a 2017 issue of the *International Journal of Environmental Research and Public Health*, evidence is emerging to show that other pathways for nature experiences—including "ingestion or inhalation of phytoncides, negative air ions, and microbes"—may be beneficial for human well-being. Whether these sensory and nonsensory pathways work in tandem or in parallel fashion, synergistically or additively, the effects on your physical and psychological well-being can be profound.

Phytoncides, which are aromatic, airborne particles with antimicrobial properties, are emitted by plants and trees to defend themselves against pests such as germs and insects. In humans, exposure to phytoncides for even a few hours has been found to decrease stress, deepen feelings of relaxation, and improve immune function. Given that phytoncides are nature's inherent source of aromatherapy, we have another compelling reason to become preservationists: to benefit from life-enhancing fragrances of pine, cedar, eucalyptus, and citrus trees. Think about it: People spend a lot of money on plant essential oils so they can soak up the scent of wellness. Well, the benefits of these aromas are readily and freely available in their original habitat—nature. Urban planners, landscapers, and health-conscious people should take note: choosing native plants that restore our landscape and ones that also emit phytoncides isn't just good for the local ecosystem; it also brings natural and systemic benefits to human health and well-being in ways that can offset some of the effects of socially determined harms to our health, such as degraded neighborhoods, poverty, and poor access to medical care.

Negative air ions are charged particles that are particularly abundant in elements of nature, including forests, waterfalls, and the seashore. Mountains have the highest levels of negative air ions, followed by rural and coastal sites. Urban environments have the lowest. Exposure to negative air ions can reduce depression and anxiety and improve mood. That's part of the reason people often say they feel and sleep better when they're near the ocean. Even during stressful tasks, exposure to negative air ions has been found to decrease the reactivity of the immune system, as well as anxiety, negative moods, and tension.

Repeated exposure to microbes—bacteria in the soil, water, and spores in the air in natural settings—can reduce inflammation, increase resilience to stress, and contribute to the maintenance of a diverse population of health-promoting gut bacteria inside us. In particular, a species of bacteria called *Mycobacterium vaccae*, which is naturally present in soil and water, raises serotonin levels, and, at least in mice (with whom we share similar neural circuitry) has positive effects on memory and arousal. Rest assured: you don't need to eat dirt to internalize these beneficial bacteria because they are present in microscopic amounts in the outdoor air we breathe.

When the noise and hectic pace of the city get to him, Peter, a forty-five-year-old globe-trotting chef who splits his time primarily between the US and Australia, ventures into the wild to spend time in fresh air and stillness. He grew up on a farm so being in the bush without any pressures from other people reminds him of his roots and what's important to him. These jaunts have "become my midlife pacifier," he says. "My crazy travel schedule doesn't leave much time for mindfulness and stillness—spending time in nature is something that absolutely keeps my mental health in check." After spending time enjoying nature's sensory treats, having time to reflect, cooking on an open fire, and shutting off from the "antisocial social world," Peter feels recharged. "When it's just me and the wild, it reminds me that I have a purpose and integrity," he adds, "and that gives me a deeper understanding of my place on this earth."

Time spent in nature doesn't need to be a wilderness experience to be beneficial. "Nearby nature," such as parks, gardens, woods, and other landscapes, can do the trick. Studies show that exposure to nearby nature can compensate for poor social connectedness, leading to reduced stress levels, lower anxiety and general psychological distress, and an improved overall sense of well-being. "People who visited nature regularly felt their lives were more worthwhile, and those who visited nature yesterday were happier," concluded a survey of 7,272 residents in the UK. In other words, small doses can make a difference and add up to greater positivity.

THE HIDDEN POWER OF BONDING WITH ANIMALS

Did you know that pet ownership is on the rise in the US, with dogs leading the way? It's true. In fact, the percentage of households with pets has increased by 21 percent since 1988, reaching an all-time high. It's no wonder when you consider how relaxed you feel when you spend time petting your dog or cat after a rough day. This effect is not only because pets lavish us with unconditional love. It's also because interacting with pets stimulates the release of oxytocin (a.k.a. the "love" or "bonding" hormone). A surge of oxytocin can improve your mood, empathy, and level of trust, while lowering the fear, anxiety, and aggression you feel. In addition to the oxytocin effect, interacting with pets or other animals can lead to a reduction in stress-related substances such as cortisol, epinephrine, and norepinephrine, as well as lower your heart rate and blood pressure.

These feelings are at least somewhat mutual: When you smile and gaze lovingly into your dogs' eyes, its oxytocin levels soar as do yours, according to research from Finland. And the nicer you are to your dog, the more oxytocin he or she will secrete, which will make you adore your pooch even more. It's a lovefest, physiologically and psychologically!

continues

These effects are so powerful that spending time with a dog can even buffer your body's stress response when you later encounter a challenging task (such as a computerized audio task that assesses someone's processing, immediate memory, and attention abilities). But it's not just time with a dog that can elicit this calming effect. With a new wellness trend called cow cuddling, people get to brush, pet, or hug bovines. With goat yoga, you can do downward dog or child's pose alongside live goats. Among the better studied forms of animal-assisted healing, equine therapy—which involves interactions between people and horses (including grooming, feeding, haltering, leading, and sometimes riding)—has been found to reduce post-traumatic stress symptoms, generalized anxiety, and symptoms of depression among some people who developed PTSD after experiencing rape or a serious accident, or who were injured in the military.

While working for a large insurance company, thirty-eight-year-old Chloe felt so anxious and frustrated that she felt like she "was slowly dying on the inside." She said, "I was very worn down by trying to be what others wanted me to be." To soothe her emotional angst, she started working with horses near her Connecticut home and immediately found the salve she was craving. "Horses are very smart animals—they can recognize verbal and nonverbal cues as well as when you are happy, sad, or mad," she explained. "They also mimic your energy so if you are frustrated and angry, they will either try to make you calm down by giving you calming signals like licking their lips or by taking a deep breath or they will walk away. This teaches you to leave your junk at the door and be truly present."

Nature may have many other pulls on us that we don't yet fully understand but that may reset our internal equilibrium, physiologically and psychologically, depending on where we are and how we live. People are craving these natural sensory experiences so much that this growing interest has given rise to businesses that feature salt caves or flotation therapy spas. Designed to simulate Himalayan salt caves, these cozy urban and suburban grottos typically contain tons of crystal salt rock and reclining chairs. During a session, a machine grinds dry salt and pumps microparticles of it into the air along with negative ions that are absorbed by your body when you inhale them. With flotation therapy, you climb inside a tank that's filled with ten inches of warm water and nearly 1,000 pounds of Epsom salt—and float in darkness and silence.

In recent years, Stephen, the Washington, DC, lawyer from chapter 3, has been going to a local salt cave periodically because "it's a forced time-out," he says. "After a session, I feel like I can breathe better because my sinuses are clear, and I feel refreshed and relaxed, like my internal equilibrium has been reset."

THE WONDERS OF AWE: BROADENING YOUR PERSPECTIVE—AND APPRECIATION

Being in nature really does help you focus on the present moment, freeing your mind from the chatter and clutter of everyday life and helping you feel like part of something larger than yourself. Gazing at the night sky, something humans have done for thousands of years, also can be emotionally therapeutic. Have you ever heard the word *noctcaelador*? It's defined as a strong interest in and psychological attachment to the night sky. People who have this quality can enter a profound state of psychological absorption—one that's akin to the state of *flow* described earlier—as they become entranced while looking at the glowing moon, twinkling stars, and bright planets at night. Night-sky watching, research shows, can be calming, tension relieving, and mood enhancing. It is linked to a healthy coping mechanism that's associated with rational problem-solving styles and openness to new experiences. You don't have to be a budding astronomer to reap these benefits; simply taking a walk at night or standing on your deck or patio and gazing at the dark sky can produce them.

These effects may stem in part from the fact that many experiences in nature—whether you're gazing at the moon, walking in the woods, or listening to the crash of waves on the beach—elicit a sense of awe, a feeling of reverential respect and wonder, which we feel in the presence of something that's majestic or powerful or that transcends our understanding of the world. Awe-eliciting experiences can feel almost spiritual. We all know that feeling of being so transfixed by something that's amazing for its vastness, mystery, or beauty—whether it's a view of the Grand Canyon or the sea from a cliff top—that we forget about ourselves and connect, however fragilely, to something larger than we are, drawing us at least for a moment into a sense of the sublime.

Looking at natural vistas gets us out of our own heads and reminds us that we're part of a larger universe. A study from the Netherlands found that when people watched an awe-inspiring slideshow of natural scenes and phenomena—featuring magnificent mountain vistas or dramatic landscapes punctuated by thunderstorms, rainbows, or sunsets—it triggered an uptick in mood, profound emotional effects (such as feeling humble), and a more positive social orientation, compared to those who viewed neutral scenes of nature, featuring everyday elements such as grass, leaves, and trees. In another study, researchers at the University of California, Irvine, examined how the experience of awe contributed to the impact of nature on the well-being of military veterans and kids from underserved communities. A week after the participants went whitewater rafting, they had lasting improvements in their well-being and stress-related symptoms, and it was the sense of awe they experienced, more than any other positive emotion, that explained this.

This transcendent feeling even shifts activity in our brains away from ourselves, as evidenced by numerous studies that show a connection between awe-inducing experiences and humility, compassion, gratitude, and optimism. In a 2019 study, researchers from the Netherlands used fMRI to obtain insights into the brain networks that are involved in the experience of awe. As participants were shown awe-eliciting videos, they were instructed to try to become fully absorbed in the scenery or to tally the number of perspective changes in the videos. In those who watched the awe-evoking videos, activity was reduced in the brain's default mode network and increased in the frontoparietal network. This finding "underlines the captivating, immersive, and attention-grabbing nature of awe stimuli that is considered to be responsible for reductions in self-reflective thought," according to the researchers.

SUMMONING AWE

Think about a time when you experienced a personal sense of awe, wonder, or amazement. Maybe it was while you were walking through a dark forest and suddenly stumbled into a sunny field of wildflowers, when you arrived on a hilltop with a sweeping view of the grand terrain, or while you were watching a wildlife documentary on a very large screen. Try to recall the sense of wonder and marvel you felt about the beauty of the greater world or how humble you felt about your own place in the universe. Try to recall how being immersed in those settings gave you the sense of time slowing down so that you could savor the present moment.

Several times per week I consciously bring to mind the time I sat on the rocky cliff at the edge of the ocean near my brother's home and enjoyed the mesmerizing sight of the sun disappearing into the horizon. Besides offering a respite from the emotional demands of the day, reliving this experience brings a profound sense of calm within minutes.

Making an effort to actively seek more everyday experiences that evoke a sense of awe and wonder will pay off. It could be as simple as getting up early and watching the sunrise or spending a few minutes pondering the stars at night. Regularly replenishing your memory bank with awe-eliciting experiences can be inspiring and transformative—and part of the antidote to emotional inflammation.

In addition to the conscious pleasures we derive from spending time in nature, we are benefitting from experiences we're not even aware of. For example, we unknowingly respond to the marvel of fractals, patterns that are resplendently abundant in nature and repeat at different scales. Picture the network of veins in a leaf, the microscopic crystals in a snowflake, patterns the wind has blown into sand dunes in the desert, or the spirals of tiny buds on Romanesco cauliflower that will make you practically giggle with pleasure at the orderliness they bring. There is a reason for this: While most of us are unaware of these repeating patterns, our eyes register them and send calming messages to the brain, suggesting that we are in a space that is orderly and predictable. This heightens our sense of safety and equilibrium. Amazingly, the visual cortex that's activated by fractals actually communicates with a part of the brain—the cerebellum—that maintains our *physical* balance.

FUN FACTS

Did you know that awe is sometimes considered an "aesthetic emotion"? *Did you even know there was such a category?* It also includes fascination, wonder, and other emotions that can arise when you perceive and evaluate something for its aesthetic appeal. These are the kinds of emotions that can give you goose bumps or a chill down your spine when you experience a stunning natural landscape or a solar eclipse, a magnificent work of art or a virtuosic music performance, a moving film, or something else that's beautiful or striking. Researchers have even developed a scale called AESTHEMOS to measure the intensity and quality of aesthetic emotions, the effects of which can range from making you feel energized or excited to peaceful or content. So in addition to spending more time soaking up nature's magical influences, treat yourself to trips to an art museum or sculpture garden or a dance or music performance to elicit different flavors of awe and wonder.

Want proof? In a study, researchers in Sweden showed thirty-five people visual stimuli with fractal properties for one minute each while monitoring their brain responses via EEG. They found that exposure to natural fractal forms induced alpha wave responses, an indicator of an alert but relaxed state. As the researchers noted, this is in keeping with ART, which maintains that the desired state for restoration is one where attention is held loosely so that the person has the mental space to reflect on other things. Reaping such restorative benefits doesn't have to be a passive experience. Gardening, for example, has been shown to lead to decreased levels of the stress hormone cortisol and to a more upbeat mood afterward. And research from Denmark found that when people with stress-related mental health conditions worked in a garden, chopping wood or collecting herbs, the experience gave them a greater sense of safety and freedom, which the sensory stimuli in the garden reinforced, as well as peace of mind and calmness in their minds and bodies. If you don't have a yard or garden of your own, consider starting or joining a community garden or even simply planting a window box of flowers or herbs and tending to it regularly.

Obtaining the restorative elements of nature doesn't have to involve a big time commitment, either. The key is to calibrate your efforts so that they work for your schedule and situation. Getting outside and walking (or moving in some other way) in a green setting for as little as five minutes at a stretch has been found to improve both mood and self-esteem; if you can do it near a body of water, it's even better. So if you work in a windowless office all day, you could go outside, ideally to a park, to eat your lunch, rather than eating at your desk. In the midafternoon, you could take a walk around the block to reset your state of mind and psyche. On the weekends, you could up the ante by taking a stroll along a river, canal, or lake—or going for a walk in the woods.

BRINGING NATURE HOME AND TO WORK

With a bit of creativity and planning, you can trick your mind into responding as if it were in a verdant, outdoor space, rather than surrounded by walls when you're at home or work. You can tune in to the healing power of nature in either setting by bringing dramatic photographs of nature (such as sun-dappled forests, majestic cliffs, or sand dunes) into your home or office or by painting a wall green. Research has found that given the choice, people show a preference for photographs of scenes that contain water, rating them as having a more powerful effect on their mood. The scientific literature is brimming with studies illustrating how viewing scenes from nature relieves stress and physical pain, enhances attention and cognition, and provides other mind-body benefits.

Here are some other ways, both large and small, that you can reclaim the gifts of nature and get them on your side wherever you live and work:

- **Incorporate elements of biophilic design.** Take a lesson from environmental psychology and create home and/or work environments that contain elements of the natural world. This can be achieved by including direct experiences from nature such as featuring natural light and air and the presence of plants and water (perhaps with a small fountain). Or you can choose furniture with curves rather than straight lines and natural materials like wood or stone rather than metal or plastic. Incorporate objects or images that showcase fractals and other elements that are evocative of nature.

  The next time you go for a walk in nature, collect long sticks with interesting curves or fragrant pine cones and place them in a vase or bowl on a table. If anyone questions your design aesthetic or actions, you might mention that incorporating biophilic design elements has been found to reduce stress, enhance creativity and clarity of thought, and improve well-being. Research shows that people recover more quickly and completely from stress—based on their heart rate, pulse, muscle tension, and skin conductance measures—when they are exposed to natural environments rather than urban settings.

- **Surround yourself with sounds of nature.** The field of psychoacoustics has provided remarkable insights into how our minds respond to sounds, including the reality that the music of moving water is immensely calming, reducing activity in the brain's fight-or-flight center, the amygdala. So go ahead and open a window or listen to sounds from nature on an app (think twittering birds, a babbling brook, the sound of wind or waves) while you're cooking at home or working. It's good for you. A study from Sweden found that after completing a series of stressful tasks, listening to sounds of nature enhanced people's physiological and psychological recovery from the stress. Among other helpful effects, nature's sounds calm the brain's amygdala. If you have trouble drifting off to sleep at night, consider using a sound machine or app on your phone (at a low volume) that features the sound of waves or the wind.

- **Grow plants indoors.** Besides adding color and texture to the environment, houseplants improve indoor air quality, namely by releasing oxygen into the air and absorbing carbon dioxide. And people who work in a "green" office space that includes plants tend to feel and be more productive than those who work in a minimalist space. (For the record, small, green, lightly scented plants have the best effects on health and well-being at work.)

- **Cultivate a sensory oasis.** Keep a book of soothing or inspiring nature-based photographs within easy reach so you can reset your mood and mind when you need a boost. Create a visual respite by placing a mini Zen rock garden on your desk. Bookmark a link to a favorite scenic slideshow on your computer and turn to it for a dose of emotional rescue when you need it.

No matter how frustrated or exasperated I sometimes feel about the state of the world, watching a video about how wolves change rivers brings me to a transcendent state. The four-and-a-half-minute video features the exhilarating sound of howling, almost unbearably beautiful images of broad landscapes, rivers, and waterfalls, and the wildly stimulating diversity of animals in action. Watching it fills me with an abundant feeling of wonder and a boundless sense of possibility and calms me with the conviction that with collective effort we can restore the (only) world we live in.

✦ ✦ ✦

The good news is, you can rekindle your relationship with the natural world by exposing yourself to awe-eliciting experiences in person and by bringing elements of nature into your everyday life. In some instances, we don't even need to look far to find it; we just need to pay attention. If you live in the suburbs, for example, making a conscious effort to listen to the music of birds when you awaken in the morning or the buzz of insects at twilight or to notice the play of shadows as the sun and wind move across the sky can be soothing ways to fulfill the human need for sensual over analytical experiences.

As previously noted, *solastalgia* is a relatively new term that refers to the emotional distress brought on by seeing or imagining irreversible damage to treasured places in the natural world. While suffering from some solastalgia may be inevitable, embracing the wonder and bounty of nature in our everyday lives, while taking steps to preserve the natural world as best we can, are deeply empowering and healing actions that can offset this distress. As you've seen, nature's riches come from many different directions and varied sources. Much of it is yours for the taking. As the great American architect Frank Lloyd Wright advised his students: "Study nature, love nature, stay close to nature. It will never fail you." That's a good lesson for us all.

THE RESTORE TO-DO LIST

☐ Revitalize your attention and emotional stamina by taking a walk in a green space, playing with your pets, or viewing images of natural environments.

☐ Bring the outdoors in by incorporating elements of nature into your home and office—with plants, pine cones in a bowl, or a window box of herbs.

☐ Give yourself a daily dose of fractals by looking at repeating patterns in leaves, branching trees, icicles, even a head of Romanesco cauliflower. Fractals provide a sense of balance to your spirit and help your brain regulate emotions.

☐ Tune in to the sounds of nature by going outdoors if you can or by listening to an app that features soothing sounds like waves rolling onto the shore or wind rustling through the trees.

☐ Gaze at the night sky, ponder the moon and stars, and tune in to the powers of awe and wonder in the universe.

CHAPTER 10

EXERCISE

YOUR POWER

Action is the

antidote to despair.

JOAN BAEZ,
American folk singer, songwriter, and activist

THE EFFECTS OF LIVING in a continuous state of high alert, helplessness, or restlessness can seep down into our deeper consciousness, with destabilizing influences on our social interactions, our psyches, and our souls. When there are big problems, as there are with many of the societal and global issues that contribute to emotional inflammation, and no one has easy answers, it's natural to wonder, *Is there anything that I can do personally that really matters?* The answer is a resounding *yes!*—for your own well-being and for the world at large. Taking any action to help make the world a more humane and equitable place can have a profound effect on your own sense of well-being and empowerment.

Indeed, one of the most effective antidotes to the frustration and sense of helplessness that many of us are feeling is to roll up our sleeves and take action in some way. In his famous *Nicomachean Ethics,* the great Greek philosopher Aristotle declared that we reach our highest purpose and our full potential when we fill our lives with meaningful action—and pursue that action with a passion to do it well. For Aristotle, this reflects moral virtue. Taking action also provides us with a sense of control. But this does *not* mean that we must accomplish a big, heroic action that "saves the day." The goal is to do what you can that's in sync with your values, skills, or talents to improve matters in some way. Each of us makes a difference every time we speak out against social injustice, assist someone who needs a hand, help to educate other people, contact lawmakers, volunteer for social outreach programs we believe in, and, in this era of climate consequences, reduce and offset our carbon footprint.

As far as you're concerned, taking action can provide an immediate mood boost and sense of relief because it lowers the effort expended in trying to bury or ignore the anxiety you're feeling. Bringing the source of anxiety out of the shadows lets you see its component parts in the light of day and turn your attention to what you can do about it. This is a homegrown version of possibility therapy, a humanistic practice that focuses on discovering or generating solutions to your challenges and fears, rather than getting hung up on the *causes* of your emotional discomfort. By taking conscious action, feelings of vulnerability can be redirected into useful, concrete remedies. Working toward upstream solutions to distressing issues can feel exhilarating, especially because positive results can improve the lives of so many. Becoming an agent of change also dials down your emotional inflammation because the positive ripple effects of being proactive offset the feeling of helplessness. An additional bonus is that the process activates the reward centers in your brain, reinforcing your desire to stay involved. The net effect: you will feel not only empowered but more psychologically resilient as well.

The inclination to take action on the enormous and varied issues we are collectively facing doesn't always come naturally. Some people tend to stay on the sidelines, as observers. This is mute testament to the power of the bystander effect. The concept of the bystander effect was popularized by social psychologists John Darley and Bibb Latané after the murder of twenty-eight-year-old Kitty Genovese in New York City in 1964. Genovese was stabbed repeatedly on the street where she lived, in front of a crowd that had gathered and witnessed the attack, but no one immediately called the police or came to her aid. The tragedy launched serious soul-searching in society, leading people to wonder, *Was the anonymity of the city, and society in general, leading us to feel so detached that we were becoming indifferent to other people's suffering?*

In studying the bystander effect, Darley and Latané came to a stunning conclusion about human behavior: in a time of crisis, the larger the crowd, the *less* likely we are to respond. In addition to the size of the crowd, other factors contribute to the bystander effect, including the diffusion of responsibility (*If we're all witnessing this, the responsibility isn't just on me*), the relative sense of anonymity in a crowd (*No one knows me*), and unconsciously deferring to other people's judgment (*No one else is acting so why should I?*). This kind of social paralysis or relinquishing of responsibility has tremendous implications not only for intervening during a crime but also for standing up and speaking out against a variety of injustices.

Anxiety-laced inaction is contagious. If it is witnessed often enough it becomes the social norm—that is, our (mostly) unconscious tendency to automatically buy into what we perceive is socially expected in given circumstances, based on what everyone else is doing. But inaction can add to our feelings of trauma because it is preventing us from doing the very things that would reduce our anxiety.

Fortunately, this herd mentality can be turned around and put to good use. Two things that help break through the bystander effect are recognizing the urgency of the situation and identifying specific, effective actions that can improve or remedy it. When we recognize the force of the herd mentality, we can turn it into an opportunity by capturing its broad power: if one person chooses to take action, others will likely follow that person's lead. Then, the script changes from *No one else is taking action, so maybe I shouldn't*, to *If I lead by example, others will follow* or *That person is taking a stand; I should, too.* In this way, the social norm is flipped so that it involves action that is expected and drives interventions to take place with the appropriate or required sense of urgency.

As proof of the power of flipping this switch, imagine what would have or could have happened if passenger Todd Beamer hadn't been on United Airlines Flight 93 on September 11, 2001, and he and a few other men hadn't formed a plan to storm the cockpit to take control of the hijacked plane. Beamer led the charge with his now-famous courageous cry, "Let's roll!" inspiring a handful of other passengers to jump in to help. So instead of hitting the intended target, the US Capitol in Washington, DC, the plane crashed into an empty Pennsylvania field. By flipping the social-norm switch, Beamer galvanized the others to wrest control of the plane from the hijackers. It cost them their lives. It saved countless others.

FUN FACT

Nonviolent protests can lead to major political and social changes, and it takes only a small proportion—3.5 percent!—of the population to make them a success, according to political scientist Erica Chenoweth, PhD, a professor in human rights and international affairs at the Harvard Kennedy School.

MOVING FROM INACTION TO ACTION

Looked at another way, a powerful remedy to these anxious, turbulent times we're experiencing is to consciously recognize and confront inaction, to move from being a bystander to being an upstander, someone who recognizes that something is wrong and speaks up or stands up to work to make it right. It's about moving from observing in silence to making *good noise.*

While the upstander concept was originally applied to children who were standing up to bullies, it can apply to taking action on any form of social or environmental injustice—from the Me Too Movement to protesting the burning of fossil fuels. As Martha Minow, a professor at Harvard Law School, explained in a 2014 lecture called "Upstanders, Whistle-Blowers, and Rescuers," "An upstander may speak out publicly against bigotry and injustice. An upstander may be a whistle-blower, who exposes wrongdoing in the hope of stopping it. An upstander may resist the temptations of silence and passivity by expressing and offering support directly to victims of bigotry and injustice."

Besides being personally empowering, becoming an upstander helps enhance the principle of *fairness* that is fundamental to a free and ordered society—and the well-being of our communities and our country. Anyone can become an upstander. In countless ways, both large and small, we have the power to take empowering actions, to speak up, or to stand up for what we believe in—without having extraordinary capabilities or trying to be a superhero.

Upstanders come from all walks of life and among their key characteristics are that they:

- Are distressed by social injustice
- Can break free of "group think"
- Move from silence or apathy to action
- View themselves as personally responsible
- Recognize dangers to society and the natural world (even when authority suggests otherwise)
- Have the foresight to see how conditions will evolve to cause harm down the road
- Are motivated by ethical or moral considerations (rather than financial ones, for example)
- Have a high degree of compassion
- Manage the anxiety at seeing harm by taking action even if this may cause personal difficulties or sacrifices

Everybody can take action. If you are taking action, you are an upstander. To inspire yourself to become an agent of change, take some time to determine what issues or concerns are close to your heart. Look back at the triggers you identified in chapter 5 that are having the biggest impact on you and review your word cloud from chapter 4. This may help you define your unvarnished feelings, which are not based on what others may think of you or what you think others want you to do, but rather on your personal, authentic emotions and interests. This, in turn, will help you find and form the personal energy and efforts that are needed to become an agent of change.

It also may be helpful to think about the planetary legacy we're leaving for our children, especially when it comes to climate issues, environmental threats, human rights erosions, and other social injustices. The next step is to evaluate how the situation is perceived and then to identify a constructive action *you* can take to address it. This two-step process is critical because it captures your attention and directs it toward action, which in turn can help relieve your anxiety.

Though her home was spared damage in the 2017 wildfires in Sonoma County, California, sixty-two-year-old artist Lily, along with just about everyone she knew in her town, was traumatized about the possibility of a recurrence. "The loss of 7,000 homes in one night to fire changed the paradigm here," she said. "No one thought that could happen in a heavily populated area—trees and forests, yes, not homes. But as we've learned, homes are better fuel bombs even than dying forests." To try to ease the grip of this anxiety, in the spring of 2019 Lily and her husband attended a disaster-preparedness fair hosted by the local fire and emergency services department. There, they got a serious education about how to better protect their home and pets, use a ham radio, outfit their home with "a trauma pack" (a specialized first-aid kit), and create a personal wildfire action plan. Lily also met neighbors she hadn't known, people who could end up becoming primary first responders if another disaster were to sweep through the area. "Between the threat of earthquakes and wildfires, the feeling of anxiety about the possibility of natural disaster never really goes away here," Lily says. "But the fair helped me to feel better prepared."

Once you have chosen the issue *you* want to act upon, read extensively about it so you feel confident that you know what you are talking about and can address opposing views. Then look for an existing group (or a local chapter of a national organization) that's working on behalf of that issue and see how you can get your feet wet by volunteering for activities the group is sponsoring. Show recognition and appreciation for the work they've been doing, learn from them, and let them know what skills you have to offer or how you can help in other ways. Sometimes volunteers come to a new group feeling uneasy about whether they can be absorbed into the culture smoothly. *Be patient!* It often takes a while for people to know that you can be depended upon.

It's an outcome worth waiting for because teamwork can be transformative. Working shoulder to shoulder with kindred spirits for a cause you believe in reduces the feeling of being alone *with* and *in* your concerns and replaces it with the uplifting feeling that comes from being, at least momentarily, a part of something bigger. In that way, teamwork is almost a version of awe.

In recent years, fifty-six-year-old Hannah, a teacher in New Hampshire, has experienced these positive effects firsthand. After the 2016 elections, she felt shaken up about what the future would bring, especially for health care, reproductive rights, voting rights, and education. "I started feeling depressed, anxious, scared, and angry—and I hated feeling that way," she said. To help herself get out of her own head, she started volunteering for Planned Parenthood, which included doing canvassing where she and other volunteers would knock on voters' doors, talk about the circumstances behind their own abortions, and ask what had shaped the voters' thinking about the issue.

"It's been life-changing," she said. "I've had some amazing, meaningful conversations, even with people who are completely against abortion. It reminds me that even the people who are against the issues I believe in aren't so very different than I am." Besides enhancing her sense of compassion and connection to others, working to try to effect positive change has been empowering for Hannah, helping her go from feeling helpless to hopeful.

In addition to having a beneficial effect on the community, volunteering can help relieve stress, anxiety, and frustration and improve one's mood. In a study involving more than 66,000 adults in the UK, researchers found that volunteering to help another person, group, or organization is an especially powerful contributor to our emotional and physical well-being. Volunteering broadens our social networks, which gives us an additional layer of social support. It gives us a feeling of accomplishment, and most precious of all, it gives us an invaluable sense of purpose. Other studies have produced similar results. What's more, volunteering on a regular basis has been found to buffer the effects of stress. Helping others—by feeding someone who is hungry, sharing your knowledge when it is needed, or being kind to someone who is down and out—brings a sense of dignity and respect to both the giver and the receiver. Plus, looking into the eyes of someone who legitimately benefits from your kindness brings a distinct kind of peace and satisfaction.

An interesting twist comes from a study by researchers at Cornell University. They found that adults who volunteer on environmental projects—what they call "environmental stewardship"—end up with more physical activity, better overall health, and fewer symptoms of depression over a period of two decades. As the researchers noted, in addition to the benefits of increased physical activity, these perks likely stem from spending more time in nature and from "a sense of generativity," working to achieve something (in this case, helping the planet) that will benefit future generations.

FUN FACTS

If you have any doubt that one person—and another courageous person who joins him or her—can start a movement, check out the YouTube video *First Follower: Leadership Lessons from Dancing Guy*. At first, a shirtless guy is dancing by himself on a grassy hill at a concert, waving his arms, kicking his legs, and spinning around, and in less than three minutes, he becomes the inspirational leader as dozens and dozens of people join him. The influence of a lone dancer becomes a phenomenon: a dancing crowd.

EMPOWERING ACTIONS, LARGE AND SMALL

Many different contributions can be made to produce a difference for the health of the planet, your community, and your own life. Every action can have traction because small changes do add up and because what *you* do sends signals to the people around you that they should do their part. Here are some small steps you can take to contribute to the issues you care about:

- Send money to a cause or nonprofit.

- Sign a petition about an issue.

- Call public officials to let them know your thoughts (or if you can manage it, take a shot at writing a letter to the editor or an opinion piece for a newspaper).

- Attend a support or protest rally.

- Calculate your carbon footprint and discover ways to reduce it (go to coolcalifornia.arb.ca.gov/calculator-households -individuals).

- Invite like-minded individuals to discuss the issue.

- Put out a yard sign that expresses your views so you can influence others.

- Take stock of your own behaviors and correct those that are inconsistent with your values.

- Buy produce that's grown locally and fruits and vegetables that are in season to reduce carbon dioxide (CO_2) emissions. Even better, plant your own garden; the soil is good for you.

- Participate in a medication take-back program to prevent contamination of waterways and land from drugs that have been improperly disposed of.

- Go plogging—and join the new movement to pick up litter while you jog.

- Support candidates who hold your values.

- Attend a campaign event and ask the candidate about his/her views on key issues (a.k.a. bird-dogging).

Here are some bigger steps:

- Start a group that's dedicated to discussing and acting on your issue.

- Launch a letter-writing campaign to elected officials in support of an issue or to pressure them to stop taking money from organizations that oppose your values.

- Weigh the pros and cons of transitioning to a job that reflects your values if your current environment doesn't.

- Build a coalition to hit up local and state representatives with calls for bills or hearings on the issue.

- Encourage your local school system to launch curricula about human rights and environmental preservation. The revival of civics classes will help more of the next generation grow up understanding their critical role.

- Take a volunteer vacation: help build houses for those in need, restore natural habitats, work in animal sanctuaries, or improve health or education programs.

- Avoid the high-carbon emissions of airline travel; slow down and take a train. It's good for *you* and having more passengers aboard drives the legitimate argument for more investment in this form of travel. (This is something I do whenever possible. I also do a cost-benefit analysis when I'm asked to travel to speak to a group, weighing the cost of my carbon emissions against the overall value of spreading the message.)

- Rejigger your work hours so you can have more time for your activism.

- Work on a get-out-the-vote campaign to improve voter turnout and/or registration.

- When it's time to replace appliances, buy energy-efficient refrigerators, dishwashers, washing machines, and the like.

- Choose renewable energy sources from your local power company.

- Talk to your workplace managers about adopting eco-friendly practices (for lighting and energy use, office products, recycling, and green cleaning products).

- Consider running for public office yourself. *Why not?*

For more ways to get involved and take action on specific issues, see "Resources."

THE DIY APPROACH

If there isn't a nearby interest group working on an issue you're passionate about, consider starting one or finding a friend or neighbor with whom you can join forces. Write a mission statement so that your goals are clearly defined. Consider the following: *What are you trying to accomplish? What do you need to do to get there? What's the timeline?* If you'd like to invite others to join you, make it an event by having an expert on the subject speak or by showing a video about it. Invite friends, neighbors, colleagues, and acquaintances who are concerned about the issue. Consider making it a potluck or dessert party, name tags provided, so people feel more invested and involved in the event, which can carry over into commitment to the cause.

If the interest is there, form a group and make it a series of meetings, with rotating agendas, responsibilities, and locations. A nominal charge for membership can be a good idea for two reasons: (1) because some studies suggest that people place more value on what they pay for than what they get for free, and (2) because you will always be able to put that money to good use for the group's mission. You could hire someone or recruit a volunteer to put together a website. You could get permits to set up a table at local events so you can spread the word and recruit more members. The possibilities are significant.

THE IMPORTANCE OF MESSAGING

One of the easiest and most effective ways to exercise your power is to speak up or stand up, to say or do something if you see something happening that's clearly wrong. That means being willing to intervene as an upstander if someone is being harassed, bullied, or abused. It means speaking up and pushing back if someone makes a racist or sexist joke or comment in your presence. Or if someone litters in front of you on the street, you could simply say, "Excuse me—you dropped something." These are small, everyday opportunities that add up and collectively create change.

Meanwhile, don't be afraid to bring distressing or frightening topics out into the open. As long as they are handled appropriately in the right company, there's more potential for benefit than harm. For example, talking to kids about their fears or concerns related to gun violence, gender politics, or other current issues can help them build their own psychological scaffolding—and learn from you as you model healthy ways to cope with or adapt to these issues.

Whether you're sharing your views with one person, five people, or a crowd, pay attention to the tone, style, and content of your message, because these factors can mean the difference between being heard and being ignored. A leading expert on persuasion, Robert Cialdini, PhD, author of *Influence: The Psychology of Persuasion*, contends that the key to getting others to listen and to foster long-lasting changes in behavior is to describe the gravity of the problem (don't sugarcoat it), using clear language and terms that are easily understood, then to pivot to what can be done about it, describing empowering actions that can offset the feeling of helplessness, ignite resolve, and promote resilience. The more likely we are to imagine a dreadful loss, the more likely we are to take action, especially if we're presented with ideas for *how* to take action. We may be reluctant to show emotion when talking to others, a phenomenon that's referred to as "affect phobia," for fear it will turn people off. But what people want to hear and what creates sustained behavioral change are most often two different things. Messages that pair *why* it's imperative to take action with the specifics of *what* we can do are most likely to lead to action.

The beauty of these approaches is that while you, as the speaker, may ratchet up other people's emotional inflammation when you discuss a particular threat or issue, you can then capture the energy of those feelings and drive it toward the solution, which lowers people's anxiety, thereby strengthening their commitment to addressing the issue. Social psychologists report that the most effective way to change *behavior* is to use messages that portray the actions we *want* to see, not what we *don't* want to see. With our innate desire to fit in, social approval reinforces our choices. So focus on how others are engaging in positive action—perhaps by noting that *more and more people are advocating for stricter gun laws* instead of saying that *too many people still don't care about gun safety and reform.* In other words, when addressing a recommended action, swing toward the positive.

But don't confuse swinging positive in order to drive other people's behavior with downplaying real threats. It's an important distinction to keep in mind. A colleague of mine once criticized me for being negative when I described climate threats, saying I should emphasize the positive. He pointed out that when American civil rights activist Dr. Martin Luther King Jr. gave his iconic speech at the 1963 March on Washington for Jobs and Freedom, he didn't say *I have a nightmare.* Dr. King didn't need to. His audience already knew the nightmare, the emotions of which he captured and directed into a galvanizing call for justice. His immortal words, "I have a dream . . ." told them what should be expected: "that one day this nation will rise up, live out the true meaning of its creed . . . that all men are created equal."

A lot can be achieved by knowing and using the power of words—and capturing other people's emotions to guide them toward collective action. Saying things once rarely works. Before a message is finally heard, it has to be repeated many times. Building the infrastructure to creating change can take a long time, but once it happens things can go quickly. There's value in repeating the message in order to change other people's actions, just as there is when trying to get kids to clean up their rooms. Don't nag and don't become shrill. Simply continue to provide the call to action, based on credible insights, so that eventually people are encouraged to join you in exercising their power.

If you can tap into and draw out other people's good natures and good intentions, it helps you find common ground and creates trust and enduring commitment to the action you're taking. As the old proverb goes, "Nothing breeds success like success," and that's true in an unpredictable world, too. Hearing stories and seeing images that connect with us emotionally, that give hope by illustrating how things are improving—such as nearly extinct animals surging back to life, illiteracy giving way to the pride of knowing how to read, and diseases being cured with ingenious, cooperatively shared research—can work like magic, restoring optimism and energy and renewing your commitment to being an agent of change. Keep your eye out for what we as human beings are doing right, and how we are and can continue turning things around.

A CALL FOR CIVILITY

These days a lot of us are struggling with emotional inflammation, and the world aches with the need for respectful discourse. Especially in these turbulent times, it's easy for us to trigger each other with rude or discourteous behavior. Whether it's related to opposing political viewpoints or simply dealing with each other on ordinary matters, the right choice of words, facial expressions, tone of voice, and body language can make people empathic, while the wrong ones can turn people off, shut them down, or make them angry.

So pay attention to these aspects of verbal and nonverbal communication in your everyday encounters. To paraphrase a key point that others have made: *Long after people forget exactly what you said, they will remember how your message made them feel.* Embrace the following as your mantra for how to behave in the world, particularly in the age of emotional inflammation: *Speak up. Tell the truth. But do it thoughtfully and with tact.*

When it comes to emotional inflammation, or anything that's distressing, taking steps to correct or modify a troubling situation is a healthy coping mechanism because it replaces the feeling of helplessness with one of empowerment. When you appreciate that taking action is therapeutic, you can begin to regain a sense of refuge that resonates for you. Instead of simply feeling vulnerable and unsteady, you can redirect your energy into working to change the upstream conditions that fuel your worries, while finding like-minded people to be at your side.

For these reasons, it's worth considering for a moment that emotional inflammation could be a hidden asset, rather than simply a burdensome weight. After all, it can set in motion your interest and inspiration to take action, in which case your passion for evoking positive change may become contagious. By seeing *you* exercise your power and put your skills to good use, others are often motivated to follow your lead, even without being aware of it. While one person can't usually make a substantial difference in changing the state of the world or humanity, our individual actions are counted together. On a personal level, by capturing the energy of your outrage, fear, and perhaps at times, despair, and channeling it into potential solutions, your life can be smoothed over with the sense of purpose that is the best salve for emotional inflammation.

As an example, consider fifty-two-year-old Tim, a science writer in Maryland. He spent years suffering from emotional inflammation, largely triggered by worries about climate change and environmental destruction, and often had images of disaster flowing through his mind. After trying to suppress them somewhat unsuccessfully, he decided to capture his anger and frustration and direct them into concrete action by becoming an activist, protesting the building of fossil fuel infrastructures, vigorously fighting fracking, and organizing communities and building coalitions to do the same. He has chosen to lead a life that reflects his values, and that knowledge provides him with considerable solace, as he continues to fight for our very survival today.

Becoming an agent of change and exercising your power to alter or modify the issues that are troubling you is a means of coming to your own emotional rescue. Rather than succumbing to your feelings of distress, forging ahead and thinking strategically about how to make things better can help change the course and quality of your life. It can provide a greater sense of meaning and a sharper sense of clarity about your values and how you want to conduct your life. Exercising these action-taking, confidence-building steps—by tactfully expressing your views and altering your behavior in life-affirming ways—produces a cycle of positive reinforcement, making it more likely that you'll continue these constructive actions and inspire others to do the same.

So keep looking up and moving forward, directing your energy and determination into thoughtful, deliberate action. Reclaiming your emotional equilibrium, and helping others to do the same, doesn't have to remain a wish or a dream. It can become your new reality, with every step you take in the right direction. You have already embarked on the journey.

THE RESTORE TO-DO LIST

☐ Break through the bystander effect; if you see something happening that seems wrong or harmful, speak up or do something to intervene.

☐ Be open to discussing upsetting political or social subjects with other people; as long as potentially sensitive or contentious topics are approached with tact and compassion, everyone can benefit from sharing their fears and concerns.

continues

☐ Calculate your carbon footprint and learn ways to reduce it by taking public transportation, buying local produce, upgrading to energy-efficient appliances, or traveling by train instead of plane.

☐ Volunteer to help a person in need or a group or organization that you believe in, whether it's on your own or with an established program.

☐ Lead by example and inspire other people to take a stand on important issues. Don't keep your efforts to take action a secret—share them!

CHAPTER 11

PERSONALIZE

YOUR RESTORE

PLAN

BY NOW, YOU SHOULD have a fairly good understanding of the various facets of your emotional inflammation and the triggers that cause it to flare up. You've read about the lifestyle factors that can contribute to, aggravate, or calm your emotional inflammation, so you know, at least in principle, how to steer yourself in the right directions or set limits with difficult people and situations. Since so many of us are in this emotional state, try to stay empathetic and compassionate toward others who may feel equally inflamed or uneasy, so that you don't inadvertently contribute to their distress. Like it or not, we're all in this together.

Now, back to you. It's time to put together your personal RESTORE plan to calm *your* emotional inflammation and reclaim your inner equilibrium. This involves a proactive approach to preventing flare-ups of emotional inflammation, as well as measures that can serve as a psychological life raft of sorts when it does get ratcheted up despite your best efforts. This may sound like a tall order, but if you approach this task in a systematic fashion, you will begin to calm the emotional flames inside you, bit by bit. Consider this an investment in yourself: a way to improve your emotional well-being, your health and vitality, and by extension, your life.

Depending on your overall reactor type or the style of emotional inflammation that distresses you most, you'll want to prioritize certain steps over others, as you'll see in the next section. So spend some time thinking about setting priorities for the strategies you'd like to try, based on what you now know from reading this book.

STRATEGIES FOR ALL REACTOR TYPES

Before we get into specific actions for each reactor type, let's start with the following essential cool-down measures since they're universally helpful for enhancing emotional regulation:

- **Put yourself on a steady sleep schedule.** Establish a consistent bedtime and awakening time that allows you to get the amount of sleep that helps you feel and function at your best (most likely something between seven and nine hours nightly). Stick with this schedule, both during the week and on the weekends. If you need to, you can vary your bedtime by an hour or two *occasionally* but try not to sleep in more than an hour (unless, of course, you're sick and need extra rest).

- **Give yourself a digital curfew.** At least ninety minutes before you plan to turn in for the night, shut down all your digital devices, dim the lights, and turn to a quiet, relaxing activity, such as reading, stretching, listening to music, or taking a warm bath. Doing this will help calm your sympathetic nervous system and set the stage for better sleep.

- **Move your body and mind.** Doing as little as ten minutes of aerobic exercise, such as brisk walking, jogging, cycling or swimming, *every* day can help prevent stress hormones from landing on the receptor sites that will make you feel tense or frayed at the edges. Remember: regular exercise also can relieve symptoms of anxiety and depression.

- **Check your emotional pulse periodically.** Try to identify how you're feeling with as much precision and specificity as possible; in other words, practice emotional granularity. Then address the way you're feeling: if you realize you're feeling tense, anxious, irritable, or downbeat, give yourself a brief time-out to engage in deep breathing exercises or meditation, to listen to soothing music, to treat yourself to a comforting scent, or to take a walk around the block.

- **Feed your gut bacteria well.** This means consuming foods with live and active cultures, foods with plenty of fiber, fermented foods, and anti-inflammatory foods, such as colorful vegetables and fruits, whole and cracked grains, beans and legumes, nuts and extra virgin olive oil, and fish and shellfish every day. Think of this as a helpful way of calming physical and emotional inflammation from the inside out. Be sure to drink plenty of noncaffeinated fluids throughout the day, too.

- **Correct your distorted thoughts.** Get in the habit of paying attention to your thoughts and when you catch them getting tangled or twisted, take a moment to question their validity. Ask yourself how likely it is that your worst fears will happen or consider whether there's evidence that the negative messages you're giving yourself are true. If your thoughts are off base, correct them and put them on a more truthful (and helpful) course.

- **Connect with nature—and awe.** Take a short walk in the woods, a garden, or a park and soak in the sensory stimuli. Focus on the magical patterns that are inherent in trees and plants. Listen to the soothing sounds of nature—the wind rustling through the trees, birds singing or chirping, water gurgling in a brook. Gaze at the stars and planets in the night sky. Make a point to appreciate the awe and wonder in the natural world—and that you're a part of it.

✦ ✦ ✦

After you've incorporated these basic measures into your everyday routine for a week or two, add specific strategies that will relieve your style of emotional inflammation. Of course, you are welcome (and encouraged) to choose and use any, or all, of the interventions recommended in this book. But the following are suggestions for strategies you may want to add to the basic priorities, depending on your reactor type.

Nervous Reactor

If you're a *nervous* reactor (meaning you have the anxious, worried, or fearful form of emotional inflammation), you'll want to take steps to calm and control your mood and behavior. To that end, it will help if you do the following:

- **Decrease your intake of stimulants.** This includes caffeine from any source (including chocolate). Also, increase your intake of calming foods that contain omega-3 fatty acids (flaxseeds, chia seeds, walnuts, and fatty fish like salmon, tuna, halibut, anchovies, and sardines) as well as magnesium (nuts, seeds, spinach, bananas, beans, and whole grains).

- **Consciously relax your body and mind.** Carve out time so you can practice progressive muscle relaxation or meditation for at least twenty minutes daily, even when you don't feel particularly nervous or agitated. By doing this consistently, you will lower the overall temperature on your emotional inflammation.

- **Put yourself on a media diet.** Choose when or how you're willing to engage with newsfeeds, newspapers, TV news, and social media—and honor those limits. This way you won't be bombarded with negative or worrisome messages all day long.

- **Write down what's eating away at you.** Not the big picture issues but the concrete, little things. Make a pledge to someone you trust to set up a plan with a timeline to address them one at a time. When you talk about them deliberately, it will help you gain control over the anxiety you are creating by holding onto these anxiety-provoking issues or letting them ricochet in your mind.

Revved Reactor

If you're a *revved* reactor (meaning you have the manic, hyperreactive form of emotional inflammation), you'll want to slow down and assess how you can best channel your energy and attention. To that end, it will help if you do the following:

- **Exercise your critical thinking skills.** Question the validity and veracity of the information you're receiving in the news or everyday life before you decide whether or not to act on it.

- **Manage your time effectively.** Delegate unnecessary time-consuming activities to other people or eliminate them from your schedule. Practice saying "no" to nonessential requests in order to conserve your valuable energy.

- **Schedule downtime.** On a daily basis, make a point to set a specific time to stop what you're doing. Then renew yourself with activities that take you away from the present—perhaps by reading the classics, watching old movies, or playing cards or word games with friends. Or take a dance class or pick up a musical instrument you used to enjoy playing.

- **Get the right colors and scents on your side.** You're already feeling revved up so try to dial down your reactivity by surrounding yourself with or wearing a serene shade of blue or green and/or by applying a dab of a soothing essential oil (such as vanilla or lavender) to the pulse points on your wrists.

Molten Reactor

If you're a *molten* reactor (meaning your emotional inflammation is largely marked by irritation, maybe even anger, and/or indignation), you'll benefit from taking your outrage and indignation and turning it into constructive action. To that end, it will help if you do the following:

- **Decrease your intake of stimulants.** That includes caffeine, chocolate, and alcohol. Meanwhile, increase your intake of calming foods that contain omega-3 fatty acids (flaxseeds, chia seeds, walnuts, and fatty fish like salmon, tuna, halibut, anchovies, and sardines) as well as magnesium (nuts, seeds, spinach, bananas, beans, and whole grains).

- **Act out your frustrations in your head.** After an upsetting encounter or event, think about what you'd really like to say or do, then go ahead and imagine (in your head) cursing that person out or acting out in another way. Doing this will help release some of the pent-up frustration (or other toxic emotions) you're feeling—without leading to negative consequences in the real world.

- **Figure out who pushes your buttons.** Then, consider how you can better deal with those people or set healthy boundaries in your engagements with them. Spend a few minutes practicing relaxation techniques (such as deep breathing or meditation) before walking into a situation that could rile you up.

- **Expose yourself to water.** If possible, go for a swim or walk the length of the pool (in the shallow end) and let the rhythmic activity calm your mind—or go for a walk near a river, lake, or pond. If you can't get to water, buy a small fountain for your home or office or invest in an app that features the sounds of waves.

Retreating Reactor

If you're a *retreating* reactor (meaning, your emotional inflammation is marked by a tendency to freeze, detach, withdraw, zone out, or numb yourself), it's important to take steps to revitalize your mood and reconnect with the world around you. To that end, it will help if you do the following:

- **Turn off the broken record.** When negative thoughts swirl through your mind on a repetitive cycle, stop your thoughts and distract yourself with a pleasant activity such as petting your dog or listening to upbeat music. Kick the tendency to ruminate, in other words, because it will only make you feel worse.

- **Think about what's good in your life.** Spend a few moments each day considering who or what you're grateful for and why. Pausing to reflect on what you appreciate in your life can improve your mood, your outlook, and your relationships (especially if you express your gratitude).

- **Do something nice for someone else.** Volunteer to help a colleague with a project or bring flowers or a meal to a sick friend or relative. Prosocial actions like these help you get out of your own head and increase positive emotions.

- **Develop a supportive social network.** Resist the urge to withdraw by identifying people in your home, workplace, or community who support you, inspire you, and have similar values. Spending time with them on a regular basis will help you gain a sense of kinship.

◆ ◆ ◆

By picking and choosing the strategies that nourish your unique blend of symptoms, you will be able to develop a personalized plan of action that suits your needs. As your emotional inflammation begins to calm down, feel free to tweak these interventions so they continue to work for you. Don't feel limited by these strategies; use them as a launching pad to try other healthy, constructive tactics that appeal to or resonate with you. Spend more time connecting with nature. Seek social support from like-minded people. Celebrate the milestones you reach as you alter your lifestyle, take action on issues you're passionate about, and begin to ease your emotional discomfort. This is *your* plan—use it, fine-tune it, own it. And appreciate the difference it makes in your state of mind over time.

As you've seen, emotional inflammation doesn't have to be an inevitable state of mind. You can take steps to calm it, tame it, and quench the flames it produces. By taking action to restore your emotional equilibrium, you'll be treating yourself to the best form of therapy there is for living in our mixed-up world. Think of the RESTORE plan as your golden ticket to arriving at a state of steady calm that allows you to feel and function better 24/7 and improve your quality of life. *You've earned it!*

EPILOGUE

I T WOULD BE A mistake to think that the world might suddenly become significantly safer, healthier, more peaceful, respectful, affordable, better preserved, and generally less stressful on its own. It would be amazing if it did, but it's magical thinking to expect such a 180-degree turn of events. So while it's true that you can't change the winds or currents in this tumultuous world, you can adjust your sails or your swimming abilities so that you can guide yourself to a safe harbor or shore. In other words, you can't always control the crises and catastrophes that are swirling around you, but you do have some sway over how you handle them and react to them emotionally.

At this point, you are in a unique position to come to your own rescue when you experience the flare-ups of emotional inflammation that are bound to happen in this chaotic world. Armed with the knowledge you've gained from reading this book and using the RESTORE plan, you now possess the tools that will help you deal with the vicissitudes and challenges of modern life. Arm yourself with those tools and wield them wisely to protect your emotional well-being and energy and to set yourself up to achieve steady calm. Continue to judiciously limit your exposure to news feeds, as well as bright lights and technological devices at night. Maintain a consistent sleep-wake schedule. Engage in regular exercise and take care of your microbiome. And keep making an effort to tame your thoughts and tension, using the techniques you've learned here. These are all essential ways to ease emotional inflammation and ward off its triggers.

Ultimately, the key to relieving the distress you've been feeling is to find the right balance between turning inward and reaching outward—that is, to untangle the complex web of emotions inside you, identify the forces that commonly trigger them, and tend to them constructively, while also engaging in meaningful activities that give you a sense of purpose, foster a sense of community, and create a spark that has the potential to ignite positive changes in the world. To paraphrase an Afghan proverb, "Drop by drop . . . it becomes a river"—meaning that every positive action you take counts. Even if you don't see the direct fruits of your efforts to improve matters, remember that there are ripple effects that come from doing the right thing on a particular issue.

Some people hesitate to take steps to bring about meaningful changes because their actions may feel paltry compared to the enormity of the problems in our world. But our personal actions *do* make a difference because the energy and initiative of one person can awaken others to follow suit; then, when they do, their actions will awaken and inspire still others to take a stand or get involved in making society a more humane and equitable place or protecting the natural world. Our actions may start off as individual ones but they are counted together and they add up—and cumulatively they can become a powerful force for change. You can lead by example—especially if you start viewing yourself as an agent of change.

Remember, though, that different people have different coping styles, and in trying times it's especially important to recognize and accept these variations—with compassion, rather than judgment. Taking a hopeful and empathetic approach to the chaos of today's world and our place in it requires courage and tenacity—qualities that come more easily when we cultivate a sense of community and solidarity. There are cultural, technological, political, ecological, and personal tipping points—pivotal points that can move the needle of change in either direction, toward progress or setbacks, on any given issue. Each and every one of us has the potential to make a difference in fostering change for the better. Once a positive tipping point is reached, progress can come more quickly than we could ever have imagined. It's about setting the wheels in motion—empowering in its own right.

As you move forward, continue to put on your own (metaphorical) oxygen mask first, especially when you feel your emotional inflammation being triggered, before trying to help or influence others. Otherwise, you'll risk depleting your own physical and emotional stamina, and you won't be able to effectively help anyone else. Human beings have a remarkable capacity to rebound from hardship and adversity, to grow and learn from their experiences. You can incorporate these hard-won lessons into your worldview, your view of yourself, and the manner in which you approach your life in ways that will help you not only survive but actually thrive. You deserve nothing less.

ACKNOWLEDGMENTS

THIS BOOK WOULD NOT HAVE BEEN POSSIBLE if the two of us hadn't met while Stacey was writing an article about anticipated trauma for *US News & World Report* and interviewed Lise. Realizing we were kindred spirits in many ways, we kept the conversation going about the emotional inflammation that so many of us are living with these days. The concept for this book arose from a very organic process, from a meeting of two minds with shared sensibilities and desires to help other people. It was made better by the insights of others, including our brilliant literary agent Heather Jackson, who was enthusiastic about this subject from day one and helped us shape the content of this book. Heather, we are incredibly grateful for all your support and wisdom—we couldn't have created this book without you.

We are also deeply indebted to our talented editor Haven Iverson, who immediately "got" the subject of emotional inflammation and brought warmth, clarity, and compassion to the topic and the process. At Sounds True, we would also like to thank Jade Lascelles, Leslie Brown, Jill Rogers, Chloe Prusiewicz, Wendy Gardner, Matt Jankauskas, Rachael Murray, and Maureen Forys for their invaluable contributions in bringing this book to life.

Of course, we want to thank our families—Jonathan, Aliza, Delaney, and Piera (on Lise's side); John, Nate, and Nick (on Stacey's)—for all of their support as we wrote this book. In particular, we want to give a shout-out to Piera, whose incredible paintings inspired the feeling we wanted to capture with the cover of *Emotional Inflammation*.

We are also grateful to the many people who shared their personal experiences with emotional inflammation and the steps they took to find relief. We hope that giving voice to your fears and anxieties and discovering that you have a great deal of company with your feelings provided a modicum of relief. When you discover that there's a name for how you've been feeling, and that you can take effective actions to restore your emotional equilibrium and change the upstream conditions that fuel your worries, it's an empowering experience—one that can move you from feeling vulnerable and victimized to strong and resilient. Writing this book has done that for us. We hope that reading it will for you, dear reader.

GLOSSARY

ACCEPTANCE AND COMMITMENT THERAPY (ACT): A newer form of psychotherapy that uses acceptance and mindfulness strategies to help people accept their feelings and change their behavior while increasing their psychological flexibility.

ALEXITHYMIA: A subclinical condition that's characterized by an inability to recognize, identify, and describe your own emotions, as well as difficulty distinguishing between emotions and bodily sensations.

ALLOSTATIC LOAD: The price the body pays for chronic or repeated exposure to elevated stress hormones; a form of long-term stress-induced wear and tear on the brain and body that increases the risk of chronic diseases and accelerates the aging process.

AMYGDALA: A structure in the brain (in the limbic system) that processes and modulates our emotions and our reactions to events. It's particularly known for processing fear and sending signals that trigger the body's fight-or-flight response.

ANTICIPATORY ANXIETY: The worry and fear you experience when you think about what could happen during an event or situation in the future.

ATTENTION RESTORATION THEORY (ART): A concept, developed by Rachel and Stephen Kaplan, professors of psychology at the University of Michigan, that suggests that people can concentrate better after spending time in nature or looking at scenes of nature.

BIOPHILIA: Love of living things (*bio* meaning "life," and *philia* meaning "love for") or nature-relatedness. Social psychologist Erich Fromm is credited with creating the term, while biologist Edward O. Wilson popularized it in his book *Biophilia*, where he offered the hypothesis that humans' affinity for nature is innate.

BRAIN-DERIVED NEUROTROPHIC FACTOR (BDNF): A protein produced inside nerve cells that plays an important role in nerve growth and survival and neuronal plasticity, which is essential for learning, memory, and other cognitive functions. Notably, levels of BDNF increase after exercise.

BYSTANDER EFFECT: A concept popularized by social psychologists John Darley and Bibb Latané after the 1964 murder of twenty-eight-year-old Kitty Genovese in New York. It refers to the tendency for some people to stay on the sidelines, observing a crisis, rather than intervening and doing something about it.

CARBON FOOTPRINT: The total amount of greenhouse gases, including carbon dioxide, that is produced and released directly and indirectly by human activities.

CIRCADIAN RHYTHM: Derived from the Latin words *circa*, which means "going around," and *diem*, for "day," this twenty-four-hour internal cycle regulates the human body's sleep-wake patterns, among many other functions.

COGNITIVE BEHAVIORAL THERAPY (CBT): A form of psychotherapy that focuses on helping people identify, challenge, and change inaccurate or unhelpful thinking patterns and develop coping strategies that help them solve problems or handle difficult situations more effectively.

COGNITIVE DISSONANCE: The experience of having two or more conflicting thoughts, beliefs, or values that trigger feelings of discomfort.

COGNITIVE DISTORTION: An exaggerated, skewed, or otherwise inaccurate thought pattern that can affect your perception of reality, typically in a negative or unhelpful way. If left unchecked, these distorted thinking patterns can contribute to depression or anxiety.

CORTISOL: Known as the primary stress hormone, cortisol is a steroid hormone that is released by the adrenal glands and is involved in regulating a wide range of processes throughout the body, including metabolism. In the right amounts, cortisol is essential for protecting your overall health and well-being, but too much can be problematic for your body and mind.

DEFAULT MODE NETWORK (DMN): An interconnected group of brain regions that appears to be less active when you're engaged in a task that requires paying attention and more active when you're not consciously focused on the outside world.

DOPAMINE: A neurotransmitter in the brain that helps perform numerous functions, including regulating movement, attention, and emotional responses. Because it mediates pleasure in the brain and stimulates us to seek rewards, dopamine plays a starring role in motivating our behavior.

DYSBIOSIS: A term for the imbalance of microbes, including bacteria, inside the body, particularly in the gut.

ECOLOGICAL GRIEF: A common response to the climate crisis that encompasses deep sorrow about experienced or anticipated environmental losses or degradation, including destruction of or damage to species, ecosystems, and meaningful natural landscapes.

EMOTIONAL GRANULARITY: The ability to experience and label emotions in a precise, nuanced manner. It is a quality that's associated with greater emotional well-being, including better emotion regulation skills and greater resilience to stress.

FLOW: A term coined by the psychologist Mihály Csíkszentmihályi that refers to an optimal state of complete absorption with or immersion in what you're doing that can cause you to lose all sense of time and space.

FOREST BATHING (SHINRIN-YOKU): A practice developed in Japan during the 1980s that involves walking slowly in a forest or under a canopy of trees and using your senses to maximize the experience. It has numerous benefits from improving immune function and reducing blood pressure to enhancing mood, attention, and energy.

FOSSIL FUELS: Sources of energy that were formed millions of years ago when plants and animals died, then were covered with soil, overgrowth, and other elements and impurities. Over time, the subsequent compression and chemical reactions brought these "fossils" to their current form—coal, oil, and gas. Burning these fossil fuels releases gases and other pollutants, which drive up global temperatures.

FRACTALS: Patterns of repeated shapes of varying sizes that have the same relative ratios. When we see fractals in nature, our eyes transmit calming messages to the brain that suggest the setting is ordered and predictable, which heightens our equilibrium and our sense of safety.

FUNCTIONAL MAGNETIC RESONANCE IMAGING (FMRI): A method for registering brain activity by measuring the increase in blood flow that's called for when more oxygen and glucose are needed as specific parts of the brain are engaged in activities such as responding to stimuli or performing a task, or during activation of the default mode network.

GHRELIN: Often called the "hunger hormone" because it stimulates appetite and food intake, ghrelin is produced and released primarily by the stomach with small amounts also released by the small intestine, pancreas, and brain. Besides influencing food consumption and fat storage, ghrelin stimulates the release of growth hormone and has protective effects on the cardiovascular system.

GREENHOUSE GASES: Gases that trap heat in the atmosphere by allowing the heat-bearing energy from the sun's rays in, while blocking the rays from exiting. This has caused the earth's temperature to increase substantially above normal, unleashing climate disruption.

GROWTH HORMONE: A small protein made by the pituitary gland and secreted into the bloodstream that promotes growth in children and maintains normal body structure and metabolism in adults. Getting enough sleep and exercising regularly increase growth hormone levels.

HYPOTHALAMUS: A small region of the brain that has a crucial role in controlling many bodily functions, including releasing hormones, maintaining body temperature, regulating sleep cycles, and contributing to other processes that are necessary for homeostasis.

LEPTIN: A hormone that's released from the fat cells and sends signals to the brain to help regulate and alter appetite, food intake, and energy expenditure over the long term, with the goal of helping the body maintain its weight. It's often thought of primarily as the hormone that signals satiety or fullness.

MELATONIN: A hormone that's released by the pineal gland and helps regulate the sleep-wake cycle. The production and release of melatonin increases when the environment is dark, making you feel sleepy, and decreases when it is light.

META-EMOTIONS: The way you feel about your feelings or react to them. In other words, meta-emotions are secondary emotions that occur in response to a primary one.

METABOLIC SYNDROME: A cluster of conditions—including high blood pressure, high blood sugar, excess abdominal fat, and abnormal cholesterol or triglyceride levels—that often occur together, increasing a person's risk of developing heart disease, stroke, and type 2 diabetes.

If at least three of these conditions occur simultaneously, the person is deemed to have metabolic syndrome.

MICROBES: Microscopic organisms—such as bacteria, viruses, and fungi—that are found in water, soil, and air. Some can make us sick, while others are good for human health.

MICROBIOME: The community of trillions of microbes—including bacteria, viruses, and fungi—that live on or within human tissues, including the gut, skin, and other areas. The gut microbiome in particular plays a critical role in human health, influencing the immune system, brain function, mood, and more.

MINDFULNESS MEDITATION: A form of meditation that centers on being present in the here and now by focusing on your breath and returning to it when your attention wanders. Research shows that mindfulness meditation reduces stress and anxiety, improves attention and memory, and promotes self-regulation and empathy.

MIRROR NEURONS: Special neurons (brain cells) that fire not only when someone performs a particular action or makes a certain facial expression but also when the person observes someone else making the same movement. Because they allow us to catch or feel someone else's emotions, these neurons play a role in empathy.

NEGATIVE AIR IONS: Invisible, charged particles in the air that are particularly abundant in elements of nature, including forests, waterfalls, and the seashore. Exposure to negative air ions has been found to reduce depression and anxiety and improve mood.

NEUROTRANSMITTERS: Chemical messengers, such as acetylcholine, dopamine, GABA, and serotonin, that send information between neurons (nerve cells) and play important roles in mood, mental health, sleep, and behavior.

NOCTCAELADOR: A strong interest in and psychological attachment to the night sky. People who possess this quality can enter a profound state of psychological absorption as they become entranced while viewing the moon, stars, and bright planets at night.

OXYTOCIN: A hormone that's produced in the hypothalamus and secreted by the pituitary gland. Often called the "love hormone" because it's released during cuddling or hugging, oxytocin fosters bonding and trust, reduces symptoms of anxiety and depression, and even quiets down the highly reactive amygdala.

PARASYMPATHETIC NERVOUS SYSTEM: Part of the involuntary nervous system that controls largely automatic processes such as digestion, respiration, and heart rate and plays a critical role in bringing bodily functions back to homeostasis and inducing the relaxation response.

PHYTONCIDES: Aromatic, airborne substances that are emitted by more than 5,000 plants to protect themselves from pests such as bacteria, fungi, and insects. Inhalation of phytoncides has been shown to reduce stress and blood pressure and improve immune function in humans.

PINEAL GLAND: A pea-sized gland in the brain that produces melatonin, which is involved in regulating sleep-wake patterns.

PREBIOTICS: Nondigestible components in certain foods such as lentils, chickpeas, garlic, and apples that, when consumed, promote the growth of good gut bacteria (probiotics).

PREFRONTAL CORTEX: A part of the brain that is involved in a variety of complex functions including planning, attention, foresight, and impulse control, and that contributes to personality development.

PRIMING EFFECT: A phenomenon where exposure to one stimulus or stressor influences and often magnifies a response to a subsequent one, without the person being aware of it.

PROBIOTICS: Beneficial bacteria or yeasts found in certain foods, including yogurt, kefir, kimchi, sauerkraut, and miso, that contribute to increasing the population of "good" bacteria in your gut.

RUMINATION: The tendency to cogitate or dwell on distressing situations so much that it can lead to an increase in anxiety, sleep disturbances, and unhealthy behaviors.

SEROTONIN: A neurotransmitter that has a wide variety of functions in the body, including stabilizing mood, promoting feelings of well-being, and facilitating communication between brain cells and other nervous system cells. It also helps with sleep and digestion.

SOCIAL JET LAG: The misalignment of a person's social and biological time-related needs—that is, the gap between how we are living and what our bodies call for at any given time.

SOLASTALGIA: Emotional distress brought on by seeing or imagining irreversible degradation or damage to treasured places in the natural world caused by climate change or industrial impacts.

SYMPATHETIC NERVOUS SYSTEM: Part of the involuntary nervous system that orchestrates the body's fight-or-flight response and helps to maintain homeostasis in the body.

TRANSCENDENTAL MEDITATION: A form of meditation that involves silently repeating a mantra (usually a word or sound) to free the mind, allowing practitioners to find a place of peace and silence. When practiced regularly, it has been found to reduce stress, chronic pain, and high blood pressure, and improve physical and emotional well-being.

TRYPTOPHAN: A naturally occurring amino acid present in many foods that has a calming effect and can help set the stage for sound sleep.

UPSTANDER: Someone who recognizes a social injustice or that something else is wrong and speaks up or stands up to work to make it right. It is the opposite of an idle bystander.

WELTSCHMERZ: A term that means "world pain" in German. It describes a world-weariness that stems from the discrepancy between how one wants the world to be and how it really is.

RESOURCES

350 An international movement of ordinary people who are working to end the age of fossil fuels and build a world of community-led renewable energy; *350.org*

The American Civil Liberties Union An organization that's dedicated to protecting immigrants' rights, human rights, privacy, racial justice, and reproductive freedom, among other key social issues; *aclu.org*

Amnesty International A global campaign for human rights with more than 7 million members; *amnesty.org/en/*

Climate Central An organization of leading scientists and journalists that's dedicated to researching and reporting the facts about climate change and its impact on the public; *climatecentral.org*

The Climate Mobilization A movement whose mission is to reverse global warming and the mass extinction of species; *theclimatemobilization.org*

Climate Psychiatry Alliance A grassroots affiliation of psychiatric professionals dedicated to informing people about the risks of climate change and its impacts on mental health; *climatepsychiatry.org*

Climate Psychology Alliance A group for psychotherapists and others who are interested in the connections between psychology and climate change; *climatepsychologyalliance.org*

Earth Day Network   An organization that aims to diversify, educate, and activate the environmental movement worldwide; *earthday.org*

Earth Justice   A nonprofit public interest environmental law organization; *earthjustice.org*

Environmental Working Group   A non-profit dedicated to protecting human health and the environment; *ewg.org*

National Wildlife Federation   The US's largest and most trusted conservation organization; *nwf.org*

Natural Resources Defense Council   An organization that's dedicated to protecting the earth, including its people, plants, animals, and natural systems; *nrdc.org*

Oceana   An international organization focused exclusively on protecting and restoring the world's oceans; *oceana.org*

Physicians for Social Responsibility   An organization that mobilizes physicians and other health professionals to advocate for climate solutions and other issues that threaten human health and survival; *psr.org*

Post Carbon Institute   An organization that provides resources to help people understand and respond to the interrelated ecological, economic, energy, and equity crises of the twenty-first century; *postcarbon.org*

The Prevention Institute   A nonprofit focused on health equity, mental health and well-being, and preventing violence, among other important topics; *preventioninstitute.org*

PsychCentral   The internet's largest and oldest independent online resource for information about mental health issues; *psychcentral.com*

Teaching Tolerance   An organization that offers educational materials and resources emphasizing social justice and anti-bias; *tolerance.org*

Transparency International   A global coalition that seeks to stop the abuse of power, bribery, and secret deals, in an effort to create a world that's free of corruption; *transparency.org*

Union of Concerned Scientists   A group of scientists, analysts, and policy and communication experts who are working to build a healthier planet and a safer world; *ucsusa.org*

The Violence Policy Center   An educational organization that's dedicated to preventing gun deaths and injuries through research, education, advocacy, and collaboration efforts; *vpc.org*

VolunteerMatch   A non-profit organization that helps people who want to volunteer connect with causes that interest them in their part of the US; *volunteermatch.org*

Woods Hole Research Center   An independent research organization where scientists study climate change and how to solve it; *whrc.org*

SELECTED BIBLIOGRAPHY

Introduction: Living on High Alert

Centers for Disease Control and Prevention. "Deaths from Prescription Pain-killer Overdoses Rise Sharply Among Women." July 2, 2013. cdc.gov/media/releases/2013/p0702-drug-overdose.html.

Coleman, Mark. "Wake Up to the Wild." *Mindful Magazine,* April 2019, 40–49.

Felter, Claire. "The U.S. Opioid Epidemic." Council on Foreign Relations. Last updated September 17, 2019. cfr.org/backgrounder/us-opioid-epidemic.

Weinberger, A.H., M. Gbedemah, A.M. Martinez, D. Nash, S. Galea, and R.D. Goodwin. "Trends in Depression Prevalence in the USA from 2005 to 2015: Widening Disparities in Vulnerable Groups." *Psychological Medicine* 48, no. 8 (June 2018): 1308–1315. ncbi.nlm.nih.gov/pubmed/29021005.

Chapter 1: Emotional Inflammation: The Name for How You've Been Feeling

Acevedo, B.P., E.N. Aron, A. Aron, M.D. Sangster, N. Collins, and L.L. Brown. "The Highly Sensitive Brain: An fMRI Study of Sensory Processing Sensi-tivity and Response to Others' Emotions." *Brain and Behavior* 4, no. 4 (July 2014): 580–594. www.ncbi.nlm.nih.gov/pmc/articles/PMC4086365/.

American Psychiatric Association. "APA Public Opinion Poll—Annual Meeting 2017." April 24–27, 2017. psychiatry.org/newsroom/apa-public-opinion-poll-annual-meeting-2017.

American Psychiatric Association. "APA Public Opinion Poll—Annual Meeting 2018." March 23–25, 2018. psychiatry.org/newsroom/apa-public-opinion-poll-annual-meeting-2018.

American Psychological Association. "Stress in America: The State of Our Nation." November 1, 2017. apa.org/news/press/releases/stress/2017 /state-nation.pdf.

Barrett, D., and M. Zapotosky. "FBI Accuses Wealthy Parents, Including Celebrities, in College-Entrance Bribery Scheme." *The Washington Post*, March 12, 2019. washingtonpost.com/world/national-security/fbi-accuses-wealthy -parents-including-celebrities-in-college-entrance-bribery-scheme/2019 /03/12/d91c9942-44d1-11e9-8aab-95b8d80a1e4f_story.html.

Berntsen, D., and D.C. Rubin. "Pretraumatic Stress Reactions in Soldiers Deployed to Afghanistan." *Clinical Psychological Science* 3, no. 5 (September 2015): 663–374. ncbi.nlm.nih.gov/pmc/articles/PMC4564108/.

Centers for Disease Control and Prevention. "Suicide Rising Across the US." *Vital Signs*, June 7, 2018. cdc.gov/vitalsigns/suicide/index.html.

Centers for Disease Control and Prevention. "Youth Risk Behavior Survey: Data Summary and Trends Report 2007–2017." cdc.gov/healthyyouth/data/yrbs /pdf/trendsreport.pdf.

Cigna. "New Cigna Study Reveals Loneliness at Epidemic Levels in America." May 1, 2018. multivu.com/players/English/8294451-cigna-us-loneliness -survey/.

Compare the Market (blog). "What's Stressing Australia?" March 1, 2016. comparethemarket.com.au/blog/health/what-is-stressing-australia/.

DiJulio, B., L. Hamel, C. Muñana, and M. Brodie. "Loneliness and Social Isolation in the United States, the United Kingdom, and Japan: An International Survey." Kaiser Family Foundation, August 30, 2018. kff.org/report-section /loneliness-and-social-isolation-in-the-united-states-the-united-kingdom -and-japan-an-international-survey-introduction/.

Engelmann, J.B., F. Meyer, E. Fehr, and C.C. Ruff. "Anticipatory Anxiety Disrupts Neural Valuation during Risky Choice." *Journal of Neuroscience* 35, no. 7 (February 18): 3085–3099. jneurosci.org/content/35/7/3085.long.

Ferreira, B. "We Asked 105 Experts What Gives Them Hope About the Future." *Motherboard, Tech By Vice*, December 5, 2018. vice.com/en_us/article /7xyewg/we-asked-105-experts-what-gives-them-hope-about-the-future.

Ford Motor Company. "Looking Further with Ford Trends Report." 2018. media.ford.com/content/dam/fordmedia/North%20America/US /2017/12/06/2018-Looking-Further-with-Ford-Trend-Report.pdf.

Forth. "Great Britain and Stress—How Bad Is It and Why Is It Happening?" February 4, 2018. forthwithlife.co.uk/blog/great-britain-and-stress/.

Gallup Global Emotions Report 2018. gallup.com/analytics/241961/gallup
-global-emotions-report-2018.aspx.

Gallup Global Emotions Report 2019. gallup.com/analytics/248906/gallup
-global-emotions-report-2019.aspx.

Gray, Alex. "What Are People in Your Country Most Worried About?" *World
Economic Forum*, February 21, 2017. weforum.org/agenda/2017/02
/what-are-people-in-your-country-most-worried-about/.

Helliwell, John F., R. Layard, and J.D. Sachs. *World Happiness Report 2019*.
worldhappiness.report/ed/2019/.

Lehrer, J., and M. Iacoboni. "The Mirror Neuron Revolution: Explaining What
Makes Humans Social." *Scientific American*, July 1, 2008. scientificamerican
.com/article/the-mirror-neuron-revolut/.

Leiserowitz, A., E. Maibach, S. Rosenthal, J. Kotcher, M. Ballew, M. Goldberg,
and A. Gustafson. "Climate Change in the American Mind: December
2018." Yale Program on Climate Change Communication Report, January
22, 2019. climatecommunication.yale.edu/publications/climate-change-in
-the-american-mind-december-2018/2/.

Newman, T. "Anxiety in the West: Is It on the Rise?" *Medical News Today*,
September 5, 2018. medicalnewstoday.com/articles/322877.php.

Norman, J. "Healthcare Once Again Tops List of Americans' Worries." Gallup,
April 1, 2019. news.gallup.com/poll/248159/healthcare-once-again-tops
-list-americans-worries.aspx.

Ophir, E., C. Nass, and A.D. Wagner. "Cognitive Control in Media Multitaskers."
Proceedings of the National Academy of Scientists USA 106, no. 37 (September
15, 2009): 15583–15587. ncbi.nlm.nih.gov/pmc/articles/PMC2747164/.

Page, Susan, and Marilyn Icsman. "Poll: For the Columbine Generation, Gun
Violence Is a Defining Fear." *USA Today*, March 22, 2018. usatoday.com
/story/news/2018/03/22/poll-columbine-generation-gun-violence
-defining-fear/441446002/.

Piff, P.K., P. Dietze, M. Feinberg, D.M. Stancato, and D. Keltner. "Awe, the Small
Self, and Prosocial Behavior." *Journal of Personality and Social Psychology*
108, no. 6 (June 2015): 883–899. ncbi.nlm.nih.gov/pubmed/25984788.

Primack, B.A., A. Shensa, J.E. Sidani, E.O. Whaite, L. Lin, D. Rosen, J.B. Colditz,
A. Radovic, and E. Miller. "Social Media Use and Perceived Social Isolation
Among Young Adults in the US." *American Journal of Preventive Medicine*
53, no. 1 (July 2017): 1–8. ajpmonline.org/article/S0749-3797(17)30016-8
/fulltext.

Ruch, Donna, A.H. Sheftall, P. Schlagbaum, J. Rausch, J.V. Campo, and J.A. Bridge. "Trends in Suicide Among Youth Aged 10 to 19 Years in the United States, 1975 to 2016." *JAMA Network Open* 2, no. 5 (2019): e193886. jamanetwork .com/journals/jamanetworkopen/fullarticle/2733430.

Tacy, J. "Technostress: A Concept Analysis." *Online Journal of Nursing Informatics* 20, no. 2 (July 2016). himss.org/library/technostress-concept -analysis.

Tsai, J., R. El-Gabalawy, W.H. Sledge, S.M. Southwick, and R.H. Pietrzak. "Post-Traumatic Growth among Veterans in the USA: Results from the National Health and Resilience in Veterans Study." *Psychological Medicine* 45, no. 1 (January 2015): 165–79. ncbi.nlm.nih.gov/pubmed/25065450.

Chapter 2: What Type of Reactor Are You?

Chester, D.S., D.R. Lynam, R. Milich, D.K. Powell, A.H. Andersen, and C.N. DeWall. "How Do Negative Emotions Impair Self-Control? A Neural Model of Negative Urgency." *Neuroimage* 15, no. 132 (May 2016): 43–50. ncbi.nlm .nih.gov/pmc/articles/PMC4851933/.

Ifeagwazi, C.M., H.E. Egberi, and J.C. Chukwuorji. "Emotional Reactivity and Blood Pressure Elevations: Anxiety as a Mediator." *Psychology, Health & Medicine* 23, no. 5 (June 2018): 585–592. ncbi.nlm.nih.gov/pubmed /29105504.

Koval, P., A. Brose, M.L. Pe, M. Houben, Y. Erbas, D. Champagne, and P. Kuppens. "Emotional Inertia and External Events: The Roles of Exposure, Reactivity, and Recovery." *Emotion* 15, no. 5 (October 2015): 625–636. ncbi.nlm.nih.gov/pubmed/25844974.

McLaughlin, K.A., L.D. Kubzansky, E.C. Dunn, R. Waldinger, G. Vaillant, and K.C. Koenen. "Childhood Social Environment, Emotional Reactivity to Stress, and Mood and Anxiety Disorders Across the Life Course." *Depression and Anxiety* 27, no. 12 (December 2010): 1087–1094. ncbi.nlm.nih.gov/pmc /articles/PMC3074636/.

Chapter 3: The Inflammatory Cascade

Amodeo, G., M.A. Trusso, and A. Fagiolini. "Depression and Inflammation: Disentangling a Clear Yet Complex and Multifaceted Link." *Neuropsychiatry* 7, no. 4 (2017). jneuropsychiatry.org/peer-review/depression-and-inflammation -disentangling-a-clear-yet-complex-and-multifaceted-link.html.

Arnsten, A., C.M. Mazure, and R. Sinha. "Everyday Stress Can Shut Down the Brain's Chief Command Center." *Scientific American*, April 9, 2012. scientificamerican.com/article/this-is-your-brain-in-meltdown/.

Cahill, L. "His Brain, Her Brain." *Scientific American*, October 1, 2012. scientificamerican.com/article/his-brain-her-brain-2012-10-23/.

Carlisle, M., B.N. Uchino, D.M. Sanbonmatsu, T.W. Smith, M.R. Cribbet, W. Birmingham, K.C. Light, and A.A. Vaughn. "Subliminal Activation of Social Ties Moderates Cardiovascular Reactivity During Acute Stress." *Health Psychology* 31, no. 2 (March 2012): 217–225. ncbi.nlm.nih.gov/pmc /articles/PMC3241848/.

Fritze, J.G., G.A. Blashki, S. Burke, and J. Wiseman. "Hope, Despair, and Trans-formation: Climate Change and the Promotion of Mental Health and Wellbeing." *International Journal of Mental Health Systems*, September 2008. ijmhs.biomedcentral.com/articles/10.1186/1752-4458-2-13.

Gump, B.B., S. Yun, and K. Kannan. "Polybrominated Diphenyl Ether (PBDE) Exposure in Children: Possible Associations with Cardiovascular and Psy-chological Functions." *Environmental Research* 132 (March 2012): 244–250. ncbi.nlm.nih.gov/pmc/articles/PMC4104497/.

Hänsel, A., and R. von Känel. "Unconscious Fearful Priming Followed by a Psychosocial Stress Test Results in Higher Cortisol Levels." *Stress and Health* 29, no. 4 (October 2013): 317–323. ncbi.nlm.nih.gov/pubmed /23086904.

Krause, N., K.I. Pargament, P.C. Hill, and G. Ironson. "Spiritual Struggles and Problem Drinking: Are Younger Adults at Greater Risk than Older Adults?" *Substance Use & Misuse* 53, no. 5 (April 16, 2018): 808–815. ncbi.nlm.nih .gov/pubmed/29172880.

Lipka, M., and C. Gecewicz. "More Americans Now Say They're Spiritual but Not Religious." *Factank: News in the Numbers*, September 6, 2017. pewresearch.org/fact-tank/2017/09/06/more-americans-now-say -theyre-spiritual-but-not-religious/.

Massar, S.A.A., J.C.J. Liu, N.B. Mohammad, and M.W.L. Chee. "Poor Habitual Sleep Efficiency Is Associated with Increased Cardiovascular and Cortisol Stress Reactivity in Men." *Psychoneuroendocrinology* 81 (July 2017): 151–156. ncbi.nlm.nih.gov/pubmed/28482312.

McEwen, Bruce S. *The End of Stress as We Know It*. New York: Dana Press, 2012.

Medina, John. *Brain Rules: 12 Principles for Surviving and Thriving at Work, Home, and School.* Seattle: Pear Press, 2014.

Miller, A.H. "Five Things to Know About Inflammation and Depression." *Psychiatric Times* 35, no. 4 (April 30, 2018). psychiatrictimes.com/special-reports/five-things-know-about-inflammation-and-depression.

Mobbs, D., C.C. Hagan, T. Dalgleish, B. Silston, and C. Prévost. "The Ecology of Human Fear: Survival Optimization and the Nervous System." *Frontiers in Neuroscience* 9, no. 55 (2015). ncbi.nlm.nih.gov/pmc/articles/PMC4364301/.

Ozbay, F., D.C. Johnson, E. Dimoulas, C.A. Morgan, III, D. Charney, and S. Southwick. "Social Support and Resilience to Stress." *Psychiatry* 4, no. 5 (May 2007): 35–40. ncbi.nlm.nih.gov/pmc/articles/PMC2921311/.

Reschke-Hernández, A.E., K.L. Okerstrom, A.B. Edwards, and D. Tranel. "Sex and Stress: Men and Women Show Different Cortisol Responses to Psychological Stress Induced by the Trier Social Stress Test and the Iowa Singing Social Stress Test." *Journal of Neuroscience Research*, November 7, 2016. onlinelibrary.wiley.com/doi/10.1002/jnr.23851.

Seo, D., A. Ahluwalia, M.N. Potenza, and R. Sinha. "Gender Differences in Neural Correlates of Stress-Induced Anxiety." *Journal of Neuroscience Research*, November 7, 2016. onlinelibrary.wiley.com/doi/10.1002/jnr.23926.

Van der Kolk, Bessel. *The Body Keeps the Score.* New York: Penguin Books, 2015.

Chapter 4: Recognize Your Feelings

Bailen, N., H.W. Hallenbeck, and R. Thompson. "How to Deal with Feeling Bad About Your Feelings." *Greater Good Magazine* 26 (2018). greatergood.berkeley.edu/article/item/how_to_deal_with_feeling_bad_about_your_feelings/.

Barrett, Lisa Feldman. *How Emotions Are Made: The Secret Life of the Brain.* New York: Mariner Books, 2018.

Brasseur, S., J. Grégoire, R. Bourdu, and Moïra Mikolajzak. "The Profile of Emotional Competence (PEC): Development and Validation of a Self-Reported Measure that Fits Dimensions of Emotional Competence Theory." *PLoS One* 8, no. 5 (2013): e62635. ncbi.nlm.nih.gov/pmc/articles/PMC3646043/.

Burklund, L.J., J.D. Creswell, M.R. Irwin, and M.D. Lieberman. "The Common and Distinct Neural Bases of Affect Labeling and Reappraisal in Healthy Adults." *Frontiers in Psychology* 5 (2014): 221. ncbi.nlm.nih.gov/pmc/articles/PMC3970015/.

Cowen, A.S., and D. Keltner. "Self-Report Captures 27 Distinct Categories of Emotion Bridged by Continuous Gradients." *Proceedings of the National Academy of Sciences of the United States of America*, September 5, 2017. pnas.org/content/early/2017/08/30/1702247114.

Edwards, E., S. Shivaji, and P. Wupperman. "The Emotion Mapping Activity: Preliminary Evaluation of a Mindfulness-Informed Exercise to Improve Emotion Labeling in Alexithymic Persons." *Scandinavian Journal of Psychology* 59, no. 3 (June 2018): 319–327. ncbi.nlm.nih.gov/pubmed /29516501.

Erbas, Y., E. Ceulemans, E.S. Blanke, L. Sels, A. Fischer, and P. Kuppens. "Emotion Differentiation Dissected: Between-Category, Within-Category, and Integral Emotion Differentiation and Their Relation to Well-Being." *Cognition & Emotion* 33, no. 2 (March 2019): 258–271. ncbi.nlm.nih.gov /pubmed/29688128.

Ford, B.Q., P. Lam, O.P. John, and I.B. Mauss. "The Psychological Health Bene-fits of Accepting Negative Emotions and Thoughts: Laboratory, Diary, and Longitudinal Evidence." *Journal of Personality and Social Psychology* 115, no. 6 (December 2018): 1075–1092. ncbi.nlm.nih.gov/pubmed/28703602.

Haradhvala, N. "Meta-Emotions in Daily Life: Associations with Emotional Awareness and Depression." *Arts & Sciences Electronic Theses and Dissertations* (2016): 978. openscholarship.wustl.edu/art_sci_etds/978.

Hunter, E.C., L.F. Katz, J.W. Shortt, B. Davis, C. Leve, N.B. Allen, and L.B. Sheeber. "How Do I Feel About Feelings? Emotion Socialization in Families of Depressed and Healthy Adolescents." *Journal of Youth and Adolescence* 40, no. 4 (April 2011): 428–441. ncbi.nlm.nih.gov/pmc/articles/PMC2992097/.

Kashdan, T.B., L.F. Barrett, and P.E. McKnight. "Unpacking Emotion Differ-entiation: Transforming Unpleasant Experience by Perceiving Distinctions in Negativity." *Current Directions in Psychological Science* 24, no. 1 (2015): 10–16. affective-science.org/pubs/2015/kashdan-et-all-unpacking-emotion -differentiation-2015.pdf.

Lee, J.Y., K.A. Lindquist, and C.S. Nam. "Emotional Granularity Effects on Event-Related Brain Potentials During Affective Picture Processing." *Frontiers in Human Neuroscience*, March 24, 2017. frontiersin.org/articles /10.3389/fnhum.2017.00133/full.

Lieberman, M.D., N.I. Eisenberg, M.J. Crockett, S.M. Tom, J.H. Pfeifer, and B.M. Way. "Putting Feelings into Words: Affect Labeling Disrupts

Amygdala Activity in Response to Affective Stimuli." *Psychological Science* 18, no. 5 (May 2007): 421–428. ncbi.nlm.nih.gov/pubmed/17576282.

McLaren, Karla. "Four Ideas That Lead Directly to Emotional Confusion." karlamclaren.com/2013/02/13/four-ideas-that-lead-directly-to-emotional-confusion/.

Medonça, D. "Emotions About Emotions." *Emotion Review* 5, no. 4 (October 2013): 390–396. deepdyve.com/lp/sage/emotions-about-emotions-p6VW9TabSb?key=dd_plugin_gs&utm_campaign=pluginGoogleScholar&utm_source=pluginGoogleScholar&utm_medium=plugin.

Memarian, N., J.B. Torre, K.E. Haltom, A.L. Stanton, and M.D. Lieberman. "Neural Activity During Affect Labeling Predicts Expressive Writing Effects on Well-Being: GLM and SVM Approaches." *Social Cognitive and Affective Neuroscience* 12, no. 9 (September 2017): 1437–1447. ncbi.nlm.nih.gov/pmc/articles/PMC5629828/.

Mikolajczak, M., H. Avalossse, S. Vancorenland, R. Verniest, M. Callens, N. van Broeck, C. Fantini-Hauwel, and A. Mierop. "A Nationally Representative Study of Emotional Competence and Health." *Emotion* 15, no. 5 (October 2015): 653–667. ncbi.nlm.nih.gov/pubmed/25893449.

Pennebaker, James W., and Joshua M. Smyth. *Opening Up by Writing It Down: How Expressive Writing Improves Health and Eases Emotional Pain.* New York: Guilford Press, 2016.

Simons, J.S., and R.M. Gaher. "The Distress Tolerance Scale Development and Validation of a Self-Report Measure." *Motivation and Emotion* 29, no. 2 (June 2005): 83–102. link.springer.com/article/10.1007/s11031-005-7955-3.

Trampe, D., J. Quoidbach, and M. Taquet. "Emotions in Everyday Life." *PLoS One* 10, no. 12 (2015): e0145450. ncbi.nlm.nih.gov/pmc/articles/PMC4689475/.

Yusuf, H., L. Vo, C. Karastury, S. Gunzburg, M. Devlin, L.F. Barrett, and K. Quigley. "Understanding Your Feelings: Emotional Granularity Influences on Coping." Research Innovation Scholarship Entrepreneurship presentation, 2018. northeastern.edu/rise/presentations/understanding-your-feelings-emotional-granularity-influences-on-coping/.

Zunhammer, M., A. Halski, P. Eichhammer, and V. Busch. "Theory of Mind and Emotional Awareness in Chronic Somatoform Pain Patients." *PLoS One* 10, no. 10 (2015): e0140016. ncbi.nlm.nih.gov/pmc/articles/PMC4596852/.

Chapter 5: Evaluate *Your* Triggers

American Psychological Association. "Stress in America: Generation Z." October 2018. apa.org/news/press/releases/stress/2018/stress-gen-z.pdf.

American Psychological Association, Climate for Health. "Mental Health and Our Changing Climate: Impacts, Implications, and Guidance." March 2017. apa.org/news/press/releases/2017/03/mental-health-climate.pdf.

Bowen, H.J., S.M. Kark, and E.A. Kensinger. "NEVER Forget: Negative Emotional Valence Enhances Recapitulation." *Psychonomic Bulletin & Review* 25, no. 3 (June 2018): 870–891. link.springer.com/article/10.3758 %2Fs13423-017-1313-9.

David, Susan. *Emotional Agility: Get Unstuck, Embrace Change, and Thrive in Work and Life*. New York: Avery, 2016.

Finan, P.H., P.J. Quartana, B. Remeniuk, E.L. Garland, J.L. Rhudy, M. Hand, M.R. Irwin, and M.T. Smith. "Partial Sleep Deprivation Attenuates the Positive Affective System: Effects Across Multiple Measurement Modalities." *Sleep* 40, no. 1 (January 1, 2017): zsw017. ncbi.nlm.nih.gov/pmc/articles/PMC6084750/.

Seider, B.H., M.N. Shiota, P. Whalen, and R.W. Levenson. "Greater Sadness Reactivity in Late Life." *Social Cognitive and Affective Neuroscience* 6, no. 2 (April 2011): 186–194. ncbi.nlm.nih.gov/pmc/articles/PMC3073392/.

Chapter 6: Steady Your Body's Natural Rhythms

Aviram, J., T. Shochat, and D. Pud. "Pain Perception in Healthy Young Men Is Modified by Time-of-Day and Is Modality Dependent." *Pain Medicine* 16, no. 6 (June 2015): 1137–1144. ncbi.nlm.nih.gov/pubmed/25545856.

Broussard, J.L., J.M. Kilkus, F. Delebecque, V. Abraham, A. Day, H.R. Whitmore, and E. Tasali. "Elevated Ghrelin Predicts Food Intake During Experimental Sleep Restriction." *Obesity* 24, no. 1 (January 2016): 132–138. ncbi.nlm.nih .gov/pmc/articles/PMC4688118/.

Csíkszentmihályi, Mihaly. *Flow: The Psychology of Optimal Experience*. New York: Harper Perennial Modern Classics, 2008.

Díaz-Morales, J.F., and C. Escribano. "Social Jetlag, Academic Achievement, and Cognitive Performance: Understanding Gender/Sex Differences." *Chronobiology International* 32, no. 6 (2015): 822–831. ncbi.nlm.nih.gov/pubmed/26061587.

Figueiro, M.G., B. Steverson, J. Heerwagen, K. Kampschroer, C.M. Hunter, K. Gonzales, B. Plitnick, and M.S. Rea. "The Impact of Daytime Light Exposures on Sleep and Mood in Office Workers." *Sleep Health*

3, no. 3 (June 2017): 204–215. sciencedirect.com/science/article/pii/
S2352721817300414?via%3Dihub.

Gooley, J.J., K. Chamberlain, K.A. Smith, S.B.S. Khalsa, S.M.W. Rajaratnam,
E. Van Reen, J.M. Zeitzer, C.A. Czeisler, and S.W. Lockley. "Exposure to
Room Light Before Bedtime Suppresses Melatonin Onset and Shortens
Melatonin Duration in Humans." *Journal of Clinical Endocrinology &
Metabolism* 96, no. 3 (March 2011): E463–E472. ncbi.nlm.nih.gov/pmc
/articles/PMC3047226/.

Haynie, D.L., D. Lewin, J.W. Luk, L.M. Lipsky, F. O'Brien, R.J. Iannotti, D.
Liu, and B.G. Simons-Morton. "Beyond Sleep Duration: Bidirectional
Associations Among Chronotype Social Jetlag, and Drinking Behaviors
in a Longitudinal Sample of U.S. High School Students." *Sleep* 41, no. 2
(February 2018): zsx 202. ncbi.nlm.nih.gov/pmc/articles/PMC6018914/.

Johns Hopkins Medicine. "Melatonin for Sleep: Does It Work?"
hopkinsmedicine.org/health/wellness-and-prevention/melatonin
-for-sleep-does-it-work.

Koopman, A.D.M., S.P. Rauh, E. van't Riet, L. Groeneveld, A.A. van der Jeijden,
P.J. Elders, J.M. Dekker, G. Nijpels, J.W. Beulens, and F. Rutters. "The Asso-
ciation Between Social Jetlag, the Metabolic Syndrome, and Type 2 Diabetes
Mellitus in the General Population: The New Hoorn Study." *Journal of
Biological Rhythms* 32, no. 4 (August 2017): 359–368. ncbi.nlm.nih.gov
/pmc/articles/PMC5564947/.

Leichtfried, V., M. Mair-Raggautz, V. Schaeffer, A. Hammerer-Lercher, G. Mair,
C. Bartenbach, M. Canazei, and W. Schobersberger. "Intense Illumination in the Morning Hours Improved Mood and Alertness but Not Mental
Performance." *Applied Ergonomics* 46, part A (January 2016): 54–59.
sciencedirect.com/science/article/pii/S0003687014001136.

Levandovski, R., G. Dantas, L.C. Fernandes, W. Caumo, I. Torres, T.
Roenneberg, M.P. Hidalgo, and K.V. Allebrandt. "Depression Scores
Associate with Chronotype and Social Jetlag in a Rural Population."
Chronobiology International 28, no. 9 (November 2011): 771–778. ncbi
.nlm.nih.gov/pubmed/21895489.

Leypunskiy, E., E. Kiciman, M. Shah, A. Rzhetsky, A.R. Dinner, and M.J. Rust.
"Geographically Resolved Rhythms in Twitter Use Reveal Social Pressures
on Daily Activity Patterns." *Current Biology*, November 15, 2018. cell.com
/current-biology/fulltext/S0960-9822(18)31345-9.

Mathew, G.M., L. Hale, and A.M. Chang. "Sex Moderates Relationships Among School Night Sleep Duration, Social Jetlag, and Depressive Symptoms in Adolescents." *Journal of Biological Rhythms* 34, no. 2 (April 2019): 205–217. ncbi.nlm.nih.gov/pubmed/30773079.

Maust, D.T., L.A. Lin, and F.C. Blow. "Benzodiazepine Use and Misuse Among Adults in the United States." *Psychiatry Online*, December 17, 2018. ps.psychiatryonline.org/doi/10.1176/appi.ps.201800321.

McGowan, N.M., B.I. Voinescu, and A.N. Coogan. "Sleep Quality, Chronotype, and Social Jetlag Differentially Associate with Symptoms of Attention Deficit Hyperactivity Disorder in Adults." *Chronobiology International* 33, no. 10 (2016): 1433–1443. ncbi.nlm.nih.gov/pubmed/27668457.

Mendoza, J. "Food Intake and Addictive-Like Eating Behaviors: Time to Think About the Circadian Clock(s)." *Neuroscience and Biobehavioral Reviews* 106 (November 2019): 122–132. ncbi.nlm.nih.gov/pubmed/29990504.

Murphy, P.J., P. Badia, B.L. Myers, M.R. Boecker, and K.P. Wright Jr. "Nonsteroidal Anti-Inflammatory Drugs Affect Normal Sleep Patterns in Humans." *Physiology & Behavior* 55, no. 6 (June 1994): 1063–1066. ncbi.nlm.nih.gov /pubmed/8047572.

Panda, Satchin. *The Circadian Code: Lose Weight, Supercharge Your Energy, and Transform Your Health from Morning to Midnight.* New York: Rodale Books, 2018.

Perrault, A.A., L. Bayer, M. Peuvrier, A. Afyouni, P. Ghisletta, C. Brockmann, M. Spiridon, S.H. Vesely, S. Perrig, S. Schwartz, and V. Sterpenich. "Imposing a Curfew on the Use of Screen Electronic Devices Improves Sleep and Daytime Vigilance in Adolescents." *bioRxiv*, March 21, 2018. biorxiv.org /content/biorxiv/early/2018/03/21/259309.full.pdf.

Piper, B.J., C.L. Ogden, O.M. Simoyan, D.Y. Chung, J.F. Caggiano, S.D. Nichols, and K.L. McCall. "Trends in Use of Prescription Stimulants in the United States and Territories, 2006 to 2016." *PLoS One*, November 28, 2018. journals.plos.org/plosone/article?id=10.1371/journal.pone.0206100.

Randler, C., and C. Vollmer. "Aggression in Young Adults—A Matter of Short Sleep and Social Jetlag?" *Psychological Reports* 113, no. 3 (December 2013): 754–765. ncbi.nlm.nih.gov/pubmed/24693810.

Rodríguez-Morilla, B., J.A. Madrid, E. Molina, J. Pérez-Navarro, and Á. Correa. "Blue-Enriched Light Enhances Alertness but Impairs Accurate Performance in Evening Chronotypes Driving in the Morning." *Frontiers in*

Psychology 9 (May 15, 2018): 688. ncbi.nlm.nih.gov/pmc/articles /PMC5962740/.

Roenneberg, T., K.V. Allebrandt, M. Merrow, and C. Vetter. "Social Jetlag and Obesity." *Current Biology* 22, no. 10 (May 22, 2012): 939–943. cell.com /current-biology/fulltext/S0960-9822(12)00325-9.

Rutters, F., S.G. Lemmens, T.C. Adams, M.A., Bremmer, P.J. Elders, G. Nijpels, and J.M. Dekker. "Is Social Jetlag Associated with an Adverse Endocrine, Behavioral, and Cardiovascular Risk Profile?" *Journal of Biological Rhythms* 29, no. 5 (October 2014): 377–383. ncbi.nlm.nih.gov/pubmed/25252710.

RxList. "Melatonin." rxlist.com/melatonin/supplements.htm.

Sahin, L., and M.G. Figueiro. "Alerting Effects of Short-Wavelength (Blue) and Long-Wavelength (Red) Lights in the Afternoon." *Physiology & Behavior* 116–117 (May 27, 2013): 1–7. sciencedirect.com/science/article/abs/pii /S0031938413000644.

Sahin, L., B.M. Wood, B. Plitnick, and M.G. Figueiro. "Daytime Light Exposure: Effects on Biomarkers, Measures of Alertness, and Performance." *Behavioural Brain Research* 274 (November 1, 2014): 176–185. sciencedirect .com/science/article/pii/S0166432814005294.

Silvester, J., and E. Konstantinou. "Lighting, Well-Being and Performance at Work." Centre for Performance at Work. cass.city.ac.uk/__data/assets/pdf _file/0004/363217/lighting-work-performance-cass.pdf.

Sleep.org. "How to Use Melatonin for Better Sleep." sleep.org/articles/use -melatonin-better-sleep/.

Smolensky, Michael, and Lynne Lamberg. *The Body Clock Guide to Better Health: How to Use Your Body's Natural Clock to Fight Illness and Achieve Maximum Health.* New York: Henry Holt and Co., 2000.

Stothard, E.R., A.W. McHill, C.M. Depner, B.R. Birks, T.M. Moehlman, H.K. Ritchie, J.R. Guzzetti, E.D. Chinoy, M.K. LeBourgeois, J. Axelsson, and K.P. Wright. "Circadian Entrainment to the Natural Light-Dark Cycle Across Seasons and the Weekend." *Current Biology* 27, no. 4 (February 20, 2017): 508–513. ncbi.nlm.nih.gov/pmc/articles/PMC5335920/.

Umemura, G.S., J.P. Pinho, B. da Silva Brandão Gonçalves, F. Furtado, and A. Forner-Cordero. "Social Jetlag Impairs Balance Control." *Scientific Reports* 8 (2018): 9406. ncbi.nlm.nih.gov/pmc/articles/PMC6010412/.

Voigt, R.M., C.B. Forsyth, S.J. Green, E. Mutlu, P. Engen, M.H. Vitaterna, F.W. Turek, and A. Keshavarzian. "Circadian Disorganization Alters Intestinal

Microbiota." *PLoS One* 9, no. 5 (2014): e97500. ncbi.nlm.nih.gov/pmc /articles/PMC4029760/.

Wehr, T.A. "In Short Photoperiods, Human Sleep Is Biphasic." *Journal of Sleep Research* 1 (1992): 103–107. onlinelibrary.wiley.com/doi/epdf/10.1111 /j.1365-2869.1992.tb00019.x.

Chapter 7: Think Yourself into a Safe Space

Akinola, M., I. Fridman, S. Mor, M.W. Morris, and A.J. Crum. "Adaptive Appraisals of Anxiety Moderate the Association Between Cortisol Reactivity and Performance in Salary Negotiations." *PLoS One* 11, no. 12 (2016): e0167977. ncbi.nlm.nih.gov/pmc/articles/PMC5161466/.

Basso, J.C., A. McHale, V. Ende, D.J. Oberlin, and W.A. Suzuki. "Brief, Daily Meditation Enhances Attention, Memory, Mood, and Emotional Regulation in Non-experienced Meditators." *Behavioural Brain Research* 356 (January 1, 2019): 208–220. ncbi.nlm.nih.gov/pubmed/30153464.

Bouygues, H.L. "3 Simple Habits to Improve Your Critical Thinking." *Harvard Business Review*, May 6, 2019. hbr.org/2019/05/3-simple-habits-to-improve -your-critical-thinking.

Chancellor, J., S. Margolis, K. Jacobs Bao, and S. Lyobomirsky. "Everyday Prosociality in the Workplace: The Reinforcing Benefits of Giving, Getting, and Glimpsing." *Emotion* 18, no. 4 (June 2018): 507–517. ncbi.nlm.nih.gov /pubmed/28581323.

Chopra, Deepak. "Why Meditate?" March 5, 2017. deepakchopra.com/blog /article/4701.

Cooney, R.E., J. Joormann, L.Y. Atlas, F. Eugène, and I.H. Gotlib. "Remembering the Good Times: Neural Correlates of Affect Regulation." *Neuroreport* 18, no. 17 (November 19, 2007): 1771–1774. ncbi.nlm.nih.gov/pubmed/18090309.

Crum, A.J., M. Akinola, A. Martin, and S. Fath. "The Role of Stress Mindset in Shaping Cognitive, Emotional, and Physiological Responses to Challenging and Threatening Stress." *Anxiety, Stress & Coping* 30, no. 4 (2017): 379–395. tandfonline.com/doi/abs/10.1080/10615806.2016.1275585?journalCode=gasc20.

Cuddy, Amy. *Presence: Bringing Your Boldest Self to Your Biggest Challenges.* New York: Little, Brown, 2018.

Cunha, L.F., L.C. Pellanda, and C.T. Reppold, "Positive Psychology and Gratitude Interventions: A Randomized Trial." *Frontiers in Psychology* 10 (2019): 584. ncbi.nlm.nih.gov/pmc/articles/PMC6437090/.

Emmons, R.A., and M.E. McCullough. "Counting Blessings Versus Burdens: An Experimental Investigation of Gratitude and Subjective Well-Being in Daily Life." *Journal of Personality and Social Psychology* 84, no. 2 (February 2003): 377–389. ncbi.nlm.nih.gov/pubmed/12585811.

The Foundation for Critical Thinking. "Critical Thinking: Where to Begin." criticalthinking.org/pages/critical-thinking-where-to-begin/796.

Fredrickson, Barbara L. *Positivity: Discover the Upward Spiral That Will Change Your Life.* New York: Harmony, 2009.

Krohne, H.W., M. Pieper, N. Knoll, and N. Breimer. "The Role of Success Versus Failure Experience and Coping Dispositions." *Cognition and Emotion* 16, no. 2 (2002): 217–243. psychologie.uni-heidelberg.de/ae/allg/mitarb/ms /Krohne.pdf.

Levitin, Daniel J. *The Organized Mind: Thinking Straight in the Age of Information.* New York: Dutton, 2015.

Lyubomirsky, Sonja. *The How of Happiness: A New Approach to Getting the Life You Want.* New York: Penguin, 2008.

Nelson, S.K., J.A.K. Fuller, I. Choi, and S. Lyubomirsky. "Beyond Self-Protection: Self-Affirmation Benefits Hedonic and Eudaimonic Well-Being." *UC Riverside Previously Published Works*, 2014. escholarship.org/uc/item/98f032gk/.

Nelson, S.K., K. Layous, S.W. Cole, and S. Lyubomirsky. "Do Unto Others or Treat Yourself? The Effects of Prosocial and Self-Focused Behavior on Psychological Flourishing." *UC Riverside Previously Published Works*, 2016. escholarship.org/uc/item/7pf57270.

O'Connell, B.H., D. O'Shea, and S. Gallagher. "Feeling Thanks and Saying Thanks: A Randomized Controlled Trial Examining If and How Socially Oriented Gratitude Journals Work." *Journal of Clinical Psychology* 73, no. 10 (October 2017): 1280–1300. ncbi.nlm.nih.gov/pubmed/28263399.

Psychology Today. "Acceptance and Commitment Therapy." psychologytoday .com/us/therapy-types/acceptance-and-commitment-therapy.

Radstaak, M., S.A. Geurts, J.F. Brosschot, and M.A. Kompier. "Music and Psychophysiological Recovery from Stress." *Psychosomatic Medicine* 76, no. 7 (September 2014): 529–537. ncbi.nlm.nih.gov/pubmed/25153936.

Reilly, L. "Why Do Our Best Ideas Come in the Shower?" *Mental Floss*, September 6, 2013. mentalfloss.com/article/52586/why-do-our-best-ideas-come-us-shower.

Ross, D. "Critical Thinking—a Critical Skill in School and for the Future of Work." *Getting Smart*, March 4, 2019. gettingsmart.com/2019/03 /critical-thinking-a-critical-skill-in-school-and-for-the-future-of-work/.

Taylor, C.T., S. Lyubomirsky, and M.B. Stein. "Upregulating the Positive Affect System in Anxiety and Depression: Outcomes of a Positive Activity Intervention." *UC Riverside Previously Published Works*, 2017. escholarship .org/uc/item/06v1w2v1.

Taylor, Jill Bolte. *My Stroke of Insight.* New York: Penguin, 2009.

Time. "The Hidden Secrets of the Creative Mind." January 16, 2006. content.time.com/time/magazine/article/0,9171,1147152,00.html.

Valdez, P., and A. Mehrabian. "Effects of Color on Emotions." *Journal of Experimental Psychology: General* 123, no. 4 (1994): 394–409. pdfs .semanticscholar.org/4711/624c0f72d8c85ea6813b8ec5e8abeedfb616.pdf.

Chapter 8: Obey Your Body

Allen, J.M., L.J. Mailing, G.M. Niemiro, R. Moore, M.D. Cook, B.A. White, H.D. Holscher, and J.A. Woods. "Exercise Alters Gut Microbiota Composition and Function in Lean and Obese Humans." *Medicine and Science in Sports and Exercise* 50, no. 4 (April 2018): 747–757. ncbi.nlm.nih.gov/pubmed/29166320.

Altena, E., J.A. Micoulaud-Franchi, P.A. Geoffroy, E. Sanz-Arigita, S. Bioulac, and P. Philip. "The Bidirectional Relation Between Emotional Reactivity and Sleep: From Disruption to Recovery." *Behavioral Neuroscience* 130, no. 3 (June 2016): 336–350. ncbi.nlm.nih.gov/pubmed/26866361.

Armstrong, L.E., M.S. Ganio, D.J. Casa, E.C. Lee, B.P. McDermott, J.F. Klau, L. Jimenez, L. LeBellego, E. Chevillotte, and H.R. Lieberman. "Mild Dehydration Affects Mood in Healthy Young Women." *The Journal of Nutrition* 142, no. 2 (February 2012): 382–388. academic.oup.com/jn/article/142 /2/382/4743487.

Babyak, M., J.A. Blumenthal, S. Herman, P. Khatri, M. Doraiswamy, K. Moore, W.E. Craighead, T.T. Baldewicz, and K.R. Krishnan. "Exercise Treatment for Major Depression: Maintenance of Therapeutic Benefit at 10 Months." *Psychosomatic Medicine* 62, no. 5 (September–October 2000): 633–638. ncbi.nlm.nih.gov/pubmed/11020092.

Bernstein, E.D., and R.J. McNally. "Exercise as a Buffer Against Difficulties with Emotion Regulation: A Pathway to Emotional Wellbeing." *Behaviour Research and Therapy* 109 (October 2018): 29–36. ncbi.nlm.nih.gov /pubmed/30081242.

Blackburn, L., S. Achor, B. Allen, N. Bauchmire, D. Dunnington, R.B. Klisovic, S.J. Naber, K. Roblee, A. Samczak, K. Tomlinson-Pinkham, and E. Chipps. "The Effect of Aromatherapy on Insomnia and Other Common Symptoms

Among Patients with Acute Leukemia." *Oncology Nursing Forum* 44, no. 4 (July 1, 2017): E185–E193. ncbi.nlm.nih.gov/pubmed/28640576.

Breus, M.J. "7 Essential Oils for Relaxation and Better Sleep." *The Sleep Doctor*, June 12, 2018. thesleepdoctor.com/2018/06/12/7-essential-oils-for -relaxation-and-better-sleep/.

Caltech. "Microbes Help Produce Serotonin in Gut." April 9, 2015. caltech.edu /about/news/microbes-help-produce-serotonin-gut-46495.

Carek, P.J., S.E. Laibstain, and S.M. Carek. "Exercise for the Treatment of Depression and Anxiety." *International Journal of Psychiatry in Medicine* 41, no. 1 (2011): 15–28. ncbi.nlm.nih.gov/pubmed/21495519.

Center for Ecogenetics & Environmental Health. "Fast Facts About the Human Microbiome." depts.washington.edu/ceeh/downloads/FF_Microbiome.pdf.

Cheung, S.G., A.R. Goldenthal, A-C. Uhlemann, J.J. Mann, J.M. Miller, and M.E. Sublette. "Systematic Review of Gut Microbiota and Major Depression." *Frontiers in Psychiatry* 10 (2019): 34. ncbi.nlm.nih.gov/pmc/articles /PMC6378305/.

Delgado, D. "Orthorexia: 10 Signs You Should Seek Help Now" *Psychology Today*, February 26, 2019. psychologytoday.com/us/blog/eating-disorders /201902/orthorexia-10-signs-you-should-seek-help-now.

Dennett, C. "The Facts About Fermented Foods." *Today's Dietitian* 20, no. 4 (April 2018): 24. todaysdietitian.com/newarchives/0418p24.shtml.

Dinan, T.G., and J.F. Cryan. "Melancholic Microbes: A Link Between Gut Microbiota and Depression?" *Neurogastroenterology and Motility* 25, no. 9 (September 2013): 713–719. ncbi.nlm.nih.gov/pubmed/23910373.

Edwards, M.K., R.E. Rhodes, and P.D. Loprinzi. "A Randomized Control Intervention Investigating the Effects of Acute Exercise on Emotional Regulation." *American Journal of Health Behavior* 41, no. 5 (September 1, 2017): 534–543. ncbi.nlm.nih.gov/pubmed/28760175.

Grewen, K.M., and K.C. Light. "Plasma Oxytocin Is Related to Lower Cardio-vascular and Sympathetic Reactivity to Stress." *Biological Psychology* 87, no. 3 (July 2011): 340–349. ncbi.nlm.nih.gov/pmc/articles/PMC3225916/.

Hackney, A.C., and E.A. Walz. "Hormonal Adaptation and the Stress of Exercise Training: The Role of Glucocorticoids." *Trends in Sport Sciences* 20, no. 4 (2013): 165–171. ncbi.nlm.nih.gov/pmc/articles/PMC5988244/.

Heijnen, S., B. Hommel, A. Kibele, and L.S. Colzato. "Neuromodulation of Aer-obic Exercise—A Review." *Frontiers in Psychology* 6 (2015): 1890. ncbi.nlm .nih.gov/pmc/articles/PMC4703784/.

Hilimire, M.R., J.E. DeVylder, and C.A. Forestell. "Fermented Foods, Neuroti-
cism, and Social Anxiety: An Interaction Model." *Psychiatry Research* 228,
no. 2 (August 15, 2015): 203–208. ncbi.nlm.nih.gov/pubmed/25998000.

Jaatinen, N., R. Korpela, R. Poussa, A. Turpeinen, S. Mustonen, J. Merilahti,
and K. Peuhkuri. "Effects of Daily Intake of Yoghurt Enriched with
Bioactive Components on Chronic Stress Responses: A Double-Blinded
Randomized Controlled Trial." *International Journal of Food Sciences
and Nutrition* 65, no. 4 (June 2014): 507–514. ncbi.nlm.nih.gov
/pubmed/24490888.

Karadag, E., S. Samancioglu, D. Ozden, and E. Bakir. "Effects of Aromatherapy
on Sleep Quality and Anxiety of Patients." *Nursing in Critical Care* 22, no.
2 (March 2017): 105–112. ncbi.nlm.nih.gov/pubmed/26211735.

Kato-Kataoka, A., K. Nishida, M. Takada, K. Suda, M. Kawai, K. Shimizu, A.
Kushiro, R. Hoshi, O. Watanabe, T. Igarashi, K. Miyazaki, Y. Kuwano, and
K. Rokutan. "Fermented Milk Containing Lactobacillus Casei Strain
Shirota Prevents the Onset of Physical Symptoms in Medical Students
Under Academic Examination Stress." *Beneficial Microbes* 7, no. 2 (2016):
153–156. ncbi.nlm.nih.gov/pubmed/26689231.

Li, L., Q. Su, B. Xie, L. Duan, W. Zhao, D. Hu, R. Wu, and H. Liu. "Gut
Microbes in Correlation with Mood: Case Study in a Closed Experimental
Human Life Support System." *Neurogastroenterology and Motility* 28, no. 8
(August 2016): 1233–1240. ncbi.nlm.nih.gov/pubmed/27027909.

Maier, L., M. Pruteanu, M. Kuhn, G. Zeller, A. Telzerow, E.E. Anderson, A.R.
Brochado, K.C. Fernandez, H. Dose, H. Mori, K.R. Patil, P. Bork, and A. Typas.
"Extensive Impact of Non-Antibiotic Drugs on Human Gut Bacteria." *Nature*
555 (March 29, 2018): 623. nature.com/articles/nature25979.epdf.

Mayo Clinic. "Relaxation Techniques: Try These Steps to Reduce Stress."
mayoclinic.org/healthy-lifestyle/stress-management/in-depth/relaxation
-technique/art-20045368.

MentalHelp.net. "Stress Management Techniques." mentalhelp.net/stress
/management-techniques/.

MentalHelp.net. "Types of Stressors (Eustress vs. Distress)." mentalhelp.net
/articles/types-of-stressors-eustress-vs-distress/.

Monda, V., I. Villano, A. Messina, A. Valenzano, T. Esposito, F. Moscatelli, A.
Viggiano, G. Cibelli, S. Chieffi, M. Monda, and G. Messina. "Exercise Mod-
ifies the Gut Microbiota with Positive Health Effects." *Oxidative Medicine
and Cellular Longevity.* ncbi.nlm.nih.gov/pmc/articles/PMC5357536/.

National Academies of Sciences, Engineering, Medicine. "Dietary Reference Intakes: Water, Potassium, Sodium, Chloride, and Sulfate." February 11, 2004. nationalacademies.org/hmd/Reports/2004/Dietary-Reference -Intakes-Water-Potassium-Sodium-Chloride-and-Sulfate.aspx.

National Eating Disorders Association. "Orthorexia." nationaleatingdisorders .org/learn/by-eating-disorder/other/orthorexia.

Perl, O., A. Arzi, L. Sela, L. Secundo, Y. Holtzman, P. Samnon, A. Oksenberg, N. Sobel, and I.S. Hairston. "Odors Enhance Slow-Wave Activity in Non-Rapid Eye Movement Sleep." *Journal of Neuropsychology* 115, no. 5 (May 1, 2016): 2294–2302. ncbi.nlm.nih.gov/pmc/articles/PMC4922455/.

Puterman, E., A. O'Donovan, N.E. Adler, A.J. Tomiyama, M. Kemeny, O.M. Wolkowitz, and E. Epel. "Physical Activity Moderates Stressor-Induced Rumination on Cortisol Reactivity." *Psychosomatic Medicine* 73, no. 7 (September 2011): 605–611. ncbi.nlm.nih.gov/pmc/articles/PMC3167008/.

Sandoui, A. "Low Oxytocin May Lead to Low Empathy, Study Finds." *Medical News Today*, November 7, 2016. medicalnewstoday.com/articles/313911.php.

ScienceDaily. "Artificial Sweeteners Have Toxic Effects on Gut Microbes." October 1, 2018. sciencedaily.com/releases/2018/10/181001101932.htm.

ScienceDaily. "Dark Chocolate Consumption Reduces Stress and Inflammation." April 24, 2018. sciencedaily.com/releases/2018/04/180424133628 .htm.

Sentürk, A., and P. Tekinsoy Kartin. "The Effect of Lavender Oil Application via Inhalation Pathway on Hemodialysis Patients' Anxiety Level and Sleep Quality." *Holistic Nursing Practice* 32, no. 6 (November/December 2018): 324–335. ncbi.nlm.nih.gov/pubmed/30320657.

Takada, M., K. Nishida, A. Kataoka-Kato, Y. Gondo, H. Ishikawa, K. Suda, M. Kawai, R. Hoshi, O. Watanabe, T. Igarashi, Y. Kuwano, K. Miyazaki, and K. Rokutan. "Probiotic Lactobacillus Casei Strain Shirota Relieves Stress-Associated Symptoms by Modulating the Gut-Brain Interaction in Human and Animal Models." *Neurogastroenterology and Motility* 28, no. 7 (July 2016): 1027–1036. ncbi.nlm.nih.gov/pubmed/26896291.

Valdes, A.M., J. Walter, E. Segal, and T.D. Spector. "Role of the Gut Microbiota in Nutrition and Health." *BMJ* 2018: 361. www.bmj.com/content/361 /bmj.k2179.

Weil, A. "Dr. Weil's Anti-Inflammatory Food Pyramid." drweil.com/diet -nutrition/anti-inflammatory-diet-pyramid/dr-weils-anti-inflammatory -food-pyramid/.

Yano, J.M., K. Yu, G.P. Donaldson, G.G. Shastri, P. Ann, L. Ma, C.R. Nagler, R.F. Ismagilov, S.K. Mazmanian, and E.Y. Hsiao. "Indigenous Bacteria from the Gut Microbiota Regulate Host Serotonin Biosynthesis." *Cell* 161, no. 2 (April 9, 2015): 264–276. ncbi.nlm.nih.gov/pmc/articles/PMC4393509/.

Chapter 9: Reclaim the Gifts of Nature

Anderson, C.L., M. Monroy, and D. Keltner. "Awe in Nature Heals: Evidence from Military Veterans, At-Risk Youth, and College Students." *Emotion* 18, no. 8 (December 2018): 1195–1202. ncbi.nlm.nih.gov/pubmed/29927260.

Annerstedt, M., P. Jönsson, M. Wallergård, G. Johansson, B. Karlson, P. Grahn, A.M. Hansen, and P. Währborg. "Inducing Physiological Stress Recovery with Sounds of Nature in a Virtual Reality Forest—Results from a Pilot Study." *Physiology & Behavior* 118 (June 13, 2013): 240–250. ncbi.nlm.nih .gov/pubmed/23688947.

Barton, J., and J. Pretty. "What Is the Best Dose of Nature and Green Exercise for Improving Mental Health? A Multi-Study Analysis." *Environmental Science & Technology* 44, no. 10 (2010): 3947–3955. pubs.acs.org/doi /10.1021/es903183r.

Basu, A., J. Duvall, and R. Kaplan. "Attention Restoration Theory: Exploring the Role of Soft Fascination and Mental Bandwidth." *Environment and Behavior*, May 16, 2018. journals.sagepub.com/doi/abs/10.1177/ 0013916518774400.

Beetz, A., K. Uvnäs-Moberg, H. Julius, and K. Kotrschal. "Psychosocial and Psychophysiological Effects of Human-Animal Interactions: The Possible Role of Oxytocin." *Frontiers in Psychology* 3 (2012): 234. ncbi.nlm.nih.gov/pmc /articles/PMC3408111/.

Berman, M.G., J. Jonides, and S. Kaplan. "The Cognitive Benefits of Interacting with Nature." *Psychological Science* 19, no. 12 (2008): 1207–1212. psych.utah.edu/_resources/documents/psych4130/The%20Cognitive %20Benefits%20of%20Interacting%20with%20Nature.pdf.

Cartwright, B.D.S., M.P. White, and T.J. Clitherow. "Nearby Nature 'Buffers' the Effect of Low Social Connectedness on Adult Subjective Wellbeing over the Last 7 Days." *International Journal of Environmental Research and Public Health* 15, no. 6 (June 2018): 1238. ncbi.nlm.nih.gov/pmc/articles/PMC6025411/.

Cools, R., A.C. Roberts, and T.W. Robbins. "Serotoninergic Regulation of Emotional and Behavioral Control Processes." *Trends in Cognitive Sciences* 12, no. 1 (January 2008): 31–40. ncbi.nlm.nih.gov/pubmed/18069045/.

Cox, D.T.C., D.F. Shanahan, H.L. Hudson, R.A. Fuller, K. Anderson, S. Hancock, and K.J. Gaston. "Doses of Nearby Nature Simultaneously Associated with Multiple Health Benefits." *International Journal of Environmental Research and Public Health* 14, no. 2 (February 2017): 172. ncbi.nlm.nih.gov /pmc/articles/PMC5334726/.

Earles, J.L., L.L. Vernon, and J.P. Yetz. "Equine-Assisted Therapy for Anxiety and Posttraumatic Stress Symptoms." *Journal of Traumatic Stress* 28, no. 2 (April 2015): 149–152. ncbi.nlm.nih.gov/pubmed/25782709.

Fiocco, A.J., and A.M. Hunse. "The Buffer Effect of Therapy Dog Exposure on Stress Reactivity in Undergraduate Students." *International Journal of Environmental Research and Public Health* 14, no. 7 (July 2017): 707. ncbi .nlm.nih.gov/pmc/articles/PMC5551145/.

Franco, L.S., D.F. Shanahan, and R.A. Fuller. "A Review of the Benefits of Nature Experiences: More than Meets the Eye." *International Journal of Environmental Research and Public Health* 14, no. 8 (August 2017): 864. ncbi.nlm.nih.gov/pmc/articles/PMC5580568/.

Gillis, K., and B. Gatersleben. "A Review of Psychological Literature on the Health and Wellbeing Benefits of Biophilic Design." *Buildings* 5, no. 3 (2015): 948–963. mdpi.com/2075-5309/5/3/948/htm.

Hagerhall, C.M., T. Laike, M. Küller, E. Marcheschi, C. Boydston, and R.P. Taylor. "Human Physiological Benefits of Viewing Nature: EEG Responses to Exact and Statistical Fractal Patterns." *Nonlinear Dynamics, Psychology, and Life Science* 19, no. 1 (January 2015): 1–12. ncbi.nlm.nih.gov/pubmed/25575556.

Joye, Y., and J.W. Bolderdijk. "An Exploratory Study into the Effects of Extraordinary Nature on Emotions, Mood, and Prosociality." *Frontiers in Psychology* 5 (2014): 1577. ncbi.nlm.nih.gov/pmc/articles/PMC4309161/.

Kaplan, S. "The Restorative Benefits of Nature: Toward an Integrative Framework." *Journal of Environmental Psychology* 15 (1995): 169–182. willsull .net/resources/KaplanS1995.pdf.

Kellert, S.R. "What Is and Is Not Biophilic Design?" *Metropolis*. metropolismag .com/architecture/what-is-and-is-not-biophilic-design/.

Kelly, W.E., and D. Daughtry. "Sleep-Length, Noctcaelador, and Watching the Night-Sky to Cope." *Individual Differences Research* 5, no. 2 (2007): 150–157. researchgate.net/profile/William_Kelly9/publication/289309723_ Sleep-length_noctcaelador_and_watching_the_night-sky_to_cope/links /56aa4e5608ae2df82166d9bc/Sleep-length-noctcaelador-and-watching-the -night-sky-to-cope.pdf.

Kelly, W.E., D. Daughtry, and K.E. Kelly. "Entranced by the Night-Sky: Psychological Absorption and Noctcaelador." *Psychology and Education* 43, no. 2 (2006): 22–27. researchgate.net/profile/William_Kelly9/publication /281641048_Entranced_by_the_Night_Sky_Psychological_Absorption _and_Noctcaelador/links/55f1ee8808aedecb69020ce4.pdf.

Louv, Richard. *Last Child in the Woods: Saving Our Children From Nature-Deficit Disorder.* Chapel Hill, NC: Algonquin, 2008.

Mala, E. "Move Over, Therapy Dogs. Hello, Therapy Cows." *The New York Times*, July 12, 2019. nytimes.com/2019/07/12/style/self-care/cow-cuddling -therapy.html.

Nakane, H., O. Asami, Y. Yamada, and H. Ohira. "Effect of Negative Air Ions on Computer Operation, Anxiety, and Salivary Chromogranin A-Like Immu-noreactivity." *International Journal of Psychophysiology* 46, no. 1 (October 2002): 85–89. ncbi.nlm.nih.gov/pubmed/12374649/.

Nelson-Coffey, S.K., P.M. Ruberton, J. Chancellor, J.E. Cornick, J. Blascovich, and S. Lyubomirsky. "The Proximal Experience of Awe." *PLoS One* 14, no. 5 (2019): e0216780. ncbi.nlm.nih.gov/pmc/articles/PMC6532958/.

Oh, B., K.J. Lee, C. Zaslawski, A. Yeung, D. Rosenthal, L. Larkey, and M. Back. "Health and Well-Being Benefits of Spending Time in Forests: Systematic Review." *Environmental Health and Preventive Medicine* 22 (2017): 71. ncbi.nlm.nih.gov/pmc/articles/PMC5664422/.

Reed, K. "7 Science-Backed Health Benefits of Having Plants at Home." *EcoWatch*, September 27, 2018. ecowatch.com/health-benefits-of-having -plants-at-home-2608386260.html.

Romaniuk, M., J. Evans, and C. Kidd. "Evaluation of an Equine-Assisted Therapy Program for Veterans Who Identify as 'Wounded, Injured, or Ill' and Their Partners." *PLoS One* 13, no. 9 (2018): e0203943. ncbi.nlm.nih.gov /pmc/articles/PMC6160012/.

Schindler, I., G. Hosoya, W. Menninghaus, U. Beermann, V. Wagner, M. Eid, and K.R. Scherer. "Measuring Aesthetic Emotions: A Review of the Literature and a New Assessment Tool." *PLoS One* 12, no. 6 (2017): e0178899. ncbi .nlm.nih.gov/pmc/articles/PMC5459466/.

Sidenius, U., U.K. Stigsdotter, D.V. Poulsen, and T. Bondas. "'I Look at My Own Forest and Fields in a Different Way': The Lived Experience of Nature-Based Therapy in a Therapy Garden When Suffering from Stress-Related Illness." *International Journal of Qualitative Studies in Health and Well-Being* 12, no. 1 (2017): 1324700. ncbi.nlm.nih.gov/pmc/articles/PMC5510200/.

Somppi, S., H. Törnqvist, J. Topál, A. Koskela, L. Hänninen, C.M. Krause, and O. Vainio. "Dogs' Visual Attention and Emotional Response Toward Positive Human Facial Expressions." *Frontiers in Psychology*, October 17, 2017. frontiersin.org/articles/10.3389/fpsyg.2017.01854/full.

Statista. "Household Penetration Rates for Pet-Ownership in the United States from 1988 to 2019." statista.com/statistics/198086/us-household-penetration -rates-for-pet-owning-since-2007/.

Stellar, J.E., A. Gordon, C.L. Anderson, P.K. Piff, G.D. McNeil, and D. Keltner. "Awe and Humility." *Journal of Personality and Social Psychology* 114, no. 2 (February 2018): 258–269. ncbi.nlm.nih.gov/pubmed/28857578.

U.S.G.S. "The Water in You: Water and the Human Body." usgs.gov/special -topic/water-science-school/science/water-you-water-and-human-body ?qt-science_center_objects=0#qt-science_center_objects.

Van Den Berg, A.E., and M.H. Custers. "Gardening Promotes Neuroendocrine and Affective Restoration from Stress." *Journal of Health Psychology* 16, no. 1 (January 2011): 3–11. ncbi.nlm.nih.gov/pubmed/20522508.

van Elk, M., M.A. Arciniegas, W. van der Zwaag, H.T. van Schie, and D. Sauter. "The Neural Correlates of the Awe Experience: Reduced Default Mode Network Activity During Feelings of Awe." *Human Brain Mapping* 40, no. 12 (August 15, 2019) 3561–3574. ncbi.nlm.nih.gov/pubmed/31062899.

White, M., A. Smith, K. Hymphryes, S. Pahl, D. Snelling, and M. Depledge. "Blue Space: The Importance of Water for Preference, Affect, and Restorativeness Ratings of Natural and Built Scenes." *Journal of Environmental Psychology* 30, no. 4 (December 2010): 482–493. sciencedirect.com/science /article/abs/pii/S0272494410000496.

White, M.P., S. Pahl, B.W. Wheeler, M.H. Depledge, and L.E. Fleming. "Natural Environments and Subjective Wellbeing: Different Types of Exposure Are Associated with Different Aspects of Wellbeing." *Health & Place* 45 (May 2017): 77–84. ncbi.nlm.nih.gov/pubmed/28319857.

Williams, Florence. *The Nature Fix: Why Nature Makes Us Happier, Healthier, and More Creative.* New York: W.W. Norton, 2018.

Willingham, A.J. "'Goat Yoga' Is a Thing—and Hundreds Are Lining Up for It." *CNN Health*, January 12, 2017. cnn.com/2017/01/12/health/goat -yoga-oregon-trnd/index.html.

Wilson, E.O. *Biophilia: The Human Bond with Other Species.* Cambridge, MA: Harvard University Press, 1984.

Yale Environment 360. "U.S. Study Shows Widening Disconnect with Nature and Potential Solutions." *E360 Digest*, April 27, 2017. e360.yale.edu/digest /u-s-study-shows-widening-disconnect-with-nature-and-potential-solutions.

Yu, C-P., C-M. Lin, M-J. Tsai, Y-C. Tsai, and C-Y. Chen. "Effects of Short Forest Bathing Program on Autonomic Nervous System Activity and Mood States in Middle-Aged and Elderly Individuals." *International Journal of Environmental Research and Public Health* 14, no. 8 (August 2017): 897. ncbi.nlm.nih.gov/pmc/articles/PMC5579495/.

Chapter 10: Exercise Your Power

Cialdini, Robert B. *Influence: The Psychology of Persuasion*. New York: Harper Business, 2006.

GoodTherapy. "Possibility Therapy." goodtherapy.org/learn-about-therapy /types/possibility-therapy.

Han, S.H., K. Kim, and J.A. Burr. "Stress-Buffering Effects of Volunteering on Daily Well-Being: Evidence from the National Study of Daily Experiences." *Journal of Gerontology, Series B, Psychological Sciences and Social Sciences*, May 6, 2019. ncbi.nlm.nih.gov/pubmed/31111935.

Minnow, M. "Upstanders, Whistle-Blowers, and Rescuers." 2014 Koningsberger Lecture, Harvard University. dash.harvard.edu/bitstream/handle/1 /17542461/rebo_rgl_minow_koningsberger_lecture_01202015.pdf ?sequence=1.

Nicholasen, M. "Nonviolent Resistance Proves Potent Weapon." *The Harvard Gazette*, February 4, 2019. news.harvard.edu/gazette/story/2019/02/why -nonviolent-resistance-beats-violent-force-in-effecting-social-political-change/.

Pillemer, K., N.M. Wells, R.H. Meador, L. Schultz, C.R. Henderson Jr., and M.T. Cope. "Engaging Older Adults in Environmental Volunteerism: The Retir- ees in Service to the Environment Program." *Gerontologist* 57, no. 2 (April 1, 2017): 367–375. ncbi.nlm.nih.gov/pmc/articles/PMC6410889/.

Sivers, D. "First Follower: Leadership Lessons from Dancing Guy." February 11, 2010. youtube.com/watch?v=fW8amMCVAJQ.

Tabassum, F., J. Mohan, and P. Smith. "Association of Volunteering with Mental Well-Being: A Lifecourse Analysis of a National Population-Based Longi- tudinal Study in the UK." *BMJ Open* 6, no. 8 (2016). bmjopen.bmj.com/ content/6/8/e011327.

INDEX

discomfort, tolerance for, 140–41

disconnection, 71–72

distraction, 6

    technology and, 28

dogs, 180–81

dopamine, 153, 229

dream hangover, 101

dysbiosis, 229

Ebert, Roger, 68

ecological grief, 91, 229

electronic devices, curfew for, 115–17,
    121, 125, 167, 214

emotion-coaching style, 81–82

emotion-dismissing style, 81–82

Emotional Agility (David), 93

emotional brain, 56

emotional competence, 72

emotional energy, conserving, 103

emotional equilibrium, 103, 118, 123,
    130, 147, 220

emotional granularity, 74, 75,
    84–85, 229

emotional hangovers (from past), 92–93

emotional hijack, 51, 102, 147

    distorted thoughts and, 135–36

emotional hyperreactivity, 6, 7, 41–42

emotional inflammation, 11–30

    age and, 102

    anticipating, 103

    balance in plan for, 222

    body, mind, and spirit effects,
        17–19, 47–64

    calming strategies for, 214–19

    cascade of effects, 50–52, 58

    chaos and crises, 20–27

    considering as asset, 208

    cooling down, 44–46, 65, 214–19

    downward spiral with, 50

    epidemic of, 24

    inflammatory cascade, 47–63

    issues out of our control, 22–23

    personal power and action, 191–210

    physical and mental effects, 49–59

    prevalence of, 13–17

    preventing, 213

    priming effect, 56–58

    reactions to, 19

    reactor types, 31–46, 216–19

    recognizing, 4

    response styles. *See* reactor types

    RESTORE plan for cooling down,
        65–220

    sharing with partner, 103

    social and spiritual effects, 59–63

    symptoms of, 3–4, 13

    types of reactors, 31–46

    understanding your own style, 33–35

    See also reactor types; RESTORE
        plan

emotional intelligence, 34, 72

emotional pulse, taking, 73, 86, 142, 214

emotional reasoning, 101

emotional regulation, deliberate,
    147–48

emotional well-being, 3, 18, 46, 49–50,
    74, 143

emotions

    acceptance of, 72, 86

    aesthetic (awe), 185

    amygdala and, 51, 54, 56, 57

    avoidance and, 70–71, 85

    awareness of, 69–71

    body experience of, 98–99, 104

    body status/equilibrium and, 102, 104

    daily fluctuation of, 69, 70

    disconnect from, 71–72

    distance from, 84

    distinguishing between, 73–74

    emotional drift, 55

    emotional granularity, 74, 75,
        84–85, 229

ABOUT THE AUTHORS

LISE VAN SUSTEREN, MD, is a general and forensic psychiatrist in Washington, DC, where she treats psychological and emotional distress on a regular basis. Previously, Dr. Van Susteren served as an assistant clinical professor of psychiatry at Georgetown University. Currently, she is the expert witness on psychological damages to children for Our Children's Trust, a landmark lawsuit (*Juliana v. the United States*) that was filed by 21 youths and climate scientist James Hansen, who are suing the federal government for inaction on climate change.

She has become a frequent commentator on anxiety and trauma for television (including CNN, GMA, NBC, VOA, Fox News, and numerous National Geographic series), radio (NPR and its local affiliates), print media (including the *Washington Post*, the *Wall Street Journal*, *Newsweek*, the *Huffington Post*, *Congressional Quarterly*, and *Global Health Now*), and websites (such as LiveScience.com, *US News & World Report*, and many others). She has also written articles for the *British Journal of Psychiatry*, *Clinical Psychiatry News*, and *Psychiatric Times*, and she has written chapters for various books, including one that's forthcoming from the Pontifical Academy of Sciences.

As a thought leader and activist, she also addresses issues related to trauma and emotional inflammation as they pertain to climate change through her previous role on the Advisory Board of the Center for Health and the Global Environment at the Harvard T.H. Chan School of Public Health and current roles with the board of Physicians for Social Responsibility and Earth Day Network. Dr. Van Susteren is the cofounder of the Climate Psychiatry Alliance (a professional group dedicated to promoting awareness and action on climate from a mental health perspective), the Climate Psychology Alliance North America, and the Interfaith Moral Action on Climate organization.

Since 2006, Dr. Van Susteren has given more than two hundred presentations around the world on the health effects and psychological aspects of climate change. In the last two years alone, she has had speaking engagements at events hosted by National Geographic, the American Public Health Association, the Pontifical Academy of Sciences (the Vatican), the American Psychiatric Association, Ohio Wesleyan University, Citizens' Climate Lobby, the Harvard Global Health Institute, the Emerging Markets Symposium (Oxford, England), EcoWatch, the California Department of Health, the University of Oregon School of Law, and the Academy of Integrative Health and Medicine.

STACEY COLINO is an award-winning writer, specializing in health and psychology. In addition to being a regular contributor to *US News & World Report* and AARP.org, her work has appeared in the *Washington Post*, *Newsweek*, *Parade*, *Cosmopolitan*, *Real Simple*, *Health*, *Prevention*, *Woman's Day*, *Harper's Bazaar*, *Parents*, and *Good Housekeeping*, among other magazines and newspapers.

She is the coauthor with David Katz, MD, of *Disease-Proof: The Remarkable Truth About What Makes Us Well* (Hudson Street Press, 2013); *Just Your Type: The Ultimate Guide to Eating and Training Right for Your Body Type* with Phil Catudal (Da Capo, 2019); *Strong Is the New Skinny: How to Eat, Live, and Move to Maximize Your Power* with Jennifer Cohen (Harmony, 2014); and *Taking Back the Month: A Personalized Solution for Managing PMS and Enhancing Your Health* with Diana Taylor, RN, PhD (Perigee, 2002). In addition, she collaborated on *The Food Therapist: Break Bad Habits, Eat with Intention, and Indulge Without Worry* by Shira Lenchewski, MS, RD (Grand

Central, 2018); *Skinny Liver: A Proven Program to Prevent and Reverse the New Silent Epidemic—Fatty Liver Disease* by Kristin Kirkpatrick, MS, RD, LD, and Ibrahim Hanouneh, MD (Da Capo, 2017); and *The Exhaustion Breakthrough: Unmask Hidden Reasons You're Tired and Beat Fatigue for Good* by Holly Phillips, MD (Rodale, 2015).

ABOUT SOUND TRUE

SOUNDS TRUE is a multimedia publisher whose mission is to inspire and support personal transformation and spiritual awakening. Founded in 1985 and located in Boulder, Colorado, we work with many of the leading spiritual teachers, thinkers, healers, and visionary artists of our time. We strive with every title to preserve the essential "living wisdom" of the author or artist. It is our goal to create products that not only provide information to a reader or listener but also embody the quality of a wisdom transmission.

For those seeking genuine transformation, Sounds True is your trusted partner. At SoundsTrue.com you will find a wealth of free resources to support your journey, including exclusive weekly audio interviews, free downloads, interactive learning tools, and other special savings on all our titles.

To learn more, please visit SoundsTrue.com/freegifts or call us toll-free at 800.333.9185.